Raffaele Cattaneo

Architecture in Italy

from the sixth to the eleventh century - historical and critical researches

Raffaele Cattaneo

Architecture in Italy
from the sixth to the eleventh century - historical and critical researches

ISBN/EAN: 9783337238179

Printed in Europe, USA, Canada, Australia, Japan

Cover: Foto ©Andreas Hilbeck / pixelio.de

More available books at **www.hansebooks.com**

Historical and Critical Researches

BY

RAFFAELE CATTANEO

TRANSLATED BY THE
CONTESSA ISABEL CURTIS-CHOLMELEY IN BERMANI

ILLUSTRATED

LONDON
T. FISHER UNWIN
M DCCC XCVI

All rights reserved.

PREFACE.

ROM the time that I first set myself in my youth, ten years ago, to study the written history of Art, I was deeply impressed by the enormous lacuna or lagoon that I found between the sixth and eleventh centuries in Italy, and by the diversity of opinion on the subject of that obscure and barbarous period and the Art that it produced. Led by a natural inclination to study the most obscure and recondite questions, I was impelled to devote myself to that field of research, and endeavour, if possible, to throw new light on the subject. Without that ingenuous boldness which youth gives, my project would undoubtedly have ended in smoke as soon as I was able to recognise its presumption; on the contrary, the desire to prosecute it took deep root, and grew into a strong passion.

My other studies, my limited resources at that time, were not of a nature to help me in so arduous a task; yet my ideal remained ever present with me, leading me on, without respite, to increase my little store of knowledge, driving, nay sometimes dragging me, half passive, to search greedily among manuscripts to copy designs, to purchase required photographs. At last came propitious opportunities and the means of frequently leaving my home to travel, to study near my monuments, to touch them with my own hands!

A large field for observation and comparison then opened up to me, and some personal discoveries, and the too-frequent blunders which I met with in certain writers, gave me confidence and courage, and I began to reason for myself.

I could not if I would narrate the slow metamorphosis that the old notions derived from books underwent in my brain. Ideas, hypotheses, old and new arguments, faced each other for the first time and did not agree. Very seldom did wisdom and prudence temper their excesses and induce them to calm discussion which might end in fraternal harmony, for mostly they insulted one another and violently squabbled in their contest for the crown: the old ones proud of their venerable age and authoritative paternity, the others haughty and strong in their freshness of youth.

It was a see-saw of alternate victories and losses; but very often the ancients were compelled to go limping out of the field amid the jeers of their prepotent rivals. Yet even these last could not always win the esteem and sympathy of their companions; so that they also sometimes came to fisticuffs, accusing one another of being systematic, vague, prejudiced, or pedantic, severe and full of affectation; and hence, among these also, sacrifices, humiliations, or exile. And harmony could never have followed if criticism and facts had not come before me which settled the question, and shed light where all had been thick darkness.

But this help did not come as quickly as I would have wished; and thus even two years ago my researches and conclusions were far from being complete, and of that I became conscious precisely when the Cavaliere Ongania proposed that I should undertake to write the architectonic history of the Basilica of S. Mark at Venice for his sumptuous publication on that wonderful monument.

By revealing itself to me in all its importance, the Basilica impressed me with a clear idea of the difficulty of my work; by degrees, as I continued to examine it with increasing patience and loving care, I discovered how many features it contained undisclosed, obscure and incomprehensible to my sight; how large a part it occupied in the history of Art in the barbarous ages, and how much study it must claim from one who fain would be its interpreter. Vainly I called the results of my past studies to my aid in unveiling the mystery of its construction and transformations; but I was not discouraged by this.

Love for the delightful Basilica upheld me, strengthened the old passion in me, and in *that* did I find impulse and vigour enough for the perfecting of those studies which I now present to the reader.

I hasten to publish them before the appearance of my work on S. Mark, because, in default of knowing the general results of my researches, the reader would be in danger of not understanding sufficiently the importance of the Basilica, and the language I adopt in describing its various parts.

The publication on S. Mark's Church has therefore hastened that of the present work, and that must be my excuse with the benevolent reader if, instead of finding the old lagoon quite filled up, he sees that it is only transformed into an archipelago. Nevertheless, I flatter myself that the green islands I have been able to evoke from it may be large, numerous, and near enough together to be easily reunited.

PUBLISHER'S NOTE.—In preparing this translation the expression "Italian-Byzantine" has invariably been used instead of "Italo-Byzantine." Proper names have been anglicised at discretion; in several instances the Latin form has been substituted for the Italian. Of the equivalents of "Ambrogio," "Ambrose" and "Ambroise," the latter has been chosen.

CONTENTS.

CHAP.		PAGE
	INTRODUCTION	17
I.	LATIN-BARBARIAN ARCHITECTURE DURING THE LOMBARD RULE	23
II.	SECOND INFLUENCE OF BYZANTINE ART ON ITALIAN ART—BYZANTINE-BARBARIAN STYLE	78
III.	ITALIAN ARCHITECTURE FROM THE END OF THE EIGHTH TO THE ELEVENTH CENTURY—ITALIAN-BYZANTINE STYLE	166
IV.	ARCHITECTURE IN THE LAGOONS OF VENETIA, FROM THE BEGINNING OF THE NINTH CENTURY TO THE YEAR 976	275
V.	ARCHITECTURE IN THE LAGOONS AND IN VENETIA, FROM THE YEAR 976 TO THE MIDDLE OF THE ELEVENTH CENTURY	314
	APPENDIX	345
	INDEX OF THE MONUMENTS DESCRIBED OR MENTIONED IN THIS VOLUME, AND OF THE CITIES OR PLACES WHERE THEY MAY BE FOUND	349
	INDEX OF THE MONUMENTS STUDIED IN THIS VOLUME ACCORDING TO THEIR CLASS AND CHRONOLOGY	357

LIST OF ILLUSTRATIONS.

FIG.		PAGE
	Frontispiece.—Parapet of the Cathedral of Torcello.	
1.	Ambo of SS. John and Paul at Ravenna.—A.D. 597	28
2.	Fragment of Ambo at the Rasponi Palace at Ravenna	30
3.	Sarcophagus at S. Apollinaris, near Ravenna	31
4.	Sarcophagus of the Archbishop, S. Felix, at S. Apollinaris, near Ravenna—A.D. 725	34
5.	Sarcophagus of an unknown person at S. Apollinaris, near Ravenna	35
6.	Plan of S. Stephen Rotunda, Rome—A.D. 468–482	37
7.	Capitals of the ancient Ciborium of S. Clement, Rome—A.D. 514–523	39
8.	Parapet and little Pilaster of S. Clement, Rome—A.D. 514 523	42
9.	Plan of S. Laurence-beyond-the-Walls at Rome	47
10.	Capital of the Galleries of S. Laurence, Rome—A.D. 578–590	53
11.	Slab of Marble at S. John's, Monza—Beginning of the VIIth Century	59
12.	Plan of the Cathedral and Baptistery of Grado—A.D. 571–586	61
13.	Capital and Open-work of Window, Cathedral of Grado—A.D. 571–586	65
14.	Plan of S. Maria of Grado—A.D. 571–586	66
15.	Crown of a Pilaster at S. Maria of Grado—A.D. 571–586	69
16.	Sarcophagus at the Church of SS. John and Paul at Venice	71
17.	Sarcophagus at the Museum of the Ducal Palace at Venice	72
18.	Balustrade of the Galleries of S. Mark at Venice—VIIth Century	83
19.	Exterior Bas-relief of Athenian Cathedral—VIIth Century	85
20.	Parapet existing in Ravenna—VIth Century	86
21.	Heading of a Door at Moudjeleia, Syria—VIIth Century	86
22.	Cymatium of a Door at Serdjilla, Syria—VIIth Century	88
23.	Cymatium of the Door of a Church at Behoih, Syria—VIIth Century	88
24.	Sculptures at a Castle near Safa, Syria—VIIth Century	89
25.	Bas-relief in the Exterior of the Cathedral at Athens	90
26.	Altar of S. Montan at Orléansville, Algeria—VIIth Century	91
27.	Details of the Porch of Cimitile—Beginning of the VIIIth Century	93
28.	Details of the Choir-screen at Cimitile—Beginning of the VIIIth Century	94
29.	Ciborium of S. George's of Valpolicella—A.D. 712	98

FIG.		PAGE
30.	Plan of the Church of S. George of Valpolicella—VIIIth and Xth Centuries (?)	101
31.	Baptistery of Calisto at Cividale—A.D. 737	103
32.	Capital of Baptistery at Cividale—A.D. 737	104
33 & 34.	Archivolts of the Baptistery at Cividale—A.D. 737	105
35.	Fragments of the Balustrades of the Baptistery at Cividale—A.D. 737	106
36.	Balustrade of Sigualdo in the Baptistery at Cividale—A.D. 762–776	107
37.	Altar of Ratchis at Cividale (posterior part)—A.D. 744–749	109
38.	Parapet of S. Maria-in-Valle at Cividale—A.D. 762–776	114
39.	Marble Door-leaves at S. Maria-in-Valle—A.D. 762–776	115
40.	Fronton of S. Maria—A.D. 762–776	116
41.	Capitals of the VIIIth Century	117
42.	Parapet found at S. Augustine at Venice—VIIIth Century	119
43.	Window near the Frescada Bridge at Venice—VIIIth Century	120
44.	Baptismal Font at the Museum at Venice—VIIth or VIIIth Century	122
45.	Principal Side of a Sarcophagus in the Cathedral of Murano—VIIIth Century	123
46.	Fragments of an Ambo at the Cathedral of Grado—VIIIth Century	124
47.	Capital at the Museum of Verona—VIIIth Century	125
48.	Plan of S. Teuteria at Verona—VIIth and XIIth Centuries	126
49.	Little Pilaster of Monselice and Fragments at the Bocchi Museum at Adria—VIIIth Century	127
50.	Arch of Ciborium in the Pieve di Bagnacavallo—VIIIth Century	129
51.	Arch of Ciborium in the Parish Church of Bagnacavallo—VIIIth Century	130
52.	Parapet in the Court of the University of Ferrara—VIIIth Century	132
53.	Arch of Ciborium over the Place S. Dominic at Bologna—VIIIth Century	133
54.	Sarcophagus of S. Agricola at S. Stephen of Bologna—XIIth Century	134
55.	Capital of SS. Peter and Paul, near S. Stephen of Bologna—XIIth Century	135
56.	Abacus of the Church of Aurona, Milan—VIIIth Century	140
57.	Pilasters of the Church of Aurona, Milan—VIIIth Century	140
58.	Small Pilasters in the Church of Aurona, Milan—VIIIth Century	141
59.	Capital of S. Vincent-in-Prato, Milan—VIIIth Century	142
60.	Capital of the Crypt in the Rotunda of Brescia—VIIIth Century	143
61.	Plan of S. Saviour's, Brescia—A.D. 753	144
62.	Capital of S. Saviour's Church, Brescia—A.D. 753	146
63.	Plan of S. Saviour's Crypt—VIIIth and XIIth Centuries	147
64.	Decorative Details of S. Saviour, Brescia—VIIIth Century	148
65.	Decorative Details of S. Saviour, Brescia—VIIIth Century	150
66.	Fragment possibly belonging to the Ambo of S. Saviour, Brescia—VIIIth Century	151
67.	Other Details of S. Saviour, Brescia—VIIIth Century	152

FIG.		PAGE
68.	Little Window of S. Saviour, Brescia—VIIIth Century	152
69.	Tomb of Theodota, Pavia—VIIIth Century	153
70.	Exterior Wall of S. Maria delle Caccie, Pavia—VIIIth Century	154
71.	Fragment of Parget found at Libarna—VIIIth Century	155
72.	Tomb at the Baptistery of Albenga—Fragments of VIIIth Century	156
73.	Capital at the Museum of Perugia—VIIIth Century	157
74.	Balustrade existing in the Belfry of the Cathedral of Spoleto—VIIIth Century	159
75.	Bas-relief at the Pinacoteca Comunale, Spoleto—VIIIth Century	159
76.	Capital in the Fieramosca Palace, Capua—VIIIth Century	161
77.	Capital in the Museum at Capua—VIIIth Century	161
78.	Bas-relief in the Museum at Capua—VIIIth Century	162
79.	Capital in the Cloister of S. Sophia at Benevento—VIIIth Century	163
80.	Plan of the Church of S. Maria-in-Cosmedin, Rome—A.D. 772–795	171
81.	Capital of S. Maria-in-Cosmedin, Rome—A.D. 772–795	173
82.	Fragment of Architrave of S. Maria-in-Cosmedin, Rome—A.D. 772–795	174
83.	Capital of the Church of S. Saba, Rome—End of the VIIIth Century	175
84.	Capital of the Portico of S. Laurence-in-Lucina, Rome—A.D. 772–795	175
85.	Mouth of the Well in the Lateran Cloister, Rome—End of the VIIIth Century	176
86.	Archivolt of the Ciborium discovered at Porto, Rome—A.D. 795–816	178
87.	Plan of the Church of S. Praxedis, Rome—A.D. 817–824	180
88.	Plan of the Chapel of S. Zenone at S. Praxedis, Rome—A.D. 817–824	181
89.	Base of Column in the Chapel of S. Zenone, Rome—A.D. 817–824	182
90.	Plan of the Church of S. Maria-in-Domnica, Rome—A.D. 817–824	183
91.	Capital of S. Maria-in-Domnica, Rome—A.D. 817–824	184
92.	Parapet of the Church of S. Sabina, Rome—A.D. 824–827	184
93.	(a) Parapet of S. Maria of Trastevere, Rome—A.D. 827	186
	(b) Parapet of S. Maria of Trastevere, Rome—A.D. 827	187
	(c) Other Parapets of S. Maria of Trastevere—A.D. 827	187
94.	Details of the Door of S. Clement on the Cœlius, Rome—IXth Century	189
95.	Parapet of S. Agnes-beyond-the-Walls, Rome—End of the VIIIth Century	190
96.	Fragment of Cross in the Roman Forum—IXth Century	190
97.	Mouth of a Well at the Office of the Minister of Agriculture, Rome—End of the VIIIth Century	191
98.	Bas-relief from the Cloister of S. Laurence-beyond-the-Walls, Rome—A.D. 1024–1033	193
99.	Fragment of Parapet in the Museum of Capua—IXth Century	194
100.	Plan of the Church of S. Michael, Capua—Xth Century (?)	194

FIG.		PAGE
101.	Capitals from S. Michael, Capua—Xth Century (?)	195
102.	Parapet found at S. Maria of the Angels, Assisi—IXth Century	197
103.	Sarcophagus of the Archbishop Gratiosus in S. Apollinaris, near Ravenna—A.D. 788	200
104.	Ciborium of S. Elucadio in S. Apollinaris, near Ravenna—A.D. 806-816	202
105.	Side of a Sarcophagus in S. Apollinaris, near Ravenna—VIth and IXth Centuries	203
106.	Cusped Archivolt in S. Apollinaris, near Ravenna—IXth Century	204
107.	Capital from the old Cathedral of Verona—A.D. 780	206
108.	Parapet of S. Peter's of Villanova—End of the VIIIth Century	208
109.	Capital of the Crypt of the Cathedral of Treviso—IXth Century	209
110.	Fragment of Baptismal Fonts at Pola—IXth Century	214
*111.	Arch of the Ciborium of the Cathedral of Cattaro—IXth Century	217
*112.	Plan of the Crypt of the Rotunda of Brescia End of the VIIIth Century	219
*113.	Capital of the Crypt of the Rotunda of Brescia—End of the VIIIth Century	220
*114.	Parapets of the old Church of S. Abbondio—IXth Century	221
*115.	Altar-front of the old Church of S. Abbondio—IXth Century	222
*116.	Epitaph of Ansperto, Archbishop of Milan	223
117.	Fragments of Doorpost in the chief Entrance of S. Ambroise, Milan—IXth Century	230
118.	Plan of S. Ambroise of Milan as it was in the IXth Century	233
119.	Parapet of S. Ambroise of Milan—IXth Century	236
120.	Archbishop's Chair in S. Ambroise of Milan—IXth Century	237
121.	Details of the Heading of the Apsis and the Presbytery in S. Ambroise of Milan—IXth Century	239
122.	Capital of the Ciborium of S. Ambroise, Milan—IXth Century	245
123.	Apsides of the Church of S. Vincent-in-Prato, Milan—IXth Century	250
124.	Capital of the Naves of S. Vincent-in-Prato, Milan—IXth Century	251
125.	Plan of the Church and of the Belfry of S. Satyrus, Milan—A.D. 879	254
126.	Capitals of the Church of S. Satyrus, Milan—A.D. 879	255
127.	Belfry of S. Satyrus, Milan—A.D. 879	256
128.	Plan of the Church and Baptistery of Alliate—A.D. 881	257
*129.	Capitals of the Crypt of Alliate—A.D. 881	258
*130.	External Wall of the chief Apsis of Alliate—A.D. 881	259
*131.	External Wall of the Baptistery of Alliate—A.D. 881	259
*132.	Plans and Elevations of the Baptistery of Biella—IXth and Xth Centuries	261
133.	Plan of the Ancient Church of S. Eustace at Milan—IXth or Xth Century	266
134.	Plan of the Church of SS. Felix and Fortunatus, near Vicenza	268

FIG.		PAGE
135.	Capital of S. Felix, near Vicenza—A.D. 985	269
136.	Plan of the Apsides of S. Stephen (inferior stage)—Xth Century (?)	271
137.	Frieze and Capital of the Balustrades of the Cathedral at Grado	283
138.	Fragment of Archivolt of the Ciborium of S. Maria at Grado—A.D. 814–818	284
139.	Cymatium, formerly above the Door of S. Mark of the Partecipazî —A.D. 829	288
140.	Parapet of S. Mark of the Partecipazî, existing in the Gallery above the Altar of S. James—A.D. 829	289
141.	Parapet of S. Mark of the Partecipazî, existing along the little Ambo Staircase—A.D. 829	290
142.	Sculpture existing formerly in the Vault of S. Mark—A.D. 829	290
143.	Lacunar of the Tomb of S. Mark in the Crypt—A.D. 829	291
144.	Parapet of S. Mark of the Partecipazî, existing in the South Transept—A.D. 829	291
145.	Cornice in the Church of S. Mark of the Partecipazî	293
146.	Bas-relief existing in the Baptistery of S. Mark of the Partecipazî —A.D. 829	294
147.	Parapet existing at Constantinople — IXth Century (after Salzemberg)	295
*148, *149, *150.	Parapets in the Church of the Mother of God at Constantinople—IXth Century (after Pulgher)	296
*151.	Parapet in the Church of the Mother of God at Constantinople— IXth Century (after Pulgher)	297
*152.	Jamb of a Door found at Athens—IXth Century (after Castellazzi)	298
*153.	Parapet found at Athens—IXth Century (after Castellazzi)	299
154.	Well-kirb belonging to M. le Chevalier Guggenheim, Venice—End of the VIIIth Century (?)	305
155.	Well-kirb formerly at Venice—Second half of the IXth Century	306
156.	Plan of the Cathedral of Torcello at the present time	308
157.	Parapet of the Cathedral of Torcello—A.D. 874	310
158.	Little Arcades forming the Base of the Choir of S. Mark's—A.D. 976	318
159.	Parapet of S. Mark, made by order of Pietro Orseolo I.—A.D. 976	321
160.	Reproduction in 1467 of a Well-ring sculptured about A.D. 1000	328
161.	Capital from the Naves of the Cathedral of Torcello—A.D. 1008	330
162.	Capital from the Naves of the Cathedral of Torcello—A.D. 1008	331
163.	Parapet of the Cathedral of Torcello—A.D. 1008	332
164.	Parapet of the Cathedral of Torcello—A.D. 1008	333
165.	Parapet of the Cathedral of Torcello—A.D. 1008	335
166.	Frieze of the Cathedral of Torcello—A.D. 1008	337
167.	Sarcophagus in a Cloister of the Convent of S. Antonio (S. Anthony) at Padua—Parapet sculptured about the year 1000	339
168.	Capital of the Crypt of the Cathedral of Aquileia—A.D. 1019–1025	341
169.	Capital of the Atrium of the Cathedral of Aquileia—A.D. 1019–1025	342

ERRATA.

PAGE				
102	. *for*	Agliate	*read*	Alliate.
215	. . „	Crose	„	Croce.
142, 150	„	Desiderio	„	Desiderius.
268	„	Fortunat	„	Fortunatus.
89, 351	„	Lokanaya	„	Kokanaya.
242	. „	Nazaro		Nazario.
351	„	Nazaire	„	Nazario.
44, 67, 179–84	„	Praxeda		Praxedis.
32	„	Vitus	„	Vitale.
68		Vita		

INTRODUCTION.

 WILL not revert to the times of the Romans and the first ages of Christianity, which are already sufficiently known; enough, too, is known, thanks to the studies of foreigners, about the works of Proto-Byzantine art * of the fifth and sixth centuries, both in the East and in the West, and I need not trouble myself about these, except when constrained to do so for the sake of later monuments; but I must attentively examine the successive centuries—centuries of decadence hitherto left in obscurity.

For precisely on account of their decadence and the scarcity of their remaining monuments, they were generally left out by all writers on Art—an omission doubly blamable since it left the chain of historic Art still broken, much to the confusion of the studious, and hindered the recovery of the knot to which successive links might be attached.

It is true that there have been a few writers who made a study of the monuments of those dark ages, such as Cordero, Ricci, Hübsch, Dartein, Selvatico, Garrucci, Mothes, and Rohault de Fleury,† but their views were too narrow, their work was limited to one fixed region or one particular class of works, or they contented themselves with glancing over the

---

* Far from siding with those who deny the existence of a Byzantine style, I so thoroughly affirm it that I find it necessary to divide it into three distinct periods (for this I shall give plain reasons in the course of this volume), and to call these periods by three distinct names—Proto-Byzantine, Barbarian-Byzantine, and Neo-Byzantine.

† See Appendix.

whole in too rapid and superficial a manner, so that all these partial studies, even when reunited, are far from offering the student even a dubious light on the subject. And yet, although some of the above-named writers sometimes so nearly approached the truth that it would seem as if they ought to have discovered it, because none of them knew how to shake off previous prejudices and trust to an artistic comparison of the monuments themselves (always the most sure guide in such researches), rather than hold faith in documents that too frequently prove fallacious, they all miserably missed the road and gained no profit for their pains.

Among all those writers there is, however, one to whom students owe more gratitude than to the rest, because he it was who first began to overthrow the preconceived opinions about the history of the monuments of the Lombard period, which had already gained ground.

As it is known, great errors were current among archaeologists and cultivators of Art-history about the origins of Lombard or Roman architecture and the period in which it prevailed, till Count Cordero de San Quintino gave to the light (in 1829) his interesting study on Italian architecture during the domination of the Lombards.*

Ill able to endure the wide lagoon that conscientious researches must have shown them to exist between the remaining monuments of the sixth century and those of the eleventh, and on the other hand being unable to account for the disappearance of nearly all the rest, they agreed to date from the Lombard ages all the monuments of Romanic style that they found in the places where chronicles, inscriptions, or popular tradition attributed them in that wretched time. It follows that, observing an immense difference of style, technique and ornament, between the Latin and Byzantine monuments of the sixth century and those believed by them to be of the seventh, and not the gradually progressive development which is wont to accompany periods of transition, they arrived at the

* "Dell'italiana Architettura durante la dominazione longobardica," Brescia, 1829.

false hypothesis that the manner of building and barbarous ornamentation, of which S. Michael of Pavia is an example (of which specimens abound in the regions once subject to the Lombards), were introduced by the Lombards themselves into Italy.

Well, Cordero rose up to say that they had all fallen into a gross blunder, and gave as final conclusion to his long discourse, "that the Lombards, being still barbarians when they descended into Italy, could not have had architects or an architecture of their own; and if old chroniclers tell us that such and such churches were erected during their domination, there is no reason to believe blindly that the church we look upon is the same construction then recorded; that, from the half of the sixth till the half of the eighth century, no other architecture was used in Italy except the Latin architecture of the preceding fourth and fifth centuries—a style which was, however, spoiled by the unskilfulness of the builders."

This was a just conclusion, but not one accepted by all, and even in our days we often hear it repeated by persons well known to fame, such as Ruskin* for example, that S. Michael of Padua dates from the seventh century. Nevertheless, such persistence in error cannot draw down much weight of blame on those who remain in it, if we only consider that, although the

* "The Stones of Venice," vol. i. p. 360. Among the rhapsodies indulged in by Ruskin in this work of transcendental æstheticism, even more than of art and of history, not least is his dream about the supposed antiquity of the Lombard style, its origin and its relation with Lombardic civilisation. In reviewing the Lombard edifices, and chiefly S. Michael of Pavia, he avers that "the Arabian feverishness infects even the Lombard in the south, showing itself, however, in endless invention, with a refreshing firmness and order directing the whole of it. The excitement is greatest in the earliest times, most of all shown in S. Michele of Pavia; and I am strongly disposed to connect much of its peculiar manifestations with the Lombard's habits of eating and drinking, especially his carnivorousness. The Lombard of early times seems to have been exactly what a tiger would be, if you could give him love of a joke, vigorous imagination, strong sense of justice, fear of hell, knowledge of northern mythology, a stone den, and a mallet and chisel: fancy him pacing up and down in the said den to digest his dinner, and striking on the wall, with a new fancy in his head, at every turn, and you have the Lombardic sculptor. As civilisation increases the supply of vegetables and shortens that of wild beasts, the excitement diminishes; it is still strong in the thirteenth century at Lyons and Rouen; it dies away gradually in the later Gothic, and is quite extinct in the fifteenth century."

conclusions of Cordero were most just, yet he knew not how to corroborate them by documents of indubitable authenticity. In fact, Cordero wove his reasoning not out of careful researches and artistic considerations, but simply out of historical discussions; and, although the reader of his pages may be led by him to exclude constructions of Romanic style from the Lombard epoch, yet he would deceive himself greatly if he imagined he could learn in those pages what sort of architecture *was* really used in Italy during that stormy period, or what were its characteristics. It is true that he points out to us certain constructions proved, so he says, by irrefutable documents to have been erected in the time of the Lombards, but a well-informed critic can accept only one of them, and as to that one even, what artistic documents could Cordero add to the historical ones, already of themselves somewhat problematic and insufficient to demonstrate that it belonged to the epoch to which he attributed it?

It is clear that Cordero's study, however precious and desirable it may have been, was only an embryo study, failing to solve definitely the problems which it raised. Yet, who would believe it? From 1829 till this present time, no one, no Italian, and fortunately no foreigner, made up his mind to continue and make perfect the work of the Count of San Quintino. One must not forget, it is true, that Selvatico, Dartein, and Garrucci, have placed in fuller view some constructions or sculptures evidently belonging to that historic period; but of what use was that whilst, for lack of necessary comparison or through carelessness of criticism, they studied to so little purpose that they confused with authentic Lombard monuments other monuments which, without doubt, belong to later centuries and to the Romanic style? Who does not see that while they did homage to Cordero's assertion in one way, they denied it in another, heaping confusion on what was already confused?

No doubt then that, while we accept Cordero's wise conclusions, we must go back to the beginning of the road so ill-trodden by him and others, to draw from it facts that admit of no question and firmly establish a system which has wavered so long.

Without further delay I set myself to the work, and in order to render such a study essentially serviceable to the history of Art, I shall follow chronological order, as far as the nature of the monuments to be examined will permit. Moreover, I am persuaded that a treatise on Art, however restricted, unless furnished with appropriate drawings, only half realises its intentions; for we might compare its effect on the reader to that which we experience when gazing on a city at night in the dim lamplight. That is why I have deemed it not only useful, but necessary, frequently to join the images of the monuments to their descriptions, and the reflections made upon them, especially in the cases of those not hitherto described. I hope to obtain in this manner a double result: to render my words clearer, and to furnish the proof of my statements.

* For the sake of justice, and that I may escape the charge of adorning myself with peacock's plumes, I frankly confess that several of the drawings that decorate the present publication are taken from the works of Vogüé, Dartein, Garrucci Jackson, Salzemberg, Pulgher and Rohault de Fleury. They are marked with an asterisk.

Chapter I.

LATIN-BARBARIAN ARCHITECTURE

DURING THE LOMBARD RULE.

IT is impossible for one to examine Italian monuments from the seventh to the eleventh century without being instantly impressed by the extraordinary decadence to which he finds all Art reduced and spontaneously asking himself what can have been the causes of it. It is chiefly attributed to the destructive Lombard conquest, and I myself do not refuse to believe that this conquest immensely contributed to the decadence. On the other hand, considering that, had this been the only cause, its sad effects would have been traceable only in those regions of Italy which were subjugated by the ferocious invaders, and one would not see the same, not to say still greater, corruption in those regions which, while they suffered indirectly by this invasion, were never victims of it, I am forced to examine whether other calamities of no less weight were not added to that of the barbarian scourge to produce such ruin of Art throughout all Italy. And we have little trouble in finding out these calamities in history, which is often reticent in recording periods of peace and joyfulness but never silent when it has to remind us of the pains and miseries of nations.

Thus we read that, about the year 566, a furious plague

afflicted all Italy and almost depopulated it.* Especially did it make havoc in Liguria (which in those times also included half Lombardy and all Piedmont), and S. Gregory the Great attests that it also desolated Rome. Such was the loss of life that, in the words of an ancient writer, only dogs were met in the streets of certain cities, and the country was in many places uninhabited, so that the animals wandered here and there without masters, and there was no one to reap corn or gather grapes.

Then in 568 the Lombards fell upon the unhappy land, and the next year there was a terrible dearth to whose effects, together with the plague alluded to above, Paolo Diacono attributes the rapid advance of those barbarians, who thus found Italy worn out and helpless. Afterwards, in 590, the whole peninsula was fearfully stricken with a pestilence among the oxen, and many people died of dysentery and smallpox. And, as if all these miseries were to be held as nothing, behold in 589 a terrible flood of waters, that in all the mountainous regions of Italy overturned and displaced the soil of the hills and so swelled up the streams in the plains that they were for the most part submerged. Whole villages were destroyed, many roads were rendered useless, and there was great loss of men and cattle. At Rome the Tiber, risen to an enormous height, did all manner of damage; in a like manner the Adige left Verona buried in great part and half ruined, rooting up and overthrowing its very walls in many places; and two months afterwards a furious conflagration reduced to ashes all that had escaped from the ruin made by the river.

After these scourges came a terrible train of plagues and famines, which deprived of life an innumerable multitude of people. Nor did misfortune end then, but till past the end of that century did not cease to strike the wretched Italians. The plague returned thrice, and was succeeded without interruption by the scourges of drought, dearth, icy cold, burning wind, and even mice and locusts that in certain regions de-

* Muratori, "Annali d'Italia."

voured the harvests of grain, the herbs of the fields, and the leaves of the trees.

Cast down by so many and so heavy misfortunes, from whence could the weakened Italians hope for help, speedily to raise and restore them? From those Lombards who had begun their reign with massacres, conflagrations, and destruction, and had made their way by robbing towns, despoiling churches, and cutting the throats of the priests? From those Lombards who, under the government of Clefis and that of the Dukes, made it their great study to murder the rich or drive them into exile, in order to confiscate their goods? From those Lombards who, ever ready to break the bounds of their own kingdom, to gorge themselves with pillage and cruelty by preying on the surrounding countries, had provoked the rage and the sanguinary vengeance of the Greeks, the Franks, and the Slaves to the harm of the unhappy peninsula? When one remembers that the bankless waters of the Adige, after the rupture described above, kept the vast plains from the Euganean hills to the ancient Po for more than two centuries in a perennial state of inundation, and that the Lombards, out of hatred to the Greeks who possessed the Lagoons, never cared to gather the flood into a new and durable bed, it may easily be understood that it would have been madness on the part of the Italians to hope for help and restoration from those barbarians.

Look now at Art and consider, that if long peace and general comfort were always requisite to insure its prosperity it must needs have all but perished in this period of invasions, wars, and calamities. Art in Italy had so much decayed during the barbaric invasions of the fifth century, that Theodoric, notwithstanding his regal encouragement, could only obtain from it very poor productions, as is proved by the monuments erected by him in Ravenna and not a few of the same style of which we find evident traces in several cities, both in northern and southern Italy. But the influence of Byzantine art, which with the Greek conquests preceded and followed the fall of the Gothic reign, though it bore in itself the germs of fresh decadence, without doubt availed to raise slightly the level of Latin art so that in the middle of the sixth century it was far removed from the barbarism into which it was to be plunged soon afterwards. Now it is precisely to this second half of the sixth century that I assign the cause and the beginning of that long decadence, or rather lethargy, of Art which, having lasted through all the period of the Lombard domination, survived it till the end of the ninth century, and. in some regions, till the tenth, and even the first half of the eleventh century, as I shall prove hereafter. The repeated plagues and famines had certainly slain or put to flight the few artists of worth that Italy would fain have cherished for their rareness; but, even had they all lived through so much ruin, who could have found the means to enable them to subsist by exercising their talent? Before occupying herself with Art, Italy had to busy herself with recovering from wounds so many and so deep, and it was much if she could employ labourers to raise up her ruined houses and mend as best might be what men and streams had spoilt—works from which Art was necessarily excluded. Therefore, when the pious Teodolinda persuaded Agilulfo to reconstruct or restore several churches destroyed or damaged in the invasions of his predecessors, Art, at least in Lombardy, had slumbered for nearly half a century.

Since the new artificers, called on to decorate these edifices with sculpture and painting, had had no chance of forming themselves in any school whatever, or indeed of exercising their mind and hand in any way, they must have felt like children with the chisel or brush in their hands, and no other guide than the remaining samples of the most recent Byzantine or Latin works —and like children they operated.

But here it would be well to try and explain another fact; that is to say. how it happened that Byzantine art, which had somewhat raised Italian art in the first half of the sixth century, was not helpful to it in the second, although the emperors of the East still possessed some of our provinces and Greek art would not so soon have decayed as the Latin. To my thinking the answer is not difficult.

It was not compassion nor magnanimity towards the wretched Italians that urged Justinian to conquer the peninsula, but simply ambition and insatiable thirst for the gold that he well knew how to wring from his subjects; and if we find him spending handsome sums to erect or complete sumptuous monuments in Italy, he did so not to succour the tottering Italian art, nor to embellish our cities, but only loudly to proclaim his powerful and fascinating opulence and greatness and high sovereignty. But after Justinian the power of the empire from day to day declined. His weak successors, partly from want of energy, partly on account of their continual molestation by the Persian Sassanidi, or by the barbarians of the North, or by internal discord, knew not how to hold ground against the impetuous hordes of the Lombards, and they remained firm only in Sicily, in the Esarchate of Ravenna, in Rome, and a few other cities. Therefore it was no longer a time when emperors could have recourse to the prestige of pompous monuments to sustain in Italy their already fallen renown. Nor was it a time in which Greek artists could be tempted to transport their tents to Italy, since the only spontaneous motive that can induce an artist to abandon his own soil is the hope of finding more abundant or more remunerative work elsewhere than his own country affords him. At this epoch the thought of Italy would more than ever dissuade him from emigration, because Italy was then a synonym for "land accursed and desolated"; Italians for miserable, impoverished slaves, and their rulers for ignorant, avaricious, cruel barbarians, destructive of the very elements of civilisation.

That the miserable Italian art was left to itself during the whole seventh century by the Byzantines, is evidently proved by the fact that even in Ravenna, which remained till the year 752 in subjection to the Greeks, who held an Esarch in that town, Art submitted rapidly to the decadence, as in the other towns of Italy.

Ravenna.—No edifice of the end of the sixth century, nor of the two succeeding ones, remains to us in Ravenna; but, to attest how Art there fell from abyss to abyss, sufficient, though not many, works of sculpture (the most potent auxiliary of the art of architecture) remain to us.

The last work of certain date that belongs to the sixth century is a parapet in the church of SS. John and Paul, which, as an incised inscription on it tells us, was ordered by Adeodato, chief of the imperial guards in the time of the Archbishop Mariniano (596-606), and precisely in the year 597.

It is composed of a slab of marble, curvilinear and slightly trilobate, whose convexity forms about the quarter of a circle, flanked by two narrow rectilineal wings. The ornamentation, like the whole, is almost copied from the ambo of the cathedral constructed in the first half of the century by Archbishop Agnello, and consists of little squares symmetrically distributed over the whole surface of the parapet and separated by crossed fillets, by striated fasces, and rosettes. Within these squares are sculptures representing symbolic animals ranged in zones—lambs, stags, peacocks, doves, and fish. The highest

FIG. 1.—Ambo of SS. John and Paul at Ravenna—A.D. 597.

squares of the wings are larger than the rest, and enclose the figures of the titular saints of the Church. The whole is terminated by a cornice of little leaves and olive moulding. In truth, even if the inscription did not proclaim the date, one might yet read at once on the wretched sculptures of this ambo the sixty years that divide it from that of the cathedral. In this latter the various figures, though flattened, have free and often elegant contours, and every animal is depicted in a form easily understood at first sight: in the ambo of SS. John and Paul, on the contrary, it is useless to seek for form and design. We distinguish the lamb from the stag only because the latter has branching horns, and the dove from the peacock because the head of this last bears a little tuft: eyes, wings, and feathers are made conspicuous by rude furrows, and the rosettes, leaves, and olives of the wretched cornice are also coarse. And what shall we say of the two figures? They do not quite come up to the horrible caricatures of the eighth century, but that fact ought not to deprive us of the right of stigmatising them as mere grotesques.

At Ravenna something still worse is to be seen in a fragment of another ambo existing in the Palace Rasponi, similar to that of the cathedral, and, indeed, in its decorations and squares approaching it more nearly than that of SS. John and Paul, though its sculptures clearly point to the seventh century. The animals are about as meritorious as those of the preceding ambo, but the figure of the saint is notably inferior, though of less squat proportions. It is a plain surface brought into relief by means of lowering the rest a few millimetres, and furrowed in its length and breadth by hard, awkward lines meant for drapery; in fact, we here have a figure inferior to those of the eighth century.

Yet, as we once before observed, while in Rome the passion for figurative sculpture was vivid even in the fifth century, so that the greater part of the sarcophagi there are covered with splendid and numerous reliefs, representing the scenes of the Old and New Testament, in Ravenna, on the contrary, it seems that such a passion was not felt, and the few sarcophagi there, dating from the fifth and following century, have only a few figures, always isolated, often in niches, and very seldom equalling those of Rome.

This shyness about human representation in sculpture was not derived from the limited skill of the artificers, but only to the immediate Greek influence to which Ravenna was subject in those ages. The Greek Christians were as little favourable to sculpture of figures as were the first Fathers of the Church; on the contrary, they neglected it, substituting for it decorations drawn from the vegetable kingdom, with capricious ornaments and Christian symbols, all representations that gave them greater opportunity to cover the marbles with splendour of intaglio and abandon themselves to the caprice of Oriental fantasy.

To this sort of sculpture they soon felt specially attracted, and it was very early introduced even in Ravenna, where the monograms of Christ, lambs, peacocks, doves, palms, crosses, or vine-branches are seen to cover the majority of the fronts of sarcophagi, the parapets and ambos of churches, and generally the capitals of columns.

But if in the sixth century the figure began to be neglected through partiality for symbolism and rich ornamentation, in the seventh it was necessarily abandoned, thanks to the absolute unskilfulness of the sculptors. The ambo of SS. John and Paul is the last sculptured work of the Lombard era by Italian hands, and of certain date, in which the human figure appears.

Fig. 2.—Fragment of Ambo at the Rasponi Palace at Ravenna.

Let us next examine a sarcophagus of some person unknown in S. Apollinaris-in-Classe, the sculptures of which, with the exception of two little pillars at the extremities of the front and of the small arches of the flanks added in the ninth century, fully accord with the end of the sixth century or the beginning of the seventh. The front view gives us, under a meagre cornice, a cross enclosed by a crown of olives with awkward ribbons

Fig. 3.—Sarcophagus at S. Apollinaris, near Ravenna.

ending in leaves and flanked by two poor sheep and the same number of palms. Three monograms of Jesus Christ surrounded by crowns of olive are seen on the cover, whose sides bear a cross between leaves and a vase with pomegranates. The worthlessness of these wretched sculptures may be easily guessed at by the reader while looking at the faithful reproduction here offered to him.

But truly, if we are to believe Cavalcaselle,* and Garrucci † and Bayet ‡ who follow him, this seventh century offers us two splendid samples of sculpture, both with figures and other decorations which must confuse all the order of progressive decadence presented by other monuments. But let the reader be neither startled nor deceived. The above-named authors contented themselves with only reading the legend engraved on these two works, and did not consider whether it agreed with the style of them or disagreed, as it does in fact. I allude to

* "Storia della Pittura in Italia," vol. i., Firenze, Le Monnier, 1875.
† "Storia dell' Arte Christiana," Prato.
‡ "L'Art Byzantin," Paris, A. Quantin.

the sarcophagus of Isaac, Esarch of the city (who died in 648), deposited near the church of S. Vitus; and to another in S. Apollinaris-in-Classe, where repose the remains of the Archbishop Theodore, who died in 688—facts attested by the legends sculptured on the respective lids. But there is so wide a difference between simply giving the name of the entombed, and certifying that the tomb was sculptured specially for him, that we may be permitted the suspicion that those sarcophagi were work of earlier centuries, perhaps abandoned for a long time, and here at last again made use of. Such a fact is by no means singular; on the contrary, in Rome, and other localities, we find various pagan sarcophagi richly sculptured, and sometimes with indecent subjects, made to serve as a place of deposit for the bodies of conspicuous Christian personages; and after the eleventh century it was usual—we have three examples here in Venice—to place the dead in tombs of the preceding Christian centuries. No wonder, therefore, that at Ravenna in the seventh century sarcophagi sculptured anteriorly should have been made use of; on the contrary, the great lack of skill in the artists of that age, who were unable to produce anything even mediocre, excuses this recurrence to preceding centuries in order to do honour to the memory of the illustrious dead, while the dispassionate examination of both the tombs in question concurs to give every appearance of likelihood to such fact. The sarcophagus of the Esarch shows us sculptured in front the Magian kings in Phrygian caps, advancing with their gifts towards Mary, who offers the child Jesus to their adoration, the miraculous star shining over her head. On one of the sides we see Daniel among the lions, on the other Jesus raising Lazarus, who, swathed like the Egyptian mummies, stands straight up on the edge of the sepulchre. The figures have just proportions and, although mutilated in many places, yet show freedom of movement, intelligence in drapery, and boldness of chisel. Thus, far from being a possible fruit of the seventh century, these groups so much resemble the very antique paintings in the catacombs of Rome, that we are induced to attribute them to the fifth century rather than to the sixth. The only part that might be of Isaac's time is the coarse, heavy, and unadorned arched lid on which Susanna, widow of the Esarch, has willed to record the acts of her husband and her own name.

We cannot say as much of the lid of Theodore's sepulchre, since both parts are without doubt synchronical and evidently of the style of the sixth century when most flourishing. The front is adorned by the monogram called "Constantine" between the Alpha and Omega, and this monogram, enclosed in olive-crowns, is thrice repeated on the convexity of the coverclo. On its sides we see two great peacocks of elegant design and workmanship, and behind these two vine-branches, rich in grapes and leaves, of graceful form and very delicate intaglio; underneath are roses and doves. A less expert but still contemporary hand is manifested by the sides, whose decoration consists of crosses, vases, plants, and heads of lions. †

What a difference between the sculpture of these two sarcophagi and the gross work of the ambos of SS. John and Paul and the Rasponi Palace! But Garrucci and Cavalcaselle did not stop here, but, seeing that these two tombs, attributed by them to the seventh century, are closed with vaulted coverings, drew therefrom argument for two utterly erroneous assertions: one, that this form of lid only came into use in that century; the second, that other sepulchres of the cathedral ought to be attributed to the same century, because they, too, have arched covercles. Having proved the first error into which these illustrious writers had fallen, no further proof is required against the two consequent ones; nevertheless, for the sake of greater clearness in the argument, and to convince those who might still be in doubt, I will say, in the first place, that the use of sepulchres with arched lids began in the fifth century, and of this there is an example in one of those attached to the Mausoleum of Galla Placidia; in the second place, that the two sarcophagi of S. Reginald and of S. Baraziano in the cathedral, rich in figures and splendid ornaments, should be considered among the finest examples of tombs of the first half of the sixth

---

* See the design in the work of Garrucci or in that of Bayet.
† See Garrucci, " L'arte Cristiana."

century in Ravenna. Those errors were rather a stumbling-block to Cavalcaselle, who had to confess that, though painting in the seventh century in and out of Rome was beyond measure decadent, sculpture in Ravenna inexplicably maintained itself in a sufficient degree of perfection.

Sculpture in Ravenna in the seventh century must have sunk to such a depth that it could not rise up again without help. There being no works assignable to the rest of that century, we pass to the succeeding one, and there meet another sarcophagus of S. Apollinaris-in-Classe, which, according to its

FIG. 4.—Sarcophagus of the Archbishop, S. Felix, at S. Apollinaris, near Ravenna—A.D. 725.

synchronical inscription, encloses the bones of the Archbishop Felix, deceased about 725. It is one of the most miserable works of sculpture ever made, looking as though the artificer had been ignorant even of square, compass, and lead, and therefore certainly of all essential art. The tomb is closed with a double sloping lid like a roof, it has crosses and circles; the front is terminated on one side by a colonette, on the other by a little fluted pilaster; then follow two candelabri with lighted candles, then two little arches from which hang crowns, then two sheep, that look like horses, with a cross over each, and in the centre a frontispiece supported by little demi-columns, under which is the monogram of Christ.

What, then, can one say of another sarcophagus of some person unknown in the same basilica, which, excepting the covercle, which seems to me a sketch of the sixth century, evidently belongs to the first half of the eighth century? The two little sheep carrying the cross (one knows not how) are such horrors that to find anything like them, one must go back to the most barbarous epochs anterior to all civilisation.

In the basilica of S. Apollinaris-in-Classe there are other

Fig. 5.—Sarcophagus of an unknown person at S. Apollinaris, near Ravenna.

tombs of the eighth and ninth centuries, but as these bear the influence of a style quite different from the indigenous one, we will leave them on one side for the present, limiting ourselves to considering how, in Ravenna in the seventh and the first half of the next century, Art fell from bad to worse, following the pattern of preceding centuries, with a variation only caused by the excessive incapacity of the artificers.

To demonstrate that Art was fallen not only in Ravenna, but throughout Italy, it is enough to examine a few works scattered here and there, to which the date of the seventh century only can be assigned.

ROME.—Here it is well to give evidence of a fact which has never been fully made known by others, and to many will seem almost strange, namely, that Proto-Byzantine art penetrated as far as Rome. And though it did not there leave samples of that daringly new and theatrical style of which we find examples in Ravenna and Milan, yet it made itself clearly known and succeeded in grafting some of its elements on Latin architecture, so that even in the seventh century they were still evident, as we may see in several of the basilicas of the city.

The most ancient examples of the influence of the Byzantine style in Rome may be seen in the church of S. Stephen on the Celio, erected by the Pontiff S. Simplicio between 468 and 482. It is a vast rotunda formed by two concentric rows of columns encircled by walls.

Some archæologists, surprised by the singular form of this church, suspected that it was once a pagan edifice, of which advantage had been taken to make a church. Some called it a temple, some a market-place, some a basilica, a slaughter-house, and even an arsenal. All these conjectures were mere dreams, because the building shows in its every part* the style of the sixth century, during which it was consecrated to Christian worship.

We are ignorant of the motives that could have induced the constructors of this church to abandon the ichnography of the basilica and adopt that only in use for baptisteries; we only know that just at that time another round church, in certain particulars similar to S. Stephen, was built in Perugia, and that, since that epoch, several others were made. For which reason

---

* With the exception of the little apsis added by Theodore I. between A.D. 642 and 649 (where the antique entrance used to be), the transversal wall of the centre, supported by great columns and pilasters, constructed, it appears, by Adrian I., the present small external portico, and the double piercing of the upper windows. The church in the fifteenth century was reduced to smaller proportions by suppressing the exterior nave, about which Francesco di Giorgio di Martino, a contemporary, left his written opinion: "less embellished than spoilt by Papa Nichola."

we may, I think, conjecture that only love of novelty incited this introduction of forms till then never used.

But besides its ichnographic originality, this Rotunda pre-

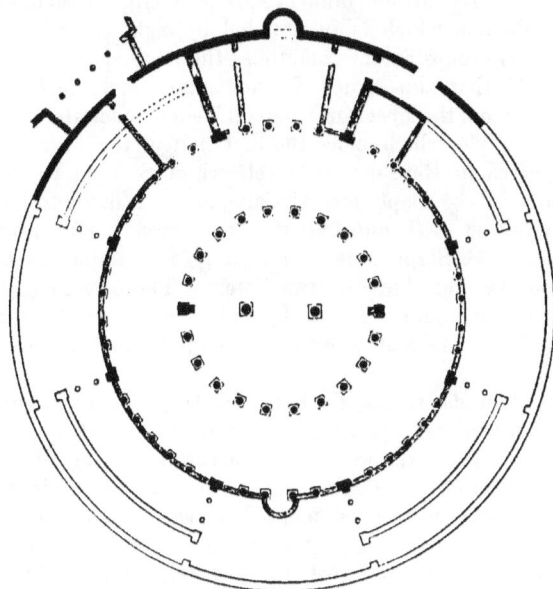

Fig. 6.— Plan of S. Stephen Rotunda, Rome — A.D. 468-482.

sents nothing that can point to an architectonic progress. That marvellous system of arches, of vaults, and cupolas that then began to make its way in the East, especially in circular constructions, was not followed or even essayed in S. Stephen; it exacted too much constructive science, too much practice, too much time and expense, to allow the poor Roman artificers of that time to make use of it, and they contented themselves with the placid and natural charm that the eye receives from the regular gyration of columns, happy to be able to follow their own old, easy and profitable way of working with materials picked up here and there. So that S. Stephen may be defined as a basilica with fine gyrating naves forming two half-circles so faced as to make one rotunda. The only detail which betrays the Byzantine influence is the large circumference of the columns, which is interrupted by eight pilasters forming as many groups as was sometimes the manner of the Greeks. I may add that the arches do not immediately rest on the capitals but on the abaci or "pulvini"—a characteristic of the Byzantine style, which, since the first half of the fifth century, had appeared in Ravenna in the church of S. John the Evangelist and in the Baptistery Ursiano, and continued to be used in Italy in the sixth and following centuries.* The profile of the abaci of S. Stephen is that of a gola of timid projection, limited below and above by two listels. Those resting on the minor Ionic columns † are plain, and those of the Corinthian that mark the ancient axis of the church, are adorned by a cross.

This rotunda seems to have displayed a truly Oriental luxury in its mosaic decorations, but specially in the incrustations of marble on the walls which, according to the Florentine Giovanni Rucellai, who saw it in 1450, were resplendent with porphyry, serpentine stones, mother-of-pearl, bunches of grapes, and other beauteous things ("gentilezze"),‡ owed, as we learn from an inscription now lost, to Pope Giovanni I. (523-536). These decorations are analogous to those of S. Vitale of Ravenna and of the Cathedral of Parenzo, Byzantine constructions of the same century.

But if the abaci of the Rotunda of S. Stephen only serve to attest the, perhaps not immediate, influence of the Byzantine style, there are works in other churches that indisputably

---

* Similar "pulvini" also support the arches of S. Angelo of Perugia, a contemporary of S. Stephen of Rome.

† All the Ionic capitals of this church, like the cornice over the columns of the smaller circle, are rough work of the time when it was erected; some are only sketched out: a manifest proof that in that time it was usual to add the decorations on the spot, as was done in later times.

‡ See the interesting and erudite pamphlet of C. De Rossi called the "La Basilica di S. Stefano Rotondo." Rome 1886.

manifest the presence of the Greek artists. The restoration in 1858 of the church of S. Clement on the Celio, famous because it caused the discovery of the true ancient basilica somewhat vaster than the actual church and situated under it, was not less famous for having brought to light a good length of architrave bearing the following inscription: "Altare tibi Deus Salvo Hormisda Papa Mercurius presbyter cum sociis of (fert). Having read this, the archæologist at once remembered two antique columns that decorate the monument to Cardinal Venerio of Recanati existing in the same church, one of which bears on its capital this other inscription: " + MERCURIUS PS SCE

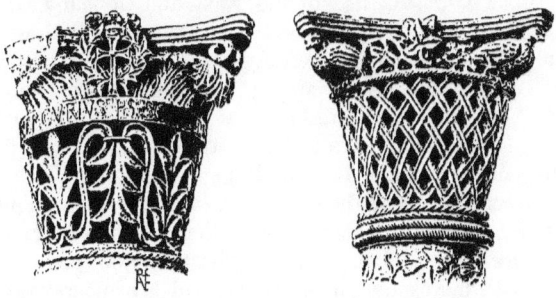

Fig. 7.—Capitals of the ancient Ciborium of S. Clement, Rome—A.D. 514-523.

E. S DNI," and came to the well-founded conclusion that the said columns and architrave must have formed part of the ciborium of the antique basilica erected during the time of Pope Hormisda (514-523) by that priest Giovanni called Mercurius, who was afterwards Pope Giovanni II. Well, those two columns arabesqued with reliefs like ivy twining round them, are without doubt Roman, but the capitals above them present the Byzantine style in its purest originality, because they are made like baskets, decorated with meanders in open-work, and with crosses and doves under their abacus. It is plain that such conceits could only issue from Greek chisels.

But that is not all. This happy discovery guided De Rossi to another not less important: it led him to the just suspicion that many of the sculptured slabs composing the chancel of the choir of the actual basilica, which bear the monogram of a Giovanni, and which had till then been attributed to the eighth Pope of that name, who reigned in the ninth century, belong to the same Giovanni called Mercurius, who constructed the above-named ciborium.* And De Rossi's suspicion can only change to certainty when we attentively observe that those parapets and many of their "pilastrini," with the exception of the additions made in the twelfth century, when they were taken from the lower to be placed in the upper church, far from presenting the style of decoration of the ninth century, clearly present that of the sixth, as it was in use in the East and in many cities of Italy.† Such are those crosses in squares and those very elegant garlands enclosing monograms and bound by floating ribbons ending in leaves of ivy and in crosses, numerous examples of which are preserved at Jerusalem, Byzantium, Thessalonica, not to speak of Pola, Parenzo, Grado, the islands of the lagoons, Ravenna, Rimini, Bologna, and all those islands where Greek influence had been powerful. Of conspicuous Byzantine character are also certain other parapets covered with woven work like matting and perforated, and certain little pilasters with leaves and pomegranates which in no way resemble the subjects employed in Roman decorations.

We should also hold the precious sculptures of the old church of S. Clement in high consideration, because these parapets, though partly mutilated, are the least incomplete type that remains to us of the chancels of the sixth century, and the architrave with the two columns mentioned above is the most ancient remnant known of an altar-ciborium. It is a pity that we know not whether, besides that mean architrave, there was some frieze or tympanum, as Rohault de Fleury ‡ supposes, or whether there was only a cornice. But however it might have been completed, it never could have been com-

* Selvatico and all the writers on Italian art continue to repeat the old error just as if De Rossi had not published his beautiful discovery.
† De Rossi, " Bullettino," 1869.
‡ " La Messe."

posed of various pyramidal orders of columns terminating with an octagonal roof or frontispiece such as may be seen in several churches of Rome and about Naples. Selvatico,* at Lenoir's † suggestion, would have us to believe it was. In fact, the kind of ciborium which he points out to us in S. George at Velabro, in S. Crisogono, in S. Laurence-beyond-the-Walls, and in the upper church of S. Clement, does not date, as he rashly asserted, from the sixth or seventh centuries, but only from the twelfth or the following century.

Other churches in Rome offer us indubitable traces of the purest Byzantine style. One of these is the old church of S. Maria in Cosmedin, which, founded by S. Damaso in 380, seems to have been restored by Belisarius in 536.‡ This tradition is sustained by the fact that, annexed to this church, there was, in the sixth century, a diaconia under the name of *Schola Græca* established there by the Greeks living in Rome, and further finds express confirmation in certain sculptures of a character absolutely Byzantine, which we will now examine, and which were not passed over in the rebuildings of the eighth century. The "Liber pontificalis" recounts that this church, before being rebuilt by Adrian I., was of very small dimensions; and that was enough for Crescimbeni § and Rohault de Fleury to think fit to consider the present crypt (a real basilica with three little naves, a little transept, and walls with niches) as the area, and even as a part of the construction of the church in the sixth century. But such a conjecture is combated—first, by the too scanty dimensions of the construction (m. 8.00 by 3.60); next, evident traces of the eighth century found therein; and lastly, by the impossibility, consequent on the narrowness of the place, to imagine it adorned, as the church of S. Damaso was without doubt, by marbles and large columns, of which there remains one capital in the superior edifice. This is the capital of the fifth column on the left, of that Byzantine composite

* "Le arti del disegno in Italia."
† In Gailhabaud's work, "Monuments anciens et modernes."
‡ See O. Mothes' work, already mentioned.
§ "L'istoria della basilica di Santa Maria in Cosmedin di Roma," 1717.

which was so familiar to the Greeks in the fifth and sixth centuries. What renders the style most characteristic is the wide chalice form, and especially the minute thorny intaglio of

Fig. 8.—Parapet and little Pilaster of S. Clement, Rome—A.D. 514-523.

the acanthus leaves, obtained with much labour of drilling. One sees similar capitals not only in the churches of Greece, but also in those of Istria, the Gulf of Venice, Ravenna, and other cities of Italy where the Byzantine influence was felt. And my assertion as to the Greek origin of this capital is validly supported by seeing it used in the edifices of Constantinople[*] from the fifth century, and the fact that it only appeared in Italy in the sixth.

But it is not only that capital that reminds one of the

[*] For example, in the church of S. John the Evangelist, still existing.

Greek S. Maria in Cosmedin of the sixth century, but also a fragment of a parapet which now serves as a "predella" at the altar of the crypt. It was adorned by foliage inscribed with squares placed angularly and framed by thin mouldings, the whole being executed in that rather hard but elegant style which characterises the chancels of S. Clement's. Four other parapets of the same style, with scantlings, discs, crosses, flowered squares, &c., closed the two extreme inter-columns of the presbytery until 1712, when they were thrown into a courtyard, where they were still to be seen in the time of Crescimbeni, who gives drawings of them.

Traces of Proto-Byzantine style also remain in the basilica of S. Saba, which rises solitarily on the summit of a hill near the Aventine—traces which, in my opinion, validly establish the date, hitherto uncertain,* of its first foundation, assigning to it the first half of the sixth century. The errors given out by Selvatico about this church are such as not to be tolerated even from the lips of a street cicerone. Starting with the assumption that the Greeks (that is to say the Basilian monks) were its probable founders, and therefore that the greater part of it, or at least its primitive part, should be Greek, he assigned to the sixth century the vestibule that precedes the courtyard of the church; declared unhesitatingly the Byzantine origin of the artist who painted two figures of saints beneath it ; alleged that the back of the high altar was analogous to the Greek *iconostasi*, and formed of antique fragments, and noticed as a somewhat rare decoration in churches of Latin origin certain " detached arcades of the interior walls." Now all this is false. The vestibule, with

* At the back of the confessional there exists an inscription bearing the name of a Pope Gregory, supposed to be Gregory the Great of the sixth century, and also supposed to allude to the period of the foundation of the church. But Oderici (see " Gasparis Aloysii Oderici Dissertationes ed Adnotationes "), observing the square C of the inscription belongs to the eighth century at least, and not the sixth or seventh, judged that it referred to one of the two Gregories who succeeded each other in the first half of the eighth century. But even Oderici had not aimed rightly; he did not observe that several A's, entirely Roman in character, could not be of earlier period than 1187, or, still better, 1227-1241 ; and my conjecture becomes a very likely one when we remember that the church itself was embellished in neo-Latin style by Roman marble-workers in the first half of the thirteenth century.

its columns, consoles, and marquetries, is work of the twelfth or following century; its pictures are uncouth work of the last century; the architectural fond of the chief altar is late work of the sixteenth or seventeenth century; it has *no* antique fragments, and was never made to remind one of the *iconostasi*; the detached arcades do not decorate all the walls, but only the northern ones; they are not detached because the columns are obviously walled, and finally, they do not simply serve for decoration because they must once have composed a real portico.

Now, how can one explain similar blunders without admitting the greatest carelessness in Selvatico? How can one believe that he had seen S. Saba before describing and analysing its details? Perhaps he never saw it, but contented himself with only looking at pictures of it and reading the studies of Lenoir, published in the work of Gailhabaud—studies wherein ignorance of history contends with want of logic. Probably the illustrious Marquis was guilty of making them too often the basis of his own opinions—thus avoiding the trouble of travelling, and sitting commodiously at his writing-table instead.

But while Lenoir and Selvatico lost themselves in seeking Greek traces where none existed, they missed finding them in one of the capitals of the left nave, which is a composite of Proto-Byzantine style of the same manner as that of S. Maria in Cosmedin.

The interesting basilica of S. Praxeda on the Esquilino can also show some Byzantine works of the sixth century. The most important is the architrave of the principal door that gives on to the public road, richly sculptured with the leaves of the wild acanthus, with roses and pomegranates, reminding one of friezes of the same kind and of the same period at Jerusalem and in the churches of Central Syria.

The same chisel may be recognised on the socles and bases of the interior columns of the chapel of S. Zenone within the same basilica, excepting in those decorations that refer to the Roman epoch, or were added, as we shall see, in the ninth century, when that chapel was constructed. To the sixth century and to Greek chisels one must also ascribe the two

Ionic capitals at the entrance of the same chapel and the little cornice that runs behind it.

The fact that the capitals are sculptured even on the sides adhering to the wall, and that the mutilated cornice is much longer than was required for the door, is a proof of these works being anterior to the ninth century; add to this the style of their sculptures, akin to those of S. Clement on Mount Cœlio.

At Rome the Greek chisels of the sixth century did not exercise themselves only in sacred buildings, since there exists a remarkable secular monument in which their style is discernible. It is the solid bridge over the Aniene on the Via Salaria, at a short distance from the city, and, according to a long inscription, was constructed in the year 565, under the Emperor Justinian, by the eunuch Narsete, after the victory over the Goths—the old bridge having been destroyed by the " most wicked " Totila.

The Byzantine style of the sixth century appears conspicuously in the parapets of the quays, which, like the parapets of the contemporaneous churches, are adorned with meagre squares enclosing imbrications, or rhombs, sometimes plain, sometimes filled, and accompanied by crosses, stars, or girandole roses. The slabs alternate with pilastrini, quadrated with mixed lines enclosing imbrications, and always crowned either by a species of square cupola or by paterae presenting concentric circles, stars, or crosses.

Among the ruins of Central Syria one finds absolutely similar ones, precisely because they are of the same family and epoch.

Works of sculpture that show the Byzantine manner are also the doors carved in nut-wood of S. Sabina on the Aventine. A tradition—we do not know if it be well founded or not—speaks of it as executed in the time of Innocent III. (1198-1216), but artistic examination is far from confirming this fancy. If Cavalcaselle, who thinks he sees in it an antique mode of working, timidly contents himself with suspecting that they were made before the eleventh century, I venture to assign to them the fifth century or the first half of the sixth.

We have seen how the sarcophagi at Ravenna of the Esarch Isaac and the Archbishop Theodore confused the opinions of Cavalcaselle about the worth of Italian sculpture in the seventh century, how he declared it to be more free from imperfections because free from the exigencies of chiaroscuro and colour to which the art of painting is always subject. But we who have seen what was really done in sculpture at Ravenna in the seventh century, and the miserable things made in Italy up to the eleventh, must conclude, in spite of his opinion, that neither painting nor mosaic work fell so low in that time as sculpture. What most confirms my opinion within the doors of S. Sabina, is the ornamentation with mouldings cut into spindles and baguets, which finely frames the various figurative compositions. The baguets especially, formed by winding vine-branches, adorned with leaves and grapes and noble and elegant open-work, remind one of similar things in the capitals, sarcophagi, and throne of S. Maximilan of Ravenna.*

Till now we have seen the Byzantine style peeping out in Rome through simple bits of decoration, but now we see it appears more freely even in certain organic portions of two sacred edifices of the same city. One is S. Laurence-beyond-the-Walls.

It was erected in the time of Constantine almost on the same level as the catacombs, for which reason it was necessary to cut down the hill that enclosed it. It bore the basilical form, covered a not very extensive area, and was decorated by ten great Corinthian, channelled columns of violet marble, without doubt taken from older edifices. Eight of them served to divide the lateral naves, and two rose in front of the apsis. The basilica was then turned towards the east, but it would be a mistake to think that it opened towards the sunrise, because the hill which surrounds and overshadows it even now by a height of three metres (which must have been greater at that time) could not permit it. The natural entrances of the

* Unfortunately, while the figures are almost all the originals, the ornaments have lately been remade. The patterns of the old ones, which had perished in course of time, have, however, been followed.

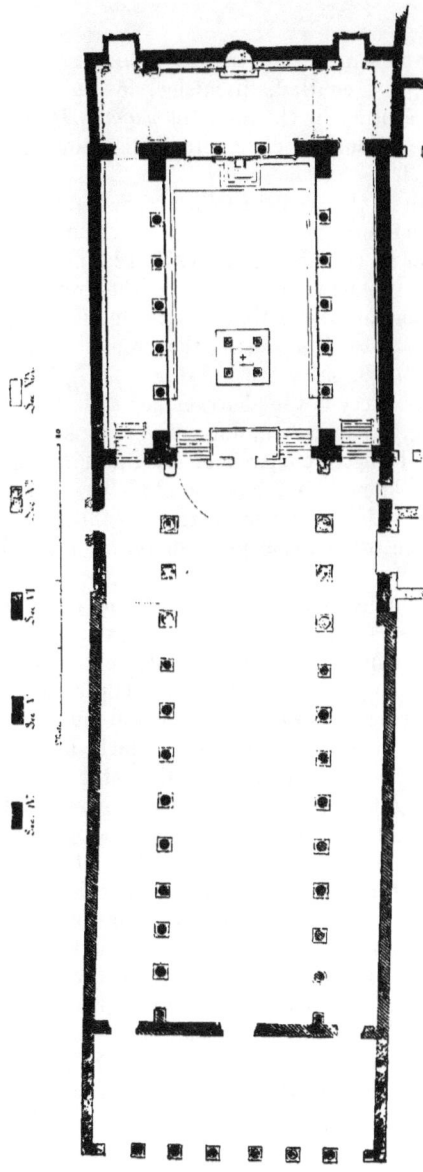

Fig. 9.—Plan of S. Laurence-beyond-the-Walls at Rome.

basilica at that time were towards the west, and there were only two of them lateral to the apsis and corresponding to the two minor naves, to which it was necessary to descend by steps. And from this side also, by a singular anomaly, the false façade of this church presented itself, probably decorated by a columned portico.

So remained the church till the pontificate of Sextus III. (432-440), who (this portico being destroyed) backed on the basilica of Constantine another and larger basilica, building it on the same plane as the street and turning it to the west, so that the apsis of each church turned its back to the apsis of the other, just like the great niches of the famous temple of Venus at Rome; and one could only arrive at the old inferior basilica by traversing the new one of Sextus III, which was also dedicated to the Virgin, and contradistinguished by the topographists of the seventh century by the name of *major*. It had three naves and sixteen columns of different diameter and quality, because derived from ancient ruins.

This is the real origin of the second basilica of S. Laurence, whose foundation, till not many years ago, was erroneously attributed to Adrian I. or to Honorius III. (1216-1227). The latter only restored the two basilicas, destroyed the two contiguous apsides, and, prolonging the sistina by six columns, made of the two edifices one vast basilica, raising the ground of that of Constantine so that it might serve as presbytery.

We owe this happy discovery to the above-named and praised De Rossi, who, according to his custom, did not fail to have it printed at once in his "Bullettino d'Archeologia Cristiana," so that the studious might know of it; but the studious are few in Italy, and not only the guides, but also the recent publications of Selvatico, Chirtani, and others, continued to repeat the old rank error.

Nevertheless, it is my opinion that except the mere stems of the columns with their respective bases, and perhaps some space of the wall, nothing remains of the church of Sextus III. Honorius III., after prolonging its naves, had sculptured all the Ionic capitals of the twenty-two columns and the four antæ of the caps, besides the modillioned cornices which he had lightened by relieving arches with stilted feet, that still appear under the lateral naves. And it is easy to persuade oneself that those Ionic capitals belong to the time of Honorius rather than to antique pagan construction, as is commonly thought, when one observes that, while they all display the same chisel and present the same design, yet at the same time they perfectly adapt themselves to all the stems of the columns, though these are of very varied dimensions, the difference between the larger and lesser ones being not less than forty centimetres. The profile of these capitals is of the same date and character as those of the porticos of SS. John and Paul and of S. George in Velabro, works of the thirteenth century (which are also

Ionic), and even the beautiful portico before the basilica of S. Laurence, indubitably the work of Honorius III. Here, then, we have a church almost entire, endowed with splendid accessories, with mosaic pavement, with ambos, pulpit, ciborium, and tombs, which we ought to value as the principal monument in Rome built in that beautiful style, true Renaissance, produced by the conjunction of Arab-Sicilian art with Lombard-Tuscan, improperly called Cosmatesco,* and which I prefer to contradistinguish by the name of neo-Latin.

But when Honorius III. united the two basilicas, the inferior one had somewhat changed. An inscription in mosaic legible on the apsis, destroyed on this occasion, praised the Pontiff Pelagio II. (578-590), who, cutting away the hill which threatened to crush the old basilica, had amplified it and given it more light. De Rossi is of opinion that the enlargement made by Pelagio was effected by prolonging the naves and the apsis—a prolongation which seems countersigned by the two columns that are shorter than the others, and have capitals with victories or trophies rather composite than Corinthian. I accept this conjecture, which is additionally supported by the fact that the cubic pedestals underneath these two short columns present mouldings and rosettes which accord well with the sixth century; but, besides that, I believe that the church was also enlarged towards the east, and precisely at the extremities of that transversal nave, or "narteci," which, closing the church in a straight line, now serves for its background. An accurate and

* I find this term unfitting for several reasons. First, I cannot comprehend why a family of artists in which only one, and not the first, bore the name of Cosimo should be called "dei Cosmati," when the grandfather, Lorenzo, and the father, Jacopo, had worked in the same style long before Cosimo was born. In the second place, even accepting the term for a moment, I do not find it just or reasonable to honour with the right to give its name to a certain style of work, a family of artists who, although they had treated that style in a praiseworthy manner for a century and a half, yet was not the only artistic family that Rome could reckon, nor the most ancient, nor the most illustrious, since they had no hand, as inscriptions plainly show, in the older and more important works of that style, such as the ciborium of S. Laurence-beyond-the-Walls, the famous cloisters of the Lateran and of S. Paul, and most probably not even in the other parts of the Basilica of S. Laurence, which, judging by similarity of form, one should rather ascribe to that Giovanni di Guido who worked in S. Maria-in-Castello at Corneto in 1209,

intimate examination recently brought by me to bear on those walls, whose design seemed to me independent of the rest of the work, made me withdraw from the idea that they could ever have formed part of the primitive basilica and persuaded me that, if not the work of Pelagio, he certainly profited by them to complete that extremity and so enlarge the basilica.

It was an important matter for Pelagio to regulate the church on this side so that the galleries placed above the naves might have a useful and easy support.

And here comes a question not yet resolved, namely, whether the use of the galleries, or "matronei," was common to the Christian basilicas of both the East and West, and which adopted it first. The fact that the primitive great Constantinian basilicas of Rome had no galleries, as also that the greater number of the oldest churches in Rome neither had nor have them, would seem to support the opinion of those who think that they were an entirely Oriental introduction. In fact, in the East, the galleries began to appear in the fourth century (see, for example, the basilica of the Calvario, erected by Constantine and fully described by Eusebius). Many basilicas of the fifth century in Syria and Greece also have them, and almost all of the Oriental churches of the succeeding centuries; thus, as it seems that, in the West, churches with galleries form an exception, and in the East churches without them are exceptional, it logically follows that we ought to believe that those galleries are nothing but a custom introduced by the Eastern Church; and that, if they have appeared in any Latin church, it is only owing to the efficacious Byzantine influence repeatedly exercised on the West. Such a conjecture would, it seems to me, assume every aspect of truth were we able to prove that the two largest basilicas in Rome which have galleries, date, like the church of S. Vitale, from the sixth or following century, and bear indubitable marks of the Byzantine school. This I will endeavour to prove.

The great columns of the lower basilica of S. Laurence do not support arches, but architraves with friezes and cornices, which, far from being sculptured on purpose for the church, present an assemblage of fragments gathered from the broken materials of old Rome and here put together as best might be. But of this came an entablature of rich but barbarous taste, where mouldings of varied profiles are made to join together, and cornices once intended to run vertically are now placed in horizontal position.

It is difficult to believe that, in the first half of the fourth century, one of the most venerated sanctuaries of the city should have been built in such an awkward way, especially since the pagan edifices, being generally, at that time, whole and well preserved, did not offer the same temptation to thieving architects and constructors as when they began to fall into ruins. Again, seeing the same work, made out of *débris*, go on without indication of later additions even in the part prolonged by Pelagio, I am more than ever persuaded that the entablature in question must be referred to the restorations made by that Pontiff. In fact, by its awkwardness it accuses the poverty and coarseness of that epoch, and makes us think sadly of the consequent abandonment and decay of the marvellous structures of Rome, which began to change the city into a mass of ruins.

Now why did the architects of Pelagio give themselves the trouble to put together all these fragments of cornices instead of putting arches between one column and the other, as was then generally done? What motive could induce them to embrace such an imperfect and, for them, arduous task, and abandon another which was easier, more natural, certainly more beautiful? In my opinion the reason was simply this—that, intending to build galleries over the naves, they foresaw that these would become too elevated if they developed arches over the already very high inferior columns. They calculated, moreover, that the want of proportion between the higher and lower series would have seemed too evident.

The entablature having thus been established at the time of the restorations made by Pelagio, and there being no other reason for the superposition of the galleries, it clearly follows that then only were they constructed.

Nor are these the only arguments that support me in this

opinion; the strongest exist in the architecture of those galleries. They are formed of channelled columns, of Greek marbles, and Corinthian columns, all taken from various pagan edifices, notwithstanding that the stems of the columns are all of the same height and diameter; between the stems the parapets are fixed, now of Serravezza marble, but once of porphyry, stolen by that egregious thief, Napoleon I. Over the same columns we have not, as below, entablature, but arches. These, however, are not planted directly on the capitals, as was the practice in the fourth century, but on a species of cushion, or abacus, in the form of a bracket which we so often see used in Byzantine constructions, and of which we have in S. Stephen's the most ancient example that remains in Rome. This architectonic member, of which the Orientals were the inventors, while it offered to the feet of the arches a base corresponding to the thickness of the wall that they supported, allowed the support underneath to be much narrower and more slender without danger to the real solidity of the edifice.

But better remains; in the smallest side of the gallery, opposite the triumphal arch, as if they had wished to utilise two short columns of very precious green porphyry, they put under them two cubic socles which recall in their whole form that of the two large lower columns. Their faces are adorned by crosses among roses and between the Alpha and Omega, and their sides by a vase with leafage and doves: reproductions after the Greek style, like those of the sixth century, to be seen in the churches of Ravenna. Finally, the two capitals of these columns are not antique Corinthians like the others, but were evidently made for the basilica in a style of sculpture entirely Byzantine, like many of Ravenna, of Parenzo, and of Venice.

We do not know if all the walls of the basilica were covered with mosaic by Pelagio II. Certainly the destroyed apsis was, and the frontal arch that is still preserved, though partly spoiled by restorations. Among the various figures of saints, that Pope is also portrayed with the model of the church in his hands; and that he was thus represented is a sign that he had made such reforms and innovations in the basilica that he might almost be considered as its second founder. The plan of the old church of S. Laurence is developed in another basilica of the same city—S. Agnes-beyond-the-Walls. The basilica of S. Agnes, which so much resembles that of S. Laurence, had a history almost parallel with it. It also was erected out of the city, and on the level of the catacombs. It seems to rise from the bowels of the earth, and to get to it it is necessary to descend many stairs.

Fig. 10.—Capital of the Galleries of S. Laurence, Rome—A.D. 578-590.

Like S. Laurence, it was built in the time of Constantine; and, therefore, probably was similarly constructed; but it is certain that, in the beginning of the seventh century, it was already so spoiled by age that Honorious I. (626-640), as soon as he assumed the Pontificate, had to think of reconstructing it. The restorations that it suffered since then do not seem to have removed from it the impression received in the seventh century. It is composed of three longitudinal and one transversal nave that precedes the others. Over the naves are galleries on three sides, and naves and galleries are formed of Corinthian columns bearing arches; one may call it a reproduction, beautiful and corrected, of the S. Laurence of Pelagio II. In S. Agnes, however, it is useless to seek anything among the capitals or the bases contemporaneous with the period of rebuilding that might give one some idea of the skill of the Roman sculptors of that day. With the exception of a few stiff and inexpressive little cornices, some naked and square abaci, adopted because they were necessary, over the little columns of the galleries, and of what belongs to later additions, all the marbles of this church appear to be remnants of pagan constructions. The apsis preserves the mosaics of the time of Honorius I., and here also, as in S. Laurence, the Pope who rebuilt the church has been represented holding a model of it in his hands.

S. Laurence and S. Agnes were perhaps the first examples of churches with galleries which Rome possessed; and if up to that time she had done without them, for what reason did she then adopt them? For æsthetic reasons? At first one would feel inclined to say yes; but afterwards, taking notice of the curious fact that each of the only two churches of Rome that had galleries presents the peculiarity of being planted very low down in the bosom of the earth, the suspicion occurs to me that only through their being rendered damp and unhealthy in the course of time, was recourse had to the galleries, which could be freely frequented by the faithful without danger to their health. And perhaps the transformations and raising of S. Laurence, effected by Honorius III., were called for from similar motives; and, in these days, since Pius IX. restored the antique level in the lower floor of the basilica, it is dangerous, notwithstanding the wide space outside, to remain there long.

To the same Honorius I. the *liber pontificalis* assigns the restoration of the church of the Four Crowned Saints, which had been erected by the Pontiff S. Leo the Great (440-461) on a vast superficies, with three naves divided by twenty-six columns and preceded by a square portico. The actual church, reduced to small proportions, and with galleries inside, must not for that reason be supposed the same as that of the seventh century, but the one Pasquale II. reconstructed in 1117 after the horrible incendiarism of Robert Guiscardo.*

* The Basilica of S. Cecilia in Trastevere, reconstructed about this period, showed galleries that were preserved till the last century. That proves that in Rome, as in

Another restoration of the seventh century was that of the church of S. George at Velabro made by Pope Leo II. (682-684). The interior with three naves formed by antique columns and capitals of various diameters and fashions may rightly be attributed to that miserable epoch, because the wretched technique of the construction of its arches and the barbarous mode in which capitals and abaci of rude and badly balanced forms are united, mark exactly the time of the most profound artistic decadence which reigned in Italy between the middle of the seventh century and the beginning of the eighth.

The *liber pontificalis* points to several other works of some importance executed in Rome in the seventh century, but the subsequent restorations that happened to those edifices, and above all their rebuilding in times nearer to us, have caused us to lose all traces of them. Yet the almost entire absence of edifices of that time in the rest of the peninsula ought to make us content to possess the two that Rome offers us: the very few contemporary traces found in other Italian cities consist only of miserable ruins, fragments of sculpture, or in arid descriptions of lost monuments.

Now, leaving the valley of the Tiber to go back to that of the Po, we hear half-way on a voice that calls us to Lucca to admire two conspicuous monuments. It is the voice of Cordero, delighted, amidst the extreme penury of edifices preserved from the Lombards' time, to read on old parchments of that city that the church of S. Frediano was erected by King Bertari in 686, and that that of S. Michael in Foro was rebuilt by Teutprando and Gumpranda in 764. He then rapidly glanced over these churches and, finding them built according to the old severe basilical rules, and noting especially that in S. Frediano various columns of the naves and many of the capitals were evidently taken from antique Roman constructions, he judged them, without any further examination, to be the actual churches erected by the above-named personages, and proposed them as

several places in and out of Italy, the custom of constructing galleries in the Byzantine style in churches was revived after the commencement of the eleventh century.

types of the sacred edifices used in Italy in the period of the Lombard domination.

Full of this flattering declaration I went to see them myself, but at first entrance experienced the greatest disillusion. With the exception of those few Roman marbles that had perhaps served also for constructions of the seventh and eighth century, everything—arches, cornices, windows, sculptures, even the very walls—showed themselves to be Tuscan-Lombard style, later than the tenth century. I found also to my satisfaction that the learned Ridolfi * had observed the error of Cordero, and stated clearly that the actual S. Frediano is but a re-edification by the Prior Rotone in 1112, and that S. Michael consequently must be held to be a work of the same century.

Therefore one must not accept even the conjecture that in these rebuildings the ichnography of the pre-existent basilicas was followed. We know this by the fact that certain excavations made about ten years ago in S. Frediano, demonstrated that the church of the seventh century arose from a plan quite different to the present.

Selvatico, justly trusting Ridolfi, disputed with Cordero the Lombard origin of these two basilicas, but did not also reject the similar assertion of the same writer in reference to the old Palatine gate at Turin that bears the name of Palazzo delle Torri.

It is a double gate flanked by two polygonal towers, and, like our well-known gate of Verona and those of Autun and Trèves, is surmounted by two small ranges of arcades adorned by little pillars and cornices. The bricks are made of excellent clay, united with a little chalk, very well baked and very large, measuring 44 cent. by 29 — a fact that, together with the style of the edifice, at once shows it to be a purely Roman fabric of the third or fourth century.

Cordero instead endeavours to demonstrate that this gate must be a Lombard work, but his long pages do not in the least succeed in proving this. That in the time of the Lombards and Carlovingians it was the custom of princes to live near or

* Guida di Lucca.

on the gates of the city, especially if those gates were large and well armed, it seems we ought to believe, on the faith of many documents quoted by Cordero himself; but from the fact of this gate having been one of these habitations, its construction by the inhabitants is by no means to be necessarily deduced.

As we must now turn our investigations towards Upper Italy, our thoughts run straight to the only important centre of population and industry that existed in the Lombard time, that is to say Pavia, which, by those barbarians, was made the capital of their own kingdom. But that city fell so often under the pickaxe of its conquerors, and was so often made a prey to the flames, that we seek in vain in it one single stone, much less a building out of the many which the Lombard kings erected there at the end of the sixth century, and in the following one. Of the royal palace there is not one stone left upon another, and the same may be said of the basilicas erected in the seventh century, not excepting that of S. Michael, of which I must say something later on.

Monza.—But the worst of it is that a similar dearth of monuments of that time is to be deplored throughout all Lombardy, whatever may be said by certain writers, according to whom some buildings erected by Queen Teodolinda are still standing. And because these gross errors, instead of being dissipated, reappear in new array in recent publications, like that of Mothes,* it is worth the trouble of halting here for a moment to consider, at least, the most famous of those edifices, namely, the church that Teodolinda erected at Monza, close to her palace,† in honour of S. John the Baptist—a church that, becoming afterwards a celebrated sanctuary, immortalised the name of the pious queen. Whoever tried to reconstruct this antique and bygone edifice in his own imagination would reasonably imagine a Latin basilica divided into naves, separated by old marble columns, terminating in the usual apsis, &c., but if we are to believe what Mabillon ‡ tells us, the church of Teodolinda

---

* Work already cited.
† See " Paolo Diacono."
‡ " Diarium Italicum."

must have had quite another form, and would be still in great part visible in the existing cathedral of Monza. He affirms that the ancient church presented the perfect figure of an equilateral cross, and that the octagon terminated at the first colonnade of the present naves, on which, he adds, still repose the remains of the old façade. He says that the altar occupied the centre of the cross, and that an atrium or quadri-portico preceded the church. In different words, Ricci, Mothes, and others repeat the same thing.

It is useless to waste more breath about it; all these authors have thought fit to refer to the time of Teodolinda those parts of the cathedral that really belong to its total rebuilding in the twelfth century, as one sees by its capitals. It is one of those many errors that we meet with in the history of Art of this period, and which I will not cease to combat till I have proscribed them all, as maintaining confusion and darkness.

The above-named writers do not stop at the interior of the church, but also consider as work of the time of Teodolinda the tympan with bas-reliefs which we see over the greater door of the façade principal, and which represents in two zones, one over the other, the baptism of the Saviour and Teodolinda who, accompanied by her children and her husband Agilulfo, offers to the Baptist the diadem of the cross. Frisi* and Ferrario,† among old writers, also believed this, and among the modern ones Selvatico and Melani,‡ but in evident error, because those figures display nothing of the style of that epoch, and present instead all the characteristics of the time when the church was rebuilt, namely, of the twelfth or following century. This my opinion is founded on a careful examination of the miserable sculpture of Ravenna, the centre of the Esarch's dominions, executed in precisely those years in which Teodolinda erected her church, and is further supported when one considers that on that tympan the queen and her husband are

* " Memorie storiche di Monza e sua Corte."
† " Il costume antico e moderno."
‡ Selvatico, work already cited; Melani, " Scultura Italiana " (Manuali Hoepli).

represented with the crown on their heads, while from what we know, the Lombard kings did not wear one.

The only sculpture that might have proceeded from the chisels which Teodolinda had at her disposal, is a slab of marble incrusted in the wall of the façade by the side of the magnificent porch, showing the monogram of Jesus Christ enclosed in a circle, flanked by two crosses, from each of which hang attached to little chains the A and the Ω, symbols (according to Mons. Barbier de Montault*) of the Trinity. These sculp-

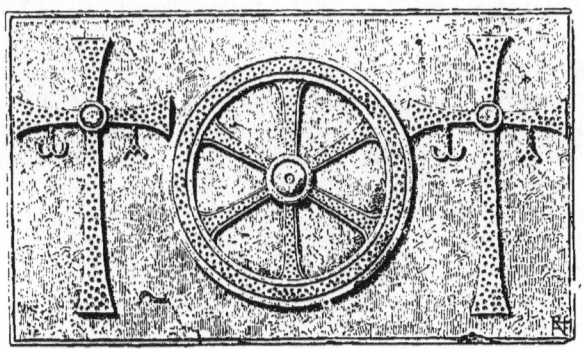

FIG. 11.—Slab of Marble at S. John's, Monza—Beginning of the VIIth Century.

tures in bas-relief, hard and coarse, childishly enriched by a multitude of drilled holes, bear testimony to the miserable condition to which the calamities before alluded to had reduced Italian art at the beginning of the seventh century.

Many are the sacred edifices of Lombardy and other countries † that, according to popular tradition, owed their origin

* " Inventaires de la Basilique royale de Monza."
† I was much surprised to read that Ricci, rejecting the tradition that ascribes the foundation of the baptistery of Florence to Theodoric, should so easily accept the one attributing it to Teodolinda. He props up his conjecture by noticing certain imperfections in the internal columns; but it is easy to see that the author has caught a monstrous crab. But quite recently the Arch. Aristide Nardini-Despotti-Mospignoti, wrote in the Florentine periodical, *Arte e Storia* (June 15, 1888), that, according to his judgment, S. John, nearly as it now appears, is not a pagan edifice, as Villani believed it to be, nor of the Lombard era, but a church belonging to primi-

to the legendary queen; but time has not spared us even one: an undoubted proof either of their infirm structure or extreme artistic imperfection, which forced succeeding generations to pull them down and substitute better fabrics in their place.

GRADO.—The Italian region to which with some profit we will now direct our researches is Venetia, where we find three edifices of the second half of the sixth century; two churches, and a baptistery of the once famous city of Grado.

Secundus, Archbishop of Aquileia, had taken refuge here, bearing with him the treasures of his church, when he found himself menaced by the terrible scourge of the Huns (A.D. 452), after which Niceta, his successor, returned to the desolated metropolis, restored modestly some of the least damaged edifices, and recalled the fugitives still living. Later on, the approach of the Goths (A.D. 480) constrained the Archbishop Marcellino to take refuge in Grado—a seat that several of his successors preferred to Aquileia. But after Friuli had been invaded by the Lombards (A.D. 568) and the archbishop Paulin had been obliged to retake the road to which misfortune had guided him, his successor, the Patriarch Elia, with the consent of the Pope, made Grado his fixed residence, and proclaimed it a metropolitan city.

It is said that in A.D. 456 Niceta had here erected a church dedicated to S. Euphemia, which, being a century afterwards embellished by Elia, was chosen by him for the cathedral. But whoever examines this church attentively will be persuaded that with the exception, perhaps, of a few

tive Christian architecture, built at the end of the fourth century or at the beginning of the fifth !

It would have been better that he should have supported this gratuitous assertion with the convincing proofs that he says he possesses, and without which no one to-day can believe him. But as I am persuaded that he is quite without such proofs, I do not fear to affirm that the interior and, in great part, the exterior of the beautiful church of S. John, in my opinion, cannot be of earlier date than the second half of the eleventh century, nor do I feel inclined to concede that the bare skeleton of the walls of the octagon could be referred to the fifth or sixth century, seeing that the size of the edifice is too far removed from the by no means colossal designs of the times of Galla Placidia and Teodolinda. I will give my reason in my " Architectonic History of the Basilica of S. Mark at Venice."

coarse Corinthian capitals of a style still Roman, which may be assigned to the fifth century, all, both the framework and such details as are not the fruit of later reparations, show the sixth century.

One must believe, then, that the work of Elia (A.D. 576-586) was an entire refabrication of the church of Niceta, which could neither be so vast nor so rich, since that archbishop built it in the anguish of exile and with the firm intention, afterwards effected, to return to Aquileia. And the mosaic inscription which we read on the fine pavement of the church speaks clearly, attributing to no other than Elia the glory of having raised this basilica; and, as every one knows, that pavement is a precious work of the sixth century.

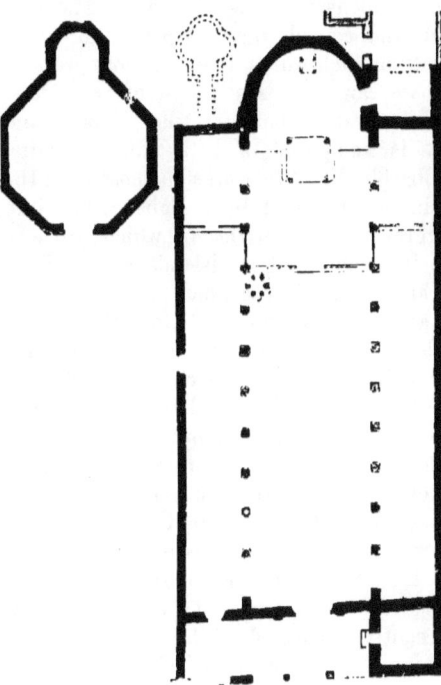

FIG. 12.—Plan of the Cathedral and Baptistery of Grado—A.D. 571-586.

This church is 46 metres long, and is composed of an exterior atrium and three separate naves divided by twenty columns of marble, several of which are of batio and others of cipollino, Greek marble, or coralline breccia. Like all Greek and Italian basilicas of the sixth century, the central nave only is terminated by an apsis which, like Byzantine ones and those of Ravenna, is curvilinear in the interior and polygonal outside. There remain no more traces of the mosaic and marble decorations that no doubt made this apsis not inferior to the splendid one of the cathedral of Parenzo, since the mosaic pavements of both churches show the same character and equal magnificence. But in compensation the Grado pavement is in great part preserved, and considering the period in which it was made and the rarity of such works, it is the most precious thing of the kind that we can see. Its design of varied and always elegant motives, partakes both of the Roman and Byzantine schools. It is composed of little bits of white, red, yellow, and black marble, like the works in mosaic on the walls; for the use of incrustations of little slabs carved into various geometrical figures, of *opus sectile*, of which we have such beautiful samples in Venice and its islands, and at Pisa, Rome, and Palermo, came from Greece much later, and only in the ninth century appeared in Italy. Before this epoch, if pavements were made in mosaic they were always, like this of Grado, in *opus vermiculatum*; in several cities considerable remains of them are to be seen. What renders this of Grado still more precious are the many inscriptions, also in mosaic, that it presents, which record the names of those that contributed with money towards its fabrication and the number of square feet of work proportionated to their respective offerings. Nor was this a speciality of the basilica of Grado, as we find it again in the remains of the church of S. Felix of Aquileia, in the few fragments of the pavement of the cathedral of Parenzo, in those recently discovered of the old cathedral of Verona, and in the remains of the ancient cathedral of Brescia. The custom, however strange, and certainly not very conformable to the evangelical humility, must have been usual, and perhaps was so simply because it was profitable, if one reflects that in all times there have been some of the faithful whose liberality was more influenced by pride than piety.

Before the apsis is the choir, raised by three low steps that perhaps were at the first only two higher ones; in the central nave it extends to the last column but two; in the lateral naves to the penultimate ones only. It must have been closed with parapets, of which one sees the remains in the pavement of the apsis and in a courtyard behind the church, and, like those of the Greek churches and of S. Clement's at Rome, it was adorned with crosses, wreaths, and ribbons. This raising of the choir must be held contemporaneous with the edification of the church, being evidently premeditated by the prudent architect. This we infer from the fact that the bases of all the columns do not immediately repose on the pavement, but on a cubic socle corresponding exactly to the elevation of the choir, so that those within the balustrades may not be too low.

Similar socles are seen to have been used in several Italian basilicas of the same century, and we therefore deduce that they were the result of a like prudence, and that those churches, especially if bearing the Byzantine character, had choirs slightly raised, though this is in discord with the Oriental rite which did not admit of any raising whatever. That in the sixth century, contrary to some opinions, very high choirs were sometimes used, is witnessed by S. Apollinaris-in-Classe, near Ravenna, which was raised by twelve steps, as is proved by the confession underneath, synchronical with the basilica.

Any artist entering this cathedral for the first time will be struck with a very strange circumstance: while the twenty capitals of the columns show various forms and diverse styles, all have on each face of their abacus an elegant rose or a sunflower; but if he looks sharply at them he will not be long in observing that it is nothing but a simple imposition of stucco-work apparently of the last century, when it was thought fit to mend with the same material certain chipped foliage or broken leaves and even entire capitals, with what taste the reader may imagine for himself. Enough to say that to one Corinthian capital volutes of a composite order were added, and those newly disguised are of the most awkward rococo in the world. But with the exception of these "sgorbs," the capitals clearly fall into two distinct classes, one anterior to the sixth century, and probably used by Elia to save time and expense, the other contemporaneous with the building of the edifice by Elia.

In the first class we have Corinthian and composite antiques in the Greek and Latin style; some of them very coarse and resembling those of S. John the Baptist at Ravenna built in the fifth century by Galla Placidia. One is bell-shaped with lily-leaves issuing from a lower circle of acanthus-leaves, like two of the capitals of S. Mark at Venice, one at Constantinople, and those of the celebrated Tower of the Winds at Athens.

The seven capitals of the second class are all of one design and from one chisel, composite, savouring of the Byzantine, with thorny acanthus-leaves of minute intaglio obtained by much use of the drill; in fact, such as we see in the Greek churches at Parenzo, Ravenna, Rome, and elsewhere. These capitals, the parapets, the pavement, the ichnography of the church, and other particulars show clearly that the constructors of this basilica were Greeks, probably called here on purpose by the Patriarch Elia, who was himself a Greek.

Where our cathedral somewhat differs from the Byzantine style is in having its arches planted on the capitals of the columns without the help of either high or low plinths. From these arches spring the high walls sustaining the bare-beamed roof, under which were numerous arched windows of medium size of which we see the traces externally, and which perhaps at one time were closed *trafori* in marble like the one which now lies behind the church. Those windows now appear flanked by truncated stones on which blind arches must originally have rested, as in S. Apollinaris-in-Classe at Ravenna, in which basilica the two graduated console-formed projections of the walls, under the lower extremities of the frontons, find their counterparts.

The atrium of the church had originally five arcades, the two lateral ones supported by piedroits, that of the centre being planted on two columns, one of which is now replaced by a terra-cotta pilaster. The only remaining one is of precious proconneso; it has no capital, but only an abacus of medium height. The three doors are rectangular; they have quite bare posts, and, above the architrave of the central one is a blind arch after the Greek fashion.

The campanile (belfry) was built much later, to the detriment of the atrium. Selvatico says it is of cylindrical form, and declares it therefore to be one of the oldest in Venetia; which is totally false. The campanile of Grado is square, and Selvatico evidently confounded it with that of the cathedral of Caorle! Yet they are miles apart.

Fig. 13.—Capital and Open-work of Window, Cathedral of Grado —A.D. 571-586.

Near the cathedral, but separated from it, rises the Baptistery, which, although now reduced to its mere mural bones, nevertheless clearly belongs to the epoch of the neighbouring basilica. It is an octagon of about 12 metres in diameter supporting a cupola *a spicchi*, and covered with an octahedron roof. It has only one door, and on the opposite side to this opens a low, deep apsis curved within and polygonal without, like that of the dome. Nothing remains of the pavement, the font, or the decorations, to give one an idea of what the edifice may have been when first built.

A few steps from the cathedral rises the church of S. Maria, which is certainly its contemporary, because it shows in its essence the same character and style of building and ornamentation. It is 20 metres long, has no atrium, and is divided by ten columns into three naves of which the central one alone terminates in the apsis.

The most conspicuous originalities presented by this church are its two chambers by the side of the apsis corresponding to modern sacristies, to which access is given by two doors pierced in the walls at the end of the lateral naves. There is no doubt of the synchronism of this part with the rest of the church, because the walls show no signs of any additions, and the mosaic pavement does not stop at the doors of these cells, but continues and covers them with the same splendour and with a design that adapts itself perfectly to the irregularity of the curve of the apsis wall. These two cells will be held by many as a singularity of our church, it being commonly believed that till towards the end of the Middle Ages all churches were unprovided with special rooms to be used as sacristies, and that the ends of the lateral naves or their apsides supplied their place.

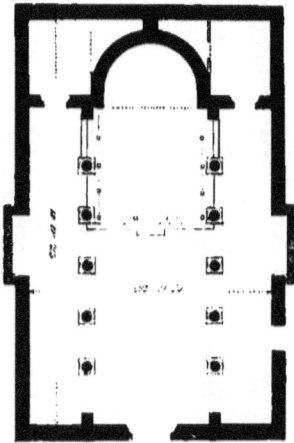

Fig. 14.—Plan of S. Maria of Grado —A.D. 571-586.

That this frequently happened, many antique churches without trace of sacristies bear witness, and S. Paul of Nola witnesses to it when he writes that in his new basilica he had disposed to the right and left two apsidioles in place of them to hold the book and objects of the sacred ministry. But that does not abolish the fact that, in the greater number of the churches of the early centuries, there were real sacristies joined to the rest of the church, but always distinct from the naves.

In large basilicas it seems that the sacristies were found near the vestibule, at the entrance of the church. The sacristy of the old church of S. Peter in the Vatican had the form of a small basilica with apsis, chapels, and columns, and was joined to the entrance-portico. At S. John Lateran, on the contrary, the oratory of S. Thomas served for sacristy, and at S. Praxeda that of S. Zenone.

In the East the churches without sacristies really form an exception. It is enough to open the very valuable work of Vogüé † to convince oneself that, in the fifth and sixth centuries, in Central Syria, at any rate, sacristies were an integral part of all churches. Of whatever form the latter may be, we always see two rectangular rooms invariably situated at the side of the apsis, with their entrance in the end of the lateral naves, and often communicating directly with the apsis itself. It is a remarkable fact that in the greater number of those churches only one of these rooms communicate with the nave by means of a door, while the other is almost a prolongation of it, because instead of a door a wide arcade opens into it. It is very probable that the closed room served to contain the sacerdotal vestments, the precious accessories, and the sacred vases, whence the names of *receptorium, restiarium, secretarium, sacrarium* or *sacristia,* and in Greek *gazophylacium, pastophorium, diaconicum;* and that the open room served simply to receive the *oblata*—that is to say, the offerings of the faithful; and the Greeks called it *prothesis* (πρόθησις).

Among the Syrian churches cited by Vogüé there are two whose plan identically reproduces that of the little church of Grado; and this, in my mind, is a new excellent proof that only Greek artists had a hand in the construction of these basilicas. But S. Maria of Grado is not the only Italian church which preserves the ancient sacristies. S. John the Evangelist, at

* Rohault de Fleury, work already cited.
† " L'Architecture civile et religieuse de la Syrie Centrale."

Ravenna, the famous S. Vita of the same city, and S. Apollinaris-in-Classe, have them to this day, and all their characteristics show that they are contemporary with this church. In the first they are rectangular, round in the second, and almost square with a little apsis in the third.

Similarly the cathedral of Ravenna of the fourth century, before it was rebuilt in modern style, had at the end of its four minor naves the same number of rectangular rooms, as we can see from authentic designs.

The basilica of S. Maria Formosa at Pola, erected in 546, of which some ruins remain, had two circular sacristies with large niches around them, and in the cathedral of Parenzo certain cells adjoining it and still existing seem to have served for sacristies.

To return to our church at Grado, its choir is raised by two high steps that occupy the last two bays of the apsis, and must have been girt with chancels of whose balusters we still see traces in several square holes, and of whose parapets some fragments remain in the pavement of the choir itself, and bear fraternal likeness to those of the cathedral. One of them presents a quadrilobe bound by ribbons, like certain others at S. Demetrius of Thessalonica. Here and there the pavements of the naves show remnants of mosaics of the same design as that of the cathedral, and, like the latter, ornamented with the usual inscriptions. The columns present the same varieties of marble as those in the cathedral, and the capitals are still more varied. There are some of Byzantine composite of minute intaglio, one Corinthian of the same style, and two basketed, with delicate ornamentation, exactly like some of those in the Greek churches at Ravenna and Istria, but unfortunately much mutilated, and therefore restored in stucco; for here, too, we have the fatal intervention of the *stucchino*, though more sparing in its sunflowers. Other capitals are either Ionic-Roman with angular volutes, or formless restorations of the centuries later than the sixth. It is to be noted that some of them have the abacus as high as those of Ravenna, and some as low as those of the eleventh century.

The rows of pilasters adherent to the apsis form a species of *cimasa* with the monogram of Jesus Christ inscribed in a circle surrounded with foliage.

These churches of Grado, though the most ancient that Venice has preserved,* escaped the misfortune common to all their sisters, even the younger ones of the cities of the plain; that is to say, they were not sunk lower, or rather the plane of the street around them was not considerably raised—a circumstance perhaps owing to the foresight of the constructors in erecting them on a higher plane (and in fact S. Maria is elevated by three or four steps), but most probably this city is not founded on the soft mud of the lagoons, but on the high, solid downs between them and the sea.

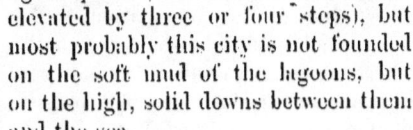
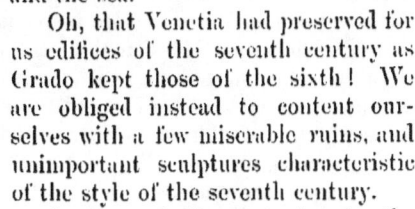
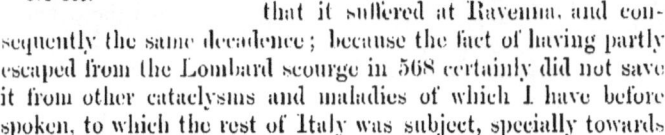

Fig. 15.—Crown of a Pilaster at S. Maria of Grado—A.D. 571-586.

Oh, that Venetia had preserved for us edifices of the seventh century as Grado kept those of the sixth! We are obliged instead to content ourselves with a few miserable ruins, and unimportant sculptures characteristic of the style of the seventh century.

It is probable that Art in the Venetian cities, especially those near the sea, suffered the same troubles that it suffered at Ravenna, and consequently the same decadence; because the fact of having partly escaped from the Lombard scourge in 568 certainly did not save it from other cataclysms and maladies of which I have before spoken, to which the rest of Italy was subject, specially towards the end of the sixth century.

VENICE.—It would be well and useful to be able to point out some work of that period belonging to this region; and I think I shall not go far from the truth in showing you three works of sculpture in Venice which seem to me indubitably to refer to

* Not reckoning the miserable remains of the ancient baptistery of Aquileia, certainly of the fourth century.

those calamitous times, and were perhaps picked up among the flaming ruins of unhappy Altino, destroyed by the Lombards in 641.

The oldest of these sculptures is a front of a sarcophagus in the atrium of the basilica of S. Mark, and which was utilised in the thirteenth century to decorate the urn of Doge Marino Morosini (who died in 1253). It presents two zones sculptured with figures; in the higher zone the Saviour is represented in the midst of His apostles; in the lower one the Virgin is depicted among male and female saints alternating with censers. The frame of the compositions is a band adorned with a cross from which issue vine-branches with grapes, leaves, and birds. These ornaments remind one much of the Byzantine style at Ravenna in the sixth century; but the figures, though in sufficient relief, are so dwarfed and deformed that even the worst of the sarcophagi at Ravenna does not equal them in badness. But, although admitting that Venetian sculptors in those times were more incompetent to reproduce figures than those of Ravenna, it is not reasonable to hold up this ugly work as an example of the sculpture of Altino in the sixth century, but only as a wretched example of the second half of this century.

Perhaps some one might hold a different opinion to mine regarding the origin of this sculpture, deeming it more likely to have been taken from Greece or Ravenna; but I would have him observe that these little figures in their unadorned costume, and their lack of symmetry are too far removed from the Oriental manner. On the contrary, they bear the Latin stamp. Moreover, the custom of subdividing the subject represented into zones does not appear in any of the sarcophagi of Ravenna, in which there exclusively obtains the custom of isolating the figures under niches, or arranging them all in a single line.

If this sculpture shows a very marked artistic decadence, another sarcophagus manifests the absolute fall of Art. It is the sarcophagus in which, in the twelfth century, the doges Giacomo and Lorenzo Tiepolo were deposited. It may be seen under an archivolt of the front of the church of SS. John and Paul.

It recalls in the *ensemble* the ordinary sarcophagi of the Pagans; that is to say, it is of oblong form, is closed with a kind of double lid, and finished at the angles with large antefixes, on which were sculptured the arms of the doges. On the front is the inscription (which has supplanted one more ancient), framed by meagre mouldings and flanked by two angels bearing censers, holding the place of the old Pagan genii. On the front side of the covercle, which is divided into three parts, is sculptured (in the centre) the cross with the two doves underneath, and (on the sides) two smaller crosses planted on globes. One notices most the coarseness of the work when looking at the two figures of the angels. There is still something of roundness in their heads, but the bodies are squat and scraggy, like the saints we saw on the ambos of Ravenna of the same date, not to mention that the lines have lost all idea of truth and taste, being simply like waves of the sea. The angles of the sarcophagi are

Fig. 16.—Sarcophagus at the Church of SS. John and Paul at Venice.

ornamented by two octagonal pilasters with capitals, with a very plain shell.

The form of these pilasters reminds us of another sarcophagus existing in the Archaeological Museum of the Ducal Palace, and which in its design and execution, and also in the characters of the inscription, points to the seventh century. We owe the preservation of this tomb also to the custom common in past centuries of using antique sarcophagi to deposit new dead, for in the sixteenth century a Soranzo was entombed in this one, as we know by the higher seal that closes the tomb.*

I have vainly attempted to read the names of the two who were first interred there; time has nearly corroded the letters: while underneath one reads without much trouble, "HANC SEDEM VIVI SIBI POSVE (runt) VNO ANIMO LABORANTES SINE VLLA QVAERELLA." However, it would not much help us to know whether their names were Peter or Paul; but we are glad to know by the inscription that the two there buried, probably brothers, knowing how to work in sculpture, with one accord set to work to make for themselves this sarcophagus.

The inscription is surrounded by a square cornice, and flanked by two little arches supported by small half-columns followed by

FIG. 17.—Sarcophagus at the Museum of the Ducal Palace at Venice.

angular pilasters. The extreme coarseness of this work appears more conspicuously from the negligence with which the vertical lines were traced. To tell the truth, they are all sloping. One

* It was in the church of S. Paul, vulgarly called S. Polo.

would think that these good artisans, like those of the sarcophagus of S. Felix in S. Apollinaris-in-Classe of Ravenna, did not know the use of square or lead; yet to confirm what they had expressed in the epigraph, and almost as if in mockery of themselves, they thought fit to sculpture an axe under the two little arches, as well as the square rule and lead which they handled so unskilfully

TORCELLO.—If I could accept all Selvatico's opinions, far from troubling myself in researches resulting in little fruit, I would at once present my readers with a multitude of works of sculpture of the sixth and seventh centuries, collected by the Venetian islanders from the ruins of Altino, Oderzo, or Concordia, and then employed to ornament their new churches and habitations. But because I know that this worthy man, while discoursing of the Art of those centuries was always working in the dark, and also because the result of my studies in nowise accords with his opinions, I willingly renounce such riches, and hold them in reserve to adorn a much later period (till now ill-used, ill-seen, and misunderstood), and meantime I shall avenge the noble Venetian-Byzantine art. This remark also refers to entire edifices, and especially to the cathedral as we see it at Torcello, which Selvatico, sword in hand, with marked passion affirmed to be throughout the same as that which was erected by the fugitives from Altino after 641, thus shutting his eyes against the historic records that declare that it was three times rebuilt. When I again speak of this precious basilica it will be seen that only deficiency of severe study, and of necessary comparisons, led Selvatico and his followers into such a false track.

In the meantime I hasten to declare that though I also am of opinion that this church was originally built in the basilical form, I cannot concede to Selvatico that its first ichnography was altogether preserved in its later rebuildings. since I perceive that the present minor naves terminate in two apsides, which was not customary in Italy before the end of the eighth century, as we shall see further on. This well-founded

* Ruskin, Mothes, and Rohault de Fleury also erroneously considered the cathedral of Torcello as an almost intact monument of the seventh century.

conjecture assumes all the appearance of truth if we only examine the plan (see Chapter IV.) and the elevation of the church. We see that the two little chapels terminated by the apsidioles have been added later, and unskilfully charged on the central apsis. This observation leads us to recognise in that central apsis the only true remains of the church of the seventh century, because we shall see that the little chapels named above, with the present perimetric walls of the basilica, the semi-annular crypt and corresponding apsis and presbyterial stairs, were indisputably constructed in 864. We have still more proof from the little windows of the crypt, evidently cut in the old wall, and from the projections of the same which we find inserted later without respect to the recurrence of the terra-cotta bricks.

The "Cronaca Altinate" tells us that this church was rich, lofty, and well-lighted. That shows that the miserable fissures of the tenebrous Lombard churches were not yet the mode, but large, wide windows were liked, copious light being considered a principal quality much to be valued. The same chronicle then mentions the pavement of the church, in the midst of which had been made a wheel of most beautiful work, without doubt in mosaic, which had aroused so much admiration that the surrounding neighbourhood took the name of *della Roda*.

If, however, a century before, as we have seen, the fugitives from Aquila who had taken refuge in Grado erected, with the help of the Greeks, churches that, for those times, were magnificent, and alternated with the marbles that they had collected those that they still knew how to carve with sufficient skill, we cannot from that infer that the miserable Altinati sheltered in Torcello were able to do the same; for though the circumstances were identical the epoch was not; and a single century of steady decadence joined to public calamities was enough to make the artificers incapable of conceiving and executing anything above the average. Hence it is that the cathedral of Torcello arose like the coeval Roman basilicas, composed of marbles and sculptures that had belonged to older edifices, picked up by those poor creatures among the ruins of their desolate country,

for certainly they had no way and no means of having recourse
to Greek artificers. And, in fact, the circular form of the large
apsis, instead of the polygonal form used by the Greeks, excludes
the intervention of Byzantine constructors. I therefore believe
that the chisel of the decorator was scarcely at all employed in
this building. Among the remains of sculpture not appertaining
to centuries later than the seventh, I. whatever Selvatico may
say, cannot find even one to which the date of 641 may be
assigned, since all show themselves to be either Byzantine, of
the sixth century, or antique Roman.

But if, from the richness of the material gathered together,
this church gained a certain splendour, it could not have had
corresponding robustness, since, according to what Dandolo says,
(lib. vii. cap. i. par. 2), the citizens of Torcello, in 697 (Diodato
being bishop), " Ecclesiam Cathedralem Sanctæ Mariæ de novo
construxerunt." One must needs think that the fugitives of
641, either through eagerness to possess an ample church, or
through not understanding the weakness of the soil on which
they built, had made very weak foundations, if only fifty-six
years were sufficient to reduce the church to such a state
that it required to be rebuilt. It may be, however, that the
rebuilding was caused by some accident, such as an earthquake
or fire, or that the so-called " rebuilding " was a simple restoration; for it is well to remember that ignorance, exaggeration,
or flattery often ascribed to mere restorations of part of an
edifice the title of radical rebuilding, so that we should accept
similar expressions with the utmost circumspection.

The chronicle referred to further says that the Tribune
of Torcello, after having raised the cathedral, built also, not
far from its atrium, a church in honour of S. John the Baptist,
in which he placed the baptismal font, remarkable for a device
through which, by small channels placed beneath, the water
flowed into the vase through the beaks of certain bronze
animals. Even to this day, in front of the principal door of
the cathedral, and divided from that by a narrow portico, there
rises a little octagonal Baptistery that Selvatico took for the
old one, or at least one rebuilt on the site of the old one. Mothes,

on the contrary, supposed it to be at the side of the church; others at once assign to it the neighbouring one of S. Fosca. But it is curious that none of those who wrote on Torcello had noticed the visible remains of the real old Baptistery, which exist now at the side of the newer one. They are two large semicircular niches, constructed of terra-cotta, that must have occupied two internal angles of the fabric, for which cause it was square outside and octagonal within, precisely like the very old baptistery of Aquileia. And, like that of Aquileia and that of Parenzo, our Baptistery also rose in front of the cathedral, and was joined to it by porticos. That proves that the Torcellesi only followed the old customs of the country, perhaps diligently reproducing in minor proportions what they had lost in their forsaken and destroyed native home.

In this period in which the exercise of Art was confined almost exclusively to the building of churches, and in which the general lack of means and extreme unskilfulness of the artificers were a continual obstacle to the development of new forms or the execution of grand conceptions, fallen Italian architecture could take no onward step. We know, or we may guess, the few forms of that time which were limited to columns or pilasters, semicircular arches, apsides, long walls and roofs with two ascents. In truth, such poor elements, finished off with the only art of which they were then capable, have little right to the name of style, and still less to the high-sounding name of architecture. And the end of the seventh century and the beginning of the eighth exactly mark the time of the most profound degradation of Italian art, without adding that the seventh century is also the poorest as regards specimens of it, so that I know not how to add any others to the few already made mention of.

But our researches in the darkness of these centuries much resemble travelling at night by unknown roads during a black tempest; the travellers run the risk of losing their way, and of imperilling themselves, unless some beneficent flash of lightning succour them with its splendour. We, too, have need of such flashes, and have them in those monuments which, boasting an age determined by authentic indisputable documents, become precious guides in the search for contemporaneous works and the endeavour to fill up certain lagoons. The eighth century at once throws much light on the subject.

Chapter II.

SECOND INFLUENCE OF BYZANTINE ART ON ITALIAN ART.

BYZANTINE-BARBARIAN STYLE.

WHAT we have seen already is not all that is left of the works indubitably completed under the *régime* of the Lombards, because there exist a considerable quantity of other works of much importance, but which require to be classed apart and seriously studied, because they are distinguished from the others by a sensible diversity of character and by less imperfection.

I said at the beginning that the influence of Byzantine art on Italian art, in the first half of the sixth century, had been able to raise the latter somewhat, but only for a very short time. It may be said, therefore, to have only retarded the total decadence that inevitably awaited it. It was like a lamp almost gone out for want of aliment, which a beneficent hand replenishes with a few drops of oil. The little flame springs up and sparkles, but very soon by degrees falls back in the first languor, crackles and dies. We have hitherto painfully watched the last agonies of poor Italian art. And if we have not yet declared it to be dead, it is because the expression seems to us too crude; but if we consider dispassionately the wretched products of which she was capable at the beginning of the eighth century—works from which not one ray of Art shines out—we shall be forced to believe that, if she was not really dead, at least she gave no sign of life.

In the midst of the seventh century she had stripped herself of the last tatters of foreign vestments, and remained in the most absolute, not to say skeleton-like, natural nudity, as we have now left her; but at the beginning of the eighth century we meet with works that strongly contrast with all that we have hitherto seen. That excessive unskilfulness and carelessness, of which certain sarcophagi of Ravenna are examples, does not appear in these; and the lines in them are traced with sufficient care and diligence. They are often even beautiful, and distributed with an evident sentiment of elegance. There is no longer a complete absence of every decoration, but a profusion of varied ornaments; no longer capitals of uncouth design and worse execution, but Corinthian and composite ones, sometimes of graceful varied shapes and accurate chiselling. Numerous animals are mixed with the leafage, but they are not invariably due, as in the past, to the symbolism of the first Christian centuries, but are often chosen and treated in a free and new manner. The human figure at last, so long proscribed by the incapacity of the artisans, here begins to reappear, though often very awkwardly. Then, in the midst of these sculptures, peep out certain strange representations of a much-veiled symbolism, and certain elements and motives of decoration that in the past had never been seen in Italy. This style—which, although never perfect or beautiful, is refreshing after the poverty of the style that preceded it—was not limited to one region alone, nor only to the Valley of the Po, as Dartein timidly said while baptizing it " Longobardian," but extended itself through all the peninsula—a fact which is proved by the traces that I found in several places.

In spite of that, I find it hard to believe, as has been believed hitherto, that these artists were Italians, for the art appears to have been completely formed in the midst of barbarism ; and, after little more than half a century, it suddenly disappeared, leaving Italian art in a state nearly as barbarous as it was before. What better argument can we have than this to prove that it was a style imported by a few artists, which naturally ceased when they died out ? Do not those fifty or sixty years of its presence in Italy seem to indicate the natural existence of those emigrants ? Those to whom my conjecture does not seem acceptable will certainly find it very difficult to reconcile the facts in any other more logical manner. I hope, however, that I am on the right tack; the more so, as the following considerations seem to me to support my conjecture.

The first and most spontaneous question that the reader will ask me will be this : If that style was an importation of foreign artists, whence did they come ? Even without analysing its characteristics, reason suggests immediately that they could not have come from the North, because the people there, being more barbarous than ourselves, often required our help; nor from the South, because the Arabs, still thirsting for Christian blood and greedy for conquests, had not devoted enough time to Art to allow it to germinate in their country. Real artists could therefore only have come from Greece—Greece alone, which, in the midst of general barbarism and poverty, had remained sufficiently rich and civilised, and where the art of ornamentation, however fallen, had never reached such depths of abasement as in Italy. Greece alone, on this occasion, could furnish us with those artificers; she alone could give lessons to Italy. And if we would postpone our judgment till the examination of those monuments, it leads us not less directly to the same conclusions. That profusion of minute ornaments, that perception of grace which reveals itself even through a rough chisel, that abundance of olives, of pearls, of plants and roses, those gemmed crosses, above all those capitals almost always composite, and with foliage of minute pointed intaglio, are all purest characteristics of the Byzantine style. Even Dartein recognised it, and this time I agree with him, whatever Selvatico may say, who, having taken it into his head to see the Latin style everywhere, sought to deny the clear Greek stamp borne by these works.

But I already hear a murmur of objection ; it will be said to me : Allowing that these works bear the signs of the Byzantine style, allowing that these not inelegant decorations are not unworthy of Greek artificers, how can we ever admit that the coarse, rude figures of animals, and the still coarser and ruder human ones, could issue from their hands ? How could Greek art have fallen so low ?

This objection is chiefly based on a prejudice arising from

the fact that people have been accustomed to indicate these works, and even superior ones, as the apogee of barbarism in Italian art. Hence the conclusion that in Greece they should know how to do much better things. But that is far from being the case. Let me give a rapid glance at certain authentic Byzantine works of these ages, from which I trust to draw light enough to elucidate the matter.

Art is the most faithful mirror of civilisation; she reflects it in all its phases, moves in parallel roads with it, and with civilisation rises, grows, becomes gigantic; or falls precipitatedly and becomes barbarous; so that the story of a people or of a nation, if not known by writings, might be guessed through its monuments and works of art. The sixth century, and especially the reign of Justinian, marked the apogee of the Byzantine power; and we see Greek art give proofs of a vigour and daring unknown previously, and touch the apex of splendour. But, after Justinian, Fortune turned her back on the empire, its possessions in Italy were reduced to small proportions; the Persians took from it a great part of Asia, and with the barbarians of the North kept it continuously employed in disastrous and often dishonourable wars. Nor did the seventh century make truce with it. On the contrary, the desert winds urged the furious Mahomedans to molest it more than ever, and take away from it nearly all its lands in Asia and Africa. Now we can surely assert that, in this tempestuous period, Greek art could neither flourish, nor maintain itself at the height it had reached. Decadence must follow without doubt; experience vouches for this; now let us see if the monuments also bear testimony to it.

But alas! it is like seeking Maria through Ravenna to turn over pages about Greece in the hope of finding monuments between the seventh and ninth centuries. Though something must be allowed for the negligence of savants in searching for monuments of the three intermediate centuries, yet the fact that none have been met with surely demonstrates how very little was achieved throughout that period, or else the want of beauty and solidity in the works which constrained posterity to reconstruct them.

In Greece, then, as in Italy, poverty in works of art seems characteristic of these centuries of decadence*; nevertheless, it may be that in some remote corner a few edifices of this period still exist, undestroyed by the wrath of time and man. But (better than the complete buildings), it is probable that many fragments of the sculptures that composed and embellished them may remain. And I have proofs of it.

In the meantime, as it has not been possible for me to travel to the East and use my own eyes in researches on the spot, let the reader content himself with what little we can find at home, and what we can learn from photographs and drawings.

Among the very numerous sculptures that the Venetians gathered from the ruins of many ancient churches of Greece, or that were at least the work of Greek chisels, and carried to Venice to make S. Mark's Church beautiful, it was not unlikely that some might belong to the epoch we are studying, and, in fact, several do seem to be of the seventh century. These are certain parapets, adorned with circles, crosses, monograms, animals, plants and other symbols, that now serve for the internal galleries of the basilica, in which, although one clearly observes a relationship with the works of the sixth century, a tendency towards novel motives and forms is also evident, that is to say, to those forms and motives which, being developed in Greece in the course of the sixth century, formed the foundation of the eighth century style, which we shall now see brought into Italy. And to the resemblance of forms and motives is coupled that of the design and the rough and careless execution.

It is well to take special notice of that parapet of the gallery in front of the chapel of the Virgin, representing an architectonic *ensemble*, with arcades and frontons, and of several sarcophagi and ambos dating from the fourth to the sixth century. Between the central columns there is a very rudely-formed vase with handles, out of which proceed two drooping vine-branches

---

* There is still another analogy. As in Italy, so also in Greece, students have attributed to this period works that should rather have been identified with the eleventh century.

with bunches of grapes sculptured in a barbarous manner. In the two lateral inter-columns are a lamb and a ram, equally primitive, at the foot of two pomegranate-trees; in the frontons are palms between doves, and, in the upper part, other vine and pomegranate branches. The style and the character of every detail of this work plainly proclaim it to be from Grecian hands; from its unskilful chiselling and incorrect and inelegant design, we perceive that it is unworthy of the fifth and sixth

Fig. 18.—Balustrade of the Galleries of S. Mark at Venice—VIIth Century.

centuries. That it cannot belong to the eighth or succeeding ones, we shall see hereafter when we learn to recognise the Byzantine art of those times; therefore it can only belong to the seventh century, that is to say to that period of decadence which prepared the style of the eighth century.

But here in S. Mark we have another work of sculpture, indubitably Byzantine, which is preserved in the Tesoro. It is that marble seat ("cattedra") which tradition declares to have been presented to the Patriarch of Grado, Primigenius, about the year 630, by the Emperor Heraclius, on account of its being supposed to be the same as that on which the Evangelist S. Mark sat in Alexandria. Selvatico laughed at that pious belief, and with his usual levity declared the "cattedra" to be a work of the tenth or eleventh century.

Several savants, versed in archæology (among whom I am glad to pay most homage to Rohault de Fleury), having submitted it to a duly serious examination, were able to give satisfactory opinions on the matter, separating in the popular tradition what was fabulous from what was probable fact. I will not here repeat the profound reasonings of these illustrious archæologists, but, gathering from them their most logical conclusions, I think we can almost take for granted, that that chair, considering the narrowness of its seat, could never have served such a purpose as was supposed, but was merely a symbol of a See. It might well belong to the church of Alexandria, and perhaps contain in the box of the seat the relics of the real ancient wooden cattedra of the Evangelist. It was never adorned or incrusted with ivory, as many have fancied, confusing it with an ivory chair in the church at Grado. Finally, as Fleury ingeniously conjectures, the Emperor Heraclius (610-641), having received it without ornament from Alexandria, either caused it to be decorated with the symbols and sculptures that we see on it; or else, as I would venture to conjecture (if the famous Sibylline inscription allows me to do so), the Emperor, having important relics from Alexandria of the wooden "cattedra," enclosed them in the marble one that he himself had executed and adorned in Byzantium, and sent them as a gift to the Patriarch of Grado. But whatever may be thought of these last conclusions, it is at any rate certain that the style of those ornaments clearly indicate either the last years of the sixth century or (more probably) the first half of the following one.

The drawing,[*] much more than a minute description, avails to give us a clear idea of the form of this seat. The interior of the back is adorned by a bas-relief representing the mystic Lamb on the hill of sacrifice, from the base of which spring the four evangelical rivers, and from the top rises the tree of life. Behind the back and on the external side of the arms are sculptured the symbols of the evangelists, each with six opened wings, and on both sides of the circular crown the cross between

[*] See Plate lxx of that splendid work "Il Tesoro di San Marco di Venezia illustrato da Antonio Pasini," published by Cav. Ongania in 1887.

two figures of saints, possibly apostles, or the evangelists themselves. Beside all this, here and there are scattered palms, rosettes, lighted tapers, and other ornaments in zigzags and squares. All these sculptures are of faint projection; the rather clumsy figures confine all delicate work to the drapery. The animals, plants, and various childish decorations, are of primitive form and careless workmanship. In fact, this work teaches us that Byzantine art in the beginning of the seventh century was fallen very low, and on the brink of falling lower still, so as to be capable of such works as I attribute to it.

But if these two sculptures, exiled far from their country, should leave some doubt in the mind of the reader, here are some others that have never seen any land but their own. The small ancient cathedral of Athens, as we see it in these days, is a work of about the eleventh century, but its exterior walls are a real museum of different styles and periods. There are fragments of antique Greek style; others of Grecian-Roman; others originate from the Christians of the eleventh century, and there are some to which we can assign no other date than the seventh or eighth century. Such are certain stones sculptured in bas-relief, representing birds, quadrupeds, &c. Two of these, of almost uniform design, show, in the lower part, two eagles fighting with two serpents, and in the higher part, two griffins climbing on a vase and pecking at a species of pine that comes out of it. Another stone represents a cross enclosed in a rectangle bordered with leaflets; the four empty spaces over and under the arms of the cross are respectively occupied by two rampant griffins and two rampant lions. Well, these sculptures are so barbarous that they would

Fig. 19.- Exterior Bas-relief of Athenian Cathedral — VIIth Century.

gain by an exchange with many of those that we shall shortly see in Italy.
They display no sense of proportion, no modelling, only a few ungraceful furrows instead of wings, feathers, and eyes. From these few examples it clearly results that, however clumsy or imperfect certain sculptural figures, on the monuments of Italy that we are about to study, may be, they do not clash with the Greek art of the eighth century, since even at home she could do no better. Yet for love of justice and truth I must here add two remarks, in extenuation of

FIG. 20.—Parapet existing in Ravenna —VIth Century.

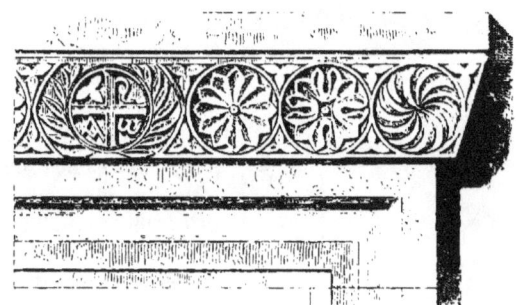

* FIG. 21.—Heading of a Door at Moudjeleia, Syria— VIIth Century.

the charge of absolute barbarism, which the reader may hastily lay at the door of all the poor Greek artists of the seventh century. The first is that the works of this style in Italy of which notice has been made in books are few, and happen to be those whose representations of figures are really barbarous; but I shall be able to indicate to the reader some others in which the human figures are much less incorrect, and those of animals really fine. We must bear in mind that in every age, amidst the vulgar mediocrity of artists, there have been some who, speaking relatively, might be termed geniuses. The other remark is, that not a few of the Greek artists who were called to Italy, or came here in the eighth century, may have been constrained by their commissioners to do figure-work, whereas in their own country they had only had practice in ornament; hence the great gulf that in some works separates the elegant decorations from the extremely barbarous figures.

But the reader wants something more from me. It is not enough, he may say to me, that you have proved that Art in Greece in the seventh or eighth centuries, brought forth wretched little monstrosities, similar to those that you will now show us in Italy; but you must also show us, with the monuments in hand, that that same style of ornament was really used even in the Byzantine Empire, without which demonstration your arguments, however solid, will never cease to revolve in a circle of mere conjecture.

Although I shall have some hard work to satisfy this desire of my reader's, yet I praise his diffident curiosity, because, in this species of study, proofs are never superfluous. It grieves me, though, not to be able to place before him a long series of the desired analogies, and it torments me not to have been able to go to those countries and make my researches in person; but let us try for the present to make up for it in other ways.

The most conspicuous ornamental characteristic of the works of the eighth century is without doubt the knot-work. Well, if in anterior epochs we find examples of this, they exist in the works of Byzantine artificers. Take, for instance, many capitals and parapets of the churches of the sixth century, principally at Ravenna and Rome (see Figs. 13 and 14). If we pass on to the monuments of the sixth and seventh centuries in Central Syria, so well illustrated by the savant Vogüé, we shall without trouble

* Fig. 22.—Cymatium of a Door at Serdjilla, Syria—VIIth Century.

find many varieties of knot-work, and also little semicircular arches so interwoven as to make pointed ones, star and also

* Fig. 23.—Cymatium of the Door of a Church at Behioh, Syria—VIIth Century.

wheel-rosettes, great profusion of beads, spindles, cords, crosses, lilies and isolated leaves—all elements characteristic of Italian works and odorous of the close influence of Persia.

See, for example, a sarcophagus of the so-called Judah's

* Fig. 24. Sculptures at a Castle near Safa, Syria—VIIth Century.

sepulchres at Jerusalem; the cymatium of a house at Mondjeleia, and of another at Serdjilla; a sarcophagus at Lokamaya, and especially the sculptures on the door of a church at Behioh, and on the doors of the castle of Kharbet-El-Beida (the White Ruin) in the neighbourhood of Safa. Vogüé, who confesses very rightly that he had not found anything similar among other ruins dating from the third to the sixth centuries, finds in it a style which, though it evinces many points of contact with old Byzantine art, possesses a new principle that strongly displays Asiatic influence. Well, those sculptures, those friezes, those circles enclosing animals in slight relief, those crosses, those roses, those beads, those complicated and ingenious knot-works, are so like what we shall soon see in Italy, as to make it impossible to doubt their common parentage of style.

The ruins of Syria, as all know, do not date further back than the seventh century, the period of the devastating Saracen conquest, which left a desert where it had found flourishing towns and cities.

But for all that Syria appears to be a too remote and Oriental region to represent in its monuments the pure Byzantine style of the seventh century, and therefore you will ask me for some other example taken from Greece itself. Here is one:—

Although publications about the Byzantine monuments of Greece do not cite any works on sculpture which can be attributed to the seventh or eighth century, yet I doubt not that many still remain in Byzantium and in various Greek cities: and this I infer from a simple photograph, in my possession, of one of the façades of the old cathedral of Athens, where, as is the case with the examples described above, the style of works made in Italy in the eighth century is quite recognisable.

Such are two fragments of frieze in interwoven circles enclosing six-leaved

Fig. 25.—Bas-relief in the Exterior of the Cathedral at Athens.

rosettes, and especially that large band placed under the fronton, into which are cut the little arches of the central double door ("bifora"). Here we ought to recognise, no less than in the Syrian remains, the same timid chisel, the same method of

ornamentation, the same bizarre and disconnected motives, and the same mingling of curved and interlaced lines that we see in Italy.

Fig. 26.—Altar of S. Montan at Orléansville, Algeria— VIIth Century.

That style was characterised by profusion of ornament, and gave free vent to the most prodigal fancy and a richness that was positively Oriental. It is not, then, wonderful that it so rapidly diffused itself through the various provinces of the Byzantine Empire, that I believe I can recognise it even in Africa on certain rude bas-reliefs among the ruins of Carthage, on the archivolts of a little ciborium found at Ain Sultan in Mauritania, adorned with windows, monograms, and rude branches of the vine; and also among the ruins of a church at Orléansville in Algeria, discovered by Villefosse, over the well-known altar of S. Montano. That minute and mincing sculpture, that frame of little squares, those rosettes, those barbarous palms, all of them seem to me to be elements characterising Greek art of the second half of the seventh century, and not of the fifth or sixth century as many have opined. This church

Rohault de Fleury, "La Messe," vol. iv.

owes its ruin to the fury of the Mahomedans which fell on that region at the end of the seventh century.

To these proofs, not many but very eloquent, which I hope my readers will receive favourably, I can add another of great weight : and it is that, though we shall meet at Venice works of Greek artificers of the ninth century, we shall still find there so many traces of the style of the eighth century that, even by that road, it will be impossible to escape from my conclusions.

But before setting ourselves to the examination of these works, it is useful to investigate the causes that may have induced several Greek artists to pass into Italy. Perhaps the continual advances of the Arabs on Syria, Armenia, and Africa put them to flight with the rest. Perhaps the improved political condition of Italy in the beginning of the eighth century encouraged certain Greek artificers to establish themselves there in the hope of finding work and profit. Or, again, the Italians themselves, having opened their eyes at last and seen with shame the miserable and unworthy state into which Art had fallen in Italy, decided to call in Greek artists or bring them with them on their return from some of their travels in Greece. All of these causes, but principally the last, may have contributed ; but in the bosom of Greece itself a potent cause was preparing, and was alone sufficient to incite that great emigration of Greek artists, to which many monuments in Italy of this eighth century bear testimony.

Everybody knows the terrible persecution of the iconoclasts initiated by the Emperor Leo III., the Isaurian, who in 726 published an edict against the worship of sacred images, and in 728 suppressed them altogether, and that the strife was not a mere religious controversy, or restricted to mere words, but produced serious disorders and revolts in Greece and in Italy, mutiny of the populace and even murders, incarcerations, and executions. We can imagine how poor Greek art suffered in such prolonged struggles, and how small were the gains of the artists. Religious art, which at that time was almost the only Art alive, was often cultivated in monasteries; and as that persecution also aimed at the weakening of monasticism, then very powerful, we may believe that many monks, as well as secular artists, took refuge in Italy, where, besides finding an asylum and protection under the Pontiff and Luitprand, who together had headed the opposition against the Emperor Leo, they hoped also to find work; nor were they disappointed, as the following monuments may prove.

CIMITILE, near Nola. — Among the most ancient examples of Byzantine-barbarous style in the eighth century that remain to us in Italy, we must certainly reckon those in the ancient basilica of S. Felix in Cimitile, near Nola, erected by the Bishop Leo the third, who, as we know, restored that church in the beginning of the eighth century. His name is sculptured on the brackets of the door of the chapel of the Holy Martyrs, and we will stop before it. The door itself (that is to say the door-posts and architrave) presents nothing artistic, and perhaps Leo had no hand in them; but what really was his work is the porch that precedes it, and which once served to protect it from the sun and the rain. It is formed of two isolated pilasters, seventy-five centimetres from the door-posts, and crowned by

FIG. 27.—Details of the Porch of Cimitile—Beginning of the VIIIth Century.

capitals that sustain two architraves proceeding from the back wall and terminating at the exterior ends in two brackets. A little vaulted arch is raised above to support the roof. We cannot fail at once to recognise in this little construction the most ancient example of porticos of this kind which Italy has preserved, and perhaps it is the first that appeared in this country. These are the porches that after the tenth century became so frequent in the churches of Rome, and those of the Lombard style in the eastern half of Upper Italy. If, however, this porch was, as I believe, the work of Oriental artists, one must admit that those artists already possessed its type in their own country; and in fact in the exterior of the church of Rouciha in Syria (sixth century), four porches exist that only differ from ours in being supported by four columns instead of pilasters, and in not possessing projecting brackets. Similar porches also protect the four lateral doors of a church of the sixth century at Baquoza.

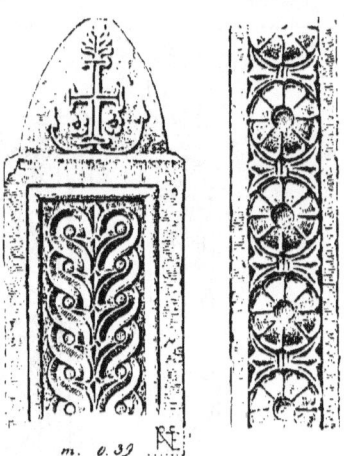

Fig. 28.—Details of the Choir-screen at Cimitile — Beginning of the VIIIth Century.

A florid decoration enriches the fronts of the pilasters of Cimitile, and as the dimensions are various, their plan being rectangular, it follows that their ornamentation is also various. The ornamentation on the narrower sides consists of spirals and leaves of entirely Byzantine style. On the wider sides are rhombs made of interwoven ribands enriched with a great number of pointed diamonds, and filled with leaves and rosettes. The capitals, which are Corinthian, have somewhat awkward forms and heavy leaves, the stalks are characteristic of the epoch;

that species of gem, which in the centre takes the place of the flower, is original. The superior brackets certainly cannot claim admiration for elegance, though they are not a barbarous conceit; their greatest value consists in the two inscriptions carved on them: "+ LEO TERTIVS — EPISCOPVS FECIT." A similar chisel, but a happier fancy is seen in several other sculptures of the old basilica,* amongst which are some parapets and pilasters, which were meant to form the chancels of a choir. Among the first the worthiest of remark is that which represents in bas-relief, and not altogether without success, two griffins on the sides of a vase, between many little branches rich in foliage. Another, mutilated more recently, bears sculptures of a lion and a bull among similar branches. More important are the pilasters, and especially that of which I offer a drawing, on account of its curious and quite Byzantine workmanship, adorned with a cross, rosettes and leaves, and its facial ornamentation. That of the principal one almost servilely copies those graceful interweavings so much used by the ancient Greeks, especially on bases and capitals of the Ionic order, and on their celebrated pottery, and afterwards imitated so often by the Romans. The narrower side shows instead an elegant decoration of alternate roses and lilies, of Asiatic character, and which anticipates by three centuries the analogous decorations by Greek artificers to be seen in Venetian palaces.

For the rest, these works of Cimitile, although belonging to the eighth century, and bearing conspicuously the Byzantine mark, are too far removed from the other works which we shall

* It is impossible to describe the miserable and unworthy condition to which they are reduced and in which they are kept. The old pictures and the venerable mosaics drop from the walls, that are covered with mould and black and swollen with the damp. The pavements are buried under heaps of mud and stones; the bas-reliefs are heaped in confusion one upon another in this or that corner amongst filth and scorpions. There is no light, no air. . . . Though I grieve for the works of Art that disappear from us to take a place in the museums beyond the Alps and beyond the sea, yet I would that these churches could be so easily transported as to tempt some stranger to acquire them, who, better able than our Government to understand the preciousness of these monuments, would preserve them with the care which is their due.

now examine. Here, for example, the study in curved and interlaced lines, that forms almost the base of the decoration of other monuments, is but slightly pronounced; and this species of capitals and profusion of diamond-points are represented only by isolated specimens among the works of the eighth century.* One might explain this anomaly by supposing that the artificer who worked in Cimitile came from a remote province of the Greek Empire, into which the new style had scarcely penetrated.

Ancona —Among the most ancient works in the Barbarous-Byzantine style existing in Italy, and one which presents the closest affinity with those of the second half of the eighth century, we must cite a monument in the church of La Misericordia, at Ancona. And this is a parapet of a semi-circular ambo, on which is carved an inscription that Rohault de Fleury read thus: "TEMPORIBVS PAPÆ SERGII, CHRISTI FAMVLVS ANDREAS FECIT . FVERAT EX VETVSTV LAPIS SET NVNC RVTILAT SPLENDENS." The style of the ambo itself prevents us from supposing that the inscription alludes to the second pope who bore the name of Sergius, or to the third or fourth; and therefore it was sculptured evidently under the pontificate of the first Sergius, that is to say between 687 and 701.

Its decoration consists of four squares framed by braids: each square encloses three compartments, divided by small channelled spiral columns crowned by rough capitals supporting a frontispiece in the centre and two archivolts at the sides. From under these one sees flexible branches of a plant proceeding from a vase, and in the central intercolumn a dry little tree furnished with rigid curling branches. The execution is very rough, and the idea in every single square borrowed from a decoration very common

* I only find in one Byzantine monument, anterior to the eighth century, diamond-points so tiny and so profuse— that is to say, on the leaves of the stucco capitals of the interior balustrades of S. Apollinaris, near Ravenna. Nor let them be suspected to be modern because they are wrought in stucco. Bas-reliefs of the same material, and well preserved, decorate many under-arches of S. Vitale at Ravenna, and the basilica of Parenzo.

on the sarcophagi of the Roman decadence and on other Latin and Byzantine ones from the fifth to the seventh century, *e.g.*, one of those in the mausoleum of the Empress Placidia, at Ravenna. One may also see the same ornamentation on ambos, like that of the Holy Spirit in the same city and on parapets, like the two existing in the interior of S. Mark's at Venice (see Fig. 18). We have seen that the latter, by their rough execution and the novelty of certain forms, show themselves to be Byzantine work of the seventh century, and already draw near to the style of the eighth century.

While this ambo, in its braiding and vine-branches, somewhat resembles the Byzantine style of the eighth century, the ciborium which I shall now show to the reader represents that style already in its full development.

S. GEORGE AT VALPOLICELLA.—There exist in the lapidary museum of Verona two small columns once belonging to the church of S. George at Valpolicella. On their convex parts, as on the legs of certain Etruscan statues, two inscriptions are engraved in barbarous characters and still more barbarous Latin:—

"+ IN N (omine) DN̄I IESV XRISTI DE DONIS SANCTI IVANNES BAPTESTE EDIFICATVS EST HANC CIVORIVS SVB TEMPORE DOMNO NOSTRO LIOPRANDO REGE ET VB (venerabile) PATERNO (pater nostro) DOMNICO EPESCOPO ET COSTODES EIVS VV̄ (venerabiles) VIDALIANO ET TANCOL PRESBITERIS ET REFOL GASTALDIO GONDELME INDIGNVS DIACONVS SCRIPSI."

And:—

"VRSVS MAGESTER CVM DISCEPOLIS SVIS IVVINTINO ET IVVIANO EDIFICAVET HANC CIVORIVM VERGONDVS TEODAL FOSCARI."

It clearly follows from these inscriptions that the ciborium was erected during the reign of Luitprand; and if we reflect that he ascended the throne the same year as Bishop Dominic died, we shall find that this work was executed precisely in 712.

Nearly all writers about mediæval Italian archæology have noticed these columns, perhaps because it was not difficult to see them in Verona, and in the works of Maffei and Venturi which portrayed them; but none of them, so far as I know, chose to go to Valpolicella and walk up the steep hill where

Fig. 29.—Ciborium of S. George's of Valpolicella—A.D. 712.

rises the little town and the church of S. George to see if nothing else remained of the old tabernacle. I would and did go there, and by good chance found rich repayment for my trouble. That is to say, I found the other two little columns with their capitals and three rich archivolts with extremities more or less mutilated, which composed the upper part of the ciborium.* Column and capital measure little less than a

* That intelligent and courteous gentleman, the Provost Don Gerolamo Arcozzi, assured me that the fourth archivolt is walled up in the central apsis, and gave me hope that one day or other it would be taken out and reunited to the other fragments, and replaced as formerly in the church.

metre in height, and the space between is not more than eighty-five centimetres, so that we ought not to imagine that the ciborium was placed on the ground, but on the table of the altar, exactly as one sees in several of the Byzantine mosaics of S. Mark's Church at Venice, and like the altar of the Greek monastery of Grottoferrata, near Frascati. The capitals of these little columns are certainly not the finest part of the ciborium. Though of regular proportions their design is rude and their chiselling careless. They may be defined as cubes with their lower corners concavely blunted. Curious channelled projections wind round below, possibly in order to recall the reverse of leaves which are not even indicated. Every corner bears a sculptured palm-leaf, and every face a cross, or a circle containing a star between two meagre caulicules with double volutes. Above, there is a little striated knot to remind one of the flower, and a very mean abacus. There was evidently an intention to imitate distantly the Corinthian capital.

The decorations of the archivolts are not so rough. Here, for the first time, we see the characteristic interweavings of osier-branches. They always wind round the arches, and often frame their upper parts. The intervening spaces are occupied either by a patera with fishes beside it or by a cross among roses, or by a peacock. One of the archivolts is framed above by rough leaves and meagre curled caulicules, which from henceforth we shall often find—a spoilt souvenir, perhaps, of the antique corridietro. One may see its prototype on a Byzantine capital of the sixth century in S. Peter of Bagnacavallo, near Ravenna. This ciborium was undoubtedly crowned by a little intaglio cornice, of which there remains a small fragment, and terminated by an octagonal roof, like many others of those times.

This cannot have been the only work which Master Orso wrought in S. George's, because there still remains the convex parapet of an ambo adorned by four simple squares framed by a baguet. On the sides we see the casements that were to fix the slabs of marble that composed the sides of the two little stairs, so that one may suppose that ambo to have resembled in its ensemble those that we see even now in Roman churches.

All these sculptures bear the indubitable mark of the Greek style, yet the artist's name is not Greek—the only name of an artificer that the many works of this style in Italy can yield us. Is that a reason for renouncing the Greek origin of that ciborium? That would be to declare all the others to be Italian works; but their style and isolation are decidedly opposed to such a conclusion. For the rest, one swallow does not make a summer, and, as many Italians of that time bore Greek names, no wonder that several Greeks should have Roman ones—the more so that the emperors of the East were well pleased to be called Romans instead of Greeks. Master Orso, then, might very well have been Greek, and for our present case it is quite sufficient that his name was not Lombard like that of Gastaldo, of the deacon, and the three other personages mentioned at the end. But though the name of the master is not Greek, some of the letters of the inscription are Greek, *e.g.*, the D, which is triangular like a *delta*, and the L, which presents precisely the form of a *lambda;* and let me remark that this, as far as I know, is the most ancient monument where such a mixture of alphabets occurs—a custom which henceforth will disappear.

But the church of S. George of Valpolicella is not only remarkable on account of these remnants, but also for many other antiquities and Roman inscriptions, for its fine belfry of the twelfth century, for a very graceful and picturesque Lombard cloister of the same epoch, and above all for itself.

It is an ancient basilica with three naves, divided partly by simple square pilasters, partly by columns; the naves are covered with woodwork,* and terminated by three apsides. At first sight one would say that the intention of adding to the ornamentation of the most sacred part of the church, that is to

* The vaults that cover them are not the real antique ones, but an unhappy work of this century.

the presbytery, raised by a step, had counselled the employment in that part of columns instead of bare stone pilasters; but that opinion must be quickly changed, that we may be able to account for a curious and particular circumstance. The façade of the church is formed in the centre not of a straight wall, but of an apsis in which is contrived the door. Certain old paintings, of which it preserves the traces internally, tell us that its construction must be antique. Of certain abbatial churches with double apsides like these, a good number are found in Germany, especially along the banks of the Rhine: but the reason adduced for it, namely, that they served at one and the

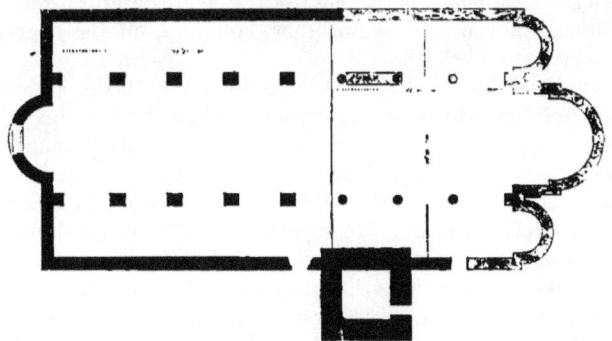

Fig. 30.—Plan of the Church of S. George's of Valpolicella—VIIIth and Xth Centuries (?).

same time for two distinct choirs, one of the abbot and the other of the prior, which choirs alternated in singing the psalms, does not apply to our church, which was never otherwise than simply collegial. It seems to be several centuries older than those of the Rhine. Taking that into consideration, it is difficult to escape from the logical and sufficiently well-founded conjecture that the apsis of the entrance, together with that part of the nave which is supported by pillars, is a portion of an ancient basilica, turned towards the east according to the liturgy of the first Christian ages, and that the rest has been added on to it later, reversing the direction, when the contrary custom prevailed. This view of the matter is supported, and I would almost say confirmed, by the number of the apsides, one only being in the more ancient part of the church, as was customary in Italy till nearly the end of the eighth century, and three in the other part, in accordance with a mode adopted from the beginning of the ninth century. If also one considers that the added portion, though more recent, is so simple and so rude that one must assign to it either the end of the ninth or the tenth century,* he may well believe that the older part belongs to the seventh century, or the time of Master Orso. Though simple in form and unadorned, we ought not to despise it; for if sculptural remains of the eighth century be numerous, buildings, on the contrary, are very rare.

FERENTILLO.—"VRSVS MAGESTER FECIT": such is the inscription which we find twice carved on the remains of an altar discovered a few years ago in the abbatial church of Ferentillo, near Spoleto, dedicated, as we learn from an inscription, to S. Peter by a certain Ilderico Dragileopa. It is known that Luitprand, coming to Spoleto in 739, put Ilderico in possession of this duchy. That made De Rossi suspect that this Duke Ilderico was the giver of the altar, and that the Master Orso there recorded was no other than the author of the ciborium of Valpolicella. The identity of the name, of the appellation, of the characters, of the style, and the coincidence of the epoch, would seem to strengthen and almost establish as a certainty the suspicion of the worthy archæologist; but still there remains a difficulty in the fact that, however rough the sculptures of the ciborium may be, those of the altar are incomparably inferior, both from their absolute absence of relief, here replaced by crude, gross furrows, and from the inelegant, childish, and barbarous distribution of the ornaments, that make the work the rudest specimen of this style remaining in Italy. Only the supposition that Orso intended merely to sketch out his design on the marble with those furrows, and had

* The fragmentary awkwardness of its supports has much in common with those of the church of Agliate, near Monza, built in 881.

no time to finish it, being perhaps prevented from doing so by death, could remove the obstacles which oppose this attribution.

The style of those "frescoes" is at any rate Byzantine in every particular : cordons, olive-branches, crosses, hexagonal

Fig. 31. Baptistery of Calisto at Cividale—A.D. 737.

roses, foliage, fans, circles, and again crosses. One also sees on it a vase flanked by two doves and grotesque figures of people praying.

CIVIDALE.—But where the most numerous and best preserved, if not the best, works of this style are to be found, in Italy is at Cividale, in Friuli.

Since about 630 the Patriarchs of Aquileia resided in

Cormons; but Calisto, disdaining that humble little place in 737, transferred his seat to Cividale, which, besides being a larger and richer city, was also the fixed residence of the Duke of Friuli. There Calisto built, amongst other things, the baptismal font which still exists, having been removed to the cathedral in the seventeenth century from the neighbouring baptistery now destroyed.

It is of octagonal form and intended for the rite of immersion. It is encircled by a parapet likewise octagonal, open on two sides, on which are raised eight slim little columns bearing the same number of semicircular archivolts, not surmounted by a cornice, but only by a band, on which is carved the inscription attesting that this *tegurio* was erected and adorned by Calisto in the reign of Luitprand.

One of the original archivolts is wanting, and is replaced by another, quite plain, with a modern inscription; one of the vases of the columns presents four leaves at the angles of the plinth, which indicates a restoration perhaps of the thirteenth century. Nor can the basement be supposed to be the true one, since it is in part made up of fragments of parapets that from their dimensions never could have belonged to it. But from the columns upwards there is no doubt that it is authentic work of the time of Calisto. The little columns have attic bases, smooth stems, high and expanded capitals, all of the usual measure and form, of a composite with two rows of leaves without ovoli with large volutes and large roses in the centre. The leaves

Fig. 32.—Capital of Baptistery at Cividale—A.D. 737.

are of two kinds, some carved like thorny acanthus, reminding one of the Byzantine capitals of the sixth century; others show a sawlike contour, a new kind for Italy, but familiar in buildings of the sixth century in Syria, where, in the conventional language of Byzantine art, it possibly stood

* Figs. 33 & 34.—Archivolts of the Baptistery at Cividale—A.D. 737.

for palm-leaves. Although the chisel is somewhat timid, yet, on the whole, I am far from defining them barbarous, as does Selvatico. I find them very elegant. Without doubt they are the best capitals that Greek artificers of the eighth century have left us in Italy. The archivolts above are also elegant, adorned by olive-moulding, vine-branches proceeding from vases, and little curls with palm-leaves. Every angle of the octagon among the arches is adorned with intaglio of circles interwoven with rich bead-work, but the part under the inscription exhibits a row of ovoli of meagre form and ineffective. In the little archivolts, and over them, among a profusion of branches, of palms, of roses full blown, or in the girandole fashion, we see animals of rude design chiselled inexpertly. The doves, peacocks, and stags, drinking at the fount, are connected with the symbolism of the first Christian ages; but those winged griffins, the two lions that are about to bite the two rabbits, and those two great fishes menacing two small ones, are entirely new representations in Western churches (though in that time they must have been in great vogue in Oriental ones), and only in the eleventh century

* Fig. 35. -Fragments of the Balustrades of the Baptistery at Cividale—A.D. 737.

did they become familiar to all the sacred buildings in Europe. The baptistery of Cividale merits, therefore, special consideration, for it offers one of the first examples in Italy of these representations of animals, which afterwards became the most conspicuous species of sculptured ornamentation of the Romanic style.

The base, as I have said, is in part composed of fragments of parapets of the same style as the archivolts, and therefore most probably by the same artificers. In the interior is a little pilaster made to serve for a cornice. Its decoration consists of a vine-branch with double row of curls of unfortunate design. On the exterior, at the left, two fragments of high parapets compose one of the sides of the base. The other

* Fig. 36.—Balustrade of Sigualdo in the Baptistery at Cividale—A.D. 762-776.

presents two squares enclosing two rude symbols of Evangelists furnished with inscriptions, and, lower down, a complicated band with curvilinear knot-work of channelled ribbons which the artificers meant for osiers. The other fragment of a parapet offers an elegant wheel formed of open lilies and some curling palm-leaves.

The first section on the right of the parapet consists only of one entire piece of marble adorned with bas-reliefs. The angles are occupied by four circles, whose borders are adorned by wreaths of little leaves and enclose the symbols of the Evangelists, of a still more barbarous design than the preceding ones and from an equally clumsy chisel. Each figure

holds a tablet, on which is carved an inscription relative to its
symbolism. The central part of the parapet is divided into two
zones. In the upper one there is a cross adorned with braidings, between two palms (below) and two roses (above), and
flanked by two candelabra shaped like many-ringed columns
with bases and small capitals. This representation, which had
appeared as early as the sixth century on monuments of Byzantine style at Rome and Ravenna, and now reappeared in Italy
through the same Byzantine influence, we shall see repeated for
a long time in Italian works of the ninth and tenth centuries.
The inferior zone of the parapet represents a tree whose upper
boughs terminate in lions' heads; below, there are two winged
griffins, and over them two doves holding bunches of grapes in
their beaks. In this quite Oriental composition, which reminds
us of those we saw on the façade of the cathedral of Athens,
Selvatico saw a reflection of the cloudy doctrines brought across
the Alps by the Lombards! This stone bears the following
carved inscription :—

+ HOC TIBI RESTITVIT SICVALD BAPTESTA
IOHANNES.

So Sigualdo, Patriarch of Aquileia, whose See dated from 762
to 776, had this parapet sculptured in substitution for one that
was ruined. That it ever belonged to the baptistery no one
can be sure of.

These poor artificers who, notwithstanding the imperfections
of their chisel, often knew how to work in ornaments with
sufficient grace, but in representing animals fell into an abyss
of unskilfulness, must have avoided, one would think, like the
pest, any occasion for representing the human figure, which, more
than that of animals, require solid artistic culture and a free
hand ; yet they did not, since we see in Cividale itself, in the
church of S. Martin, an altar of their making, covered on three
sides by figures with sacred subjects. The inscription that
encircles it says that it was ordered by King Ratchis (744–749),
the son of Pemone, Duke of Friuli. The reader may imagine
what sort of thing could issue from such hands. If the coarse-

ness of the times did not justify the presence of these wretched things, one would think they were gross caricatures; they are such horrors that they can only be compared to those *sgorbi* that the uneducated children of the populace often trace upon

* Fig. 37.—Altar of Ratchis at Cividale (posterior part)—A.D. 744-749.

the walls of our houses, especially if newly painted and whitewashed. Truly, if all the sacred images that the eighth century offered to the veneration of the faithful had been of this stamp, one would almost find even the fury of the iconoclasts reasonable.

On the front of the altar Jesus Christ is represented in the act of benediction. A seraph with six wings is on each side of Him. Observe a peculiarity of these wings. They are dowered with a great number of human eyes, certainly in order to follow scrupulously the descriptions made by Ezekiel and S. John. This singularity, unique in Italy, must have been common in Greece, as we can still see at Constantinople in the interior of the ancient church of S. Ireno, a capital that seems to date from the eleventh century, having four seraphim under the angles of the abacus with their wings similarly spotted with eyes. Four palm-branches borne by as many angels enclose in an oval the Saviour and the seraphim. One side of the altar represents the visitation of S. Elizabeth; the other the adoration of the Magi; and at the back are two great jewelled crosses of an entirely Greek character. Each face of the altar is framed by plaits, cordons, spindles, or by several bands formed by the letters SS uniting at their heads like chain-work. Palms, roses, and lilies, are copiously used.

But another monument waits for us in Cividale where, for nearly twenty years, writers on Art are wont to guide Art-students to comfort and recreate themselves with the sight of some fine *stucchi*. It is the little church of S. Maria-in-Valle, of which a chronicle written in 1533 would have us believe that it is the same as that which was adorned by Pertrude, wife of the Duke of Friuli in the time of the Patriarch Sigualdo. It tells us that Pertrude, having founded a monastery there, deposited relics of saints in costly cases in that little church, and built a most beautiful choir surrounded by several marble tablets and by columns also of marble supporting the vault. It also mentions the majestic door of the church adorned internally by a vine, and above by six images of saints. All that we can see even now, so that the work of Pertrude remains to us perfectly and wonderfully preserved.

Lenoir was the first to make this church known to us through the work of Gailhabaud, who blindly bowed to the chronicle and gave us this little church for an example of decoration and sculpture of the eighth century. Dartein and Selvatico confirmed his conclusion, but not without some doubts, and they were followed by Cavallucci * Bayet † and many others. But it is sufficient to glance at the date of that chronicle to make us cautious in giving faith to such opinions; and, if we

---

* "Manuale di Storia della Scultura," Lœscher, 1884.
† "L'Art Byzantin," Paris, Quantin.

proceed to examine the monument in a diligent and dispassionate way, they must be at last altogether rejected.

It is composed of a square cell of solid masonry, covered by a solid vault of crosier pattern, and followed by a little presbytery subdivided into three small chapels by some columns supporting architraves, on which curve three vaults whose arches are slightly raised. The first two columns, because they serve to support the wall above, are larger than the others; their capitals, though not as elegant as those of the baptistery of Calisto, remind one of their style. The choir is closed by a chancel formed by two slabs of marble with a simple fillet, and by two slender little pilasters supporting a little wooden cornice whose capitals still more resemble the accurate chiselling of those of the above-mentioned baptistery. There is one door surmounted by a blind arch which is repeated on the two lateral walls; and blind arches in curved windows also decorate the outer flanks of the little church. A rich and elegant decoration in stucco covers the internal front of the edifice, and consists of two demi-columns (which have now almost disappeared) supporting a light archivolt of vine-branches, spindles, and roses curving over the entrance; of a band of interlaced SS that runs over the architrave; of two cornices in rosework; of a window embellished with little columns and a rich archivolt, and finally of six statues in high relief representing saints in vestments rich in ornaments and pearls, of a character absolutely Byzantine.

In face of the infantile and barbarous figures of the baptistery of Calisto and the altar of Ratchis, how can we attribute to the same epoch, in the same city, these six statues which, though somewhat too long and wooden, and leaving something to be desired in the drapery, are nevertheless as superior to the others as the sun is to the moon? That elegant archivolt of proportions so just, and of an effect so lovely, so enchanting that any artist might be proud of having imagined it, is it not the most beautiful thing of the kind that exists in the world? These were the first and most spontaneous considerations that made me doubt the authenticity of the chronicle; but there is more yet. The beautiful decoration in stucco, now limited to the sole internal façade, must originally have been repeated on all the other walls and even under the little chapels, as is evidently shown by the existence of remnants here and there. Now, why is it that the chronicler who describes the work of Pertrude, mentions only the wall which is still preserved? If, as he asserts, he really drew it from authentic sources, why did not his description also include the things now lost? Selvatico, sustaining the veracity of that chronicle, says we must not think that the chronicler of that monastery was only guided by the foolish vanity of making the little church appear very antique. This time the critic is really too indulgent! Of these foolish vanities the history of Art has many specimens, and Selvatico himself often fell into them unawares; but who is unable to see that here vanity was not so much in question as the ignorance of the chronicler, in whose time there was not even a faintly dawning twilight of critical history of Art, especially mediaeval Art? Indeed one may swear that no one then would have dreamt of doubting the pretended antiquity of that church. I never could understand how the aforesaid worthy historians of the edifice under discussion, although tormented by the doubts that leak out of their pages * had not the courage once for all to emancipate themselves from that mendacious chronicle. But note the power of analogy! Notwithstanding that everything here gave them cause for doubting it, that chronicle was not repudiated, because the capitals resembled those of Calisto's baptistery. That is why they have taken the whole for the part. I, on the contrary, would have picked out the part and left the rest.

In fact, it is not only the stucco decoration that in my opinion cannot be attributed to the eighth century, but the whole ensemble of the edifice. As far as I am concerned the present church is only a refabrication of that adorned by Pertrude, perhaps in the same place and on the same foundations, but with a very different design, worked out about the

* The only one who did not limit himself to mere doubt, but curtly refused to believe that the statues mentioned above belong to the eighth century, was the excellent Professor Melani in his little volume on the " Scultura Italiana " (Hœpli). But he held back at the figures, continuing to regard and point out the beautiful ornaments as examples of architectonic decoration of the eighth century.

year 1100. In the eleventh or twelfth century that solid vault of crosier pattern was built; they were then capable of building it, and it is not necessary, as Dartein and Selvatico wish, to revert to the Roman epoch in witnessing the technical inexperience of artificers of the seventh and eighth centuries. In the eleventh or twelfth century those blind external and internal arches found their place, and especially those vaults with arches raised on, and projecting from, great brackets springing from the capitals—a mode that in Venice, in Italy, and even in Greece was not familiar to architects before the tenth century. But as there is nothing in this fabric that belongs to the Lombard style and, on the contrary, the Neo-Byzantine style is evident in every part of it, we must needs believe it to be the work of some Greek artist, who required simple forms and bare walls as a field for the splendid stucco decorations that he wished to lavish upon them. By all who have any knowledge of mediæval Art, the Greek hand has been recognised in these works. Those graceful motives of ornamentation, that beauty of form and elegance of conceit, those tall figures with beautiful small heads and Oriental vestures, while they retain all the impression of Grecian art, do not find their counterparts in any other authentically Italian work. In only one other part of Italy have I seen similar things. I refer to certain bas-reliefs in stucco that adorn the ciborium of the high altar, or adorned the presbytery of S. Ambroise of Milan; and why we ought to consider them as Greek and contemporaneous with the stuccoes of Cividale we shall see in the following chapter.

Some of the champions of the chronicle referred to tried to explain the great superiority of these reliefs in stucco to those in marble on the altar of Ratchis, not so much by supposing greater power in the artist, as by insisting on the facility offered by the material he employed, more docile to inspiration and more susceptible to skill. But this idea is erroneous, because, ordinarily, just the reverse occurs; that is to say, works in stucco always turn out rougher than works in marble of the same epoch, so much so that the eye cannot easily miss the fact. And I firmly hold that the man who adorned

S. Maria-in-Vallo in certain particulars—as, for example, in the capitals—would have been a much finer and more fortunate worker if he had had to do with hard stone. But whatever one may think of the epoch of those figures and those ornaments, this is certain—that they breathe forth the renaissance of Byzantine art in the tenth century. Before then sculpture sinned rather by heaviness than lightness; afterwards just the reverse was the case; and those saints seem copied from some of those many bas-reliefs in ivory, that were then produced by thousands in Greece, and circulated through the whole world.

But here is the most eloquent proof that neither the stucco decorations nor the existing edifice can be attributed to the

Fig. 38.—Parapet of S. Maria-in-Valle at Cividale—A.D. 762-776.

eighth century. In the wall of the façade of the little church (the same that holds the figures and the archivolts) one saw, some years ago, certain slabs of marble in fragments adorned by ornamental bas-reliefs, set there not for decoration, but simply to economise other material. One of them was even used as the tablet of a window over the door (now walled), and it was necessary to chip away its corners in order to remove it. More of these stones were found scattered here and there in the contiguous cloister, and together with the first were, by a happy thought, adapted to the walls of the atrium of the church. Well, it is here that I find chiselling of Sigualdo's time, and here alone may we see the remnants of Pertrude's work.

One of these slabs, of a rectangular form, is adorned above and below with two borders of foliage of various designs that remind one of the little pilaster seen by us in the interior of the baptistery of Calisto; the central space is divided into three compartments, one occupied by a wheel with rays, another by a girandole-wheel, the third by slender leaves, probably intended for lilies. Two bands of vine-branches separate these compartments, and spindles and cords are used everywhere. No doubt this was a parapet meant to form part of the chancel of the Sanctuary, and its companion must have been that other, of identical design and measure, of which mutilated remnants are to be found in the pavement of the little presbytery. When measured, they are found to correspond perfectly with the dimensions of the simple modern ones, substituted in the restoration. A sarcophagus lying in the presbytery and, according to popular tradition, enclosing the ashes of the pious duchess, is formed by two slabs of ornamented marble of rectangular form, one of whose smaller sides, somewhat inclined in each slab, terminates at the summit in a

FIG. 39.—Marble Door-leaves at S. Maria-in-Valle—A.D. 762-776.

smooth pineapple. These slabs are neither more nor less than the marble doors of the antique chancel; their decoration consists below of two little arcades, with a palm-tree or a vine, and above of little squares, sometimes filled up by roses, and always framed by braids or twists of leafage and birds.

Fig. 40.—Fronton of S. Maria—A.D. 762-776.

Not less interesting are three other slabs of marble, taking the form of a fronton. The smaller one, with rather steep inclination, seems an unfinished work, and offers an embarrassed design in circles, with palms and braidings. Perhaps it once decorated the entrance of the little church. The other two, of equal dimensions and better proportions, are identical in their framings, and varied only in their tympanum; the horizontal bands are adorned by fine gyres with rosettes of conspicuously Greek pattern; and the inclined bands show SS fronting each other and bound together,[*] and are terminated by rampant leaves. One tympanum shows the usual decorations of rectangles and wheels rich in roses, lilies and palms, and in one corner a cock; the other a great wheel, with knot-work flanked by a bull and a lion, followed by two little animals of the same

[*] These ornaments evidently served as models for the worker in stucco of the twelfth century, who copied them several times in his decorations.

species. These are figures worthy of those in the baptistery. These two frontons united to other horizontal ornaments, of which abundant fragments remain, perhaps served, supported

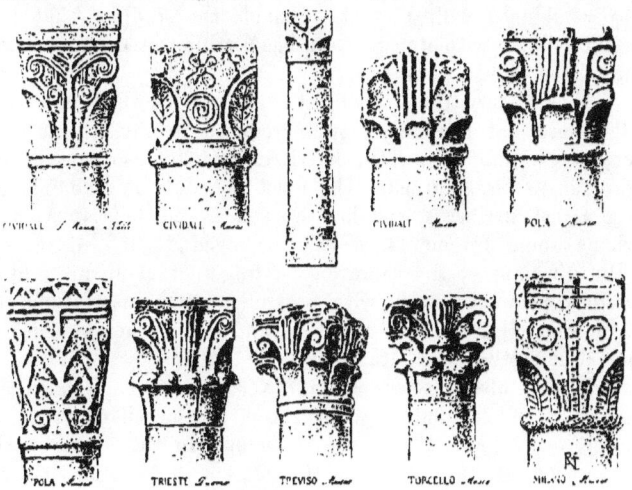

Fig. 41.—Capitals of the VIIIth Century.

by small columns, to cover, like a ciborium, the altar of the little church. I cannot imagine any other place for them.

Several other fragments in the same style, friezes, parapets, and a disc which was perhaps the table of a round monostyle altar, are gathered together on these walls. In the interior also, besides the two little capitals on the pilasters of the chancel and the before-mentioned fragments, the little column with a capital (see Fig. 41) and ornamented pedestal that, in the centre, serves to bear the reading-desk, shows seventh-century work. in addition to the two great capitals that now lie upside down in the presbytery, and serve as pole-bearers.

Their accurate work reminds me of those of the baptistery much more than the others that support the vaults of the present chapels, which, perhaps, may be an imitative work of the time when the church was rebuilt.

The consideration that all these marbles of the eighth century could not have been placed in the little modern church without demolishing it, joined to the reasons which I have already adduced, will, I trust, persuade the studious that the present edifice, with its stuccoes, has nothing in common with that of the eighth century.

The baptistery, the altar, and the decorations of S. Maria-in-Valle, were not the only works produced in Cividale at that time, as it is known that the Patriarch Calisto also caused the cathedral to be enlarged. He must certainly have employed those Greek artificers who had worked in the baptistery, and perhaps some fragments of this belonged to it. Moreover, in the museum of the same city, a fragment of an arch of a ciborium is to be seen with bas-reliefs and inscriptions of the identical style of the baptistery, and some other bits in the same style as that of S. Maria-in-Valle.

One can also observe certain very rough capitals, that, presenting much analogy with those of the ciborium of S. George of Valpolicella, evidently belong to the same epoch. The conceit of the cube with the cut corners is there clearly seen, and the artist has often given it the semblance of leafage.

Guided by these things, we shall recognise similar ones in several other places.

TRIESTE.—We see two slight columns in the cathedral of Trieste of more slender proportions, but of analogous taste, employed as best might be in a restoration of the eleventh century, but evidently belonging to the eighth. In the lower part they have a row of coarse leaves, here each cut in three different directions; higher up is the usual cutting of the corners, and on the front a channelled convexity with meagre honeysuckle ornaments supporting the abacus.

POLA.—Of the same kind, but wrought by a coarser and less correct hand, is a little capital in the museum of Pola, and also another somewhat different but of the same style.

TREVISO.—The museum of Treviso has a rectangular basin, adorned with fine, large, and original leaves of wild acanthus, that shows the style of the eighth century, and so does a little broken column with capital, that seems to belong to the same family as the above-described.

TORCELLO.—Several are to be seen in the museum of

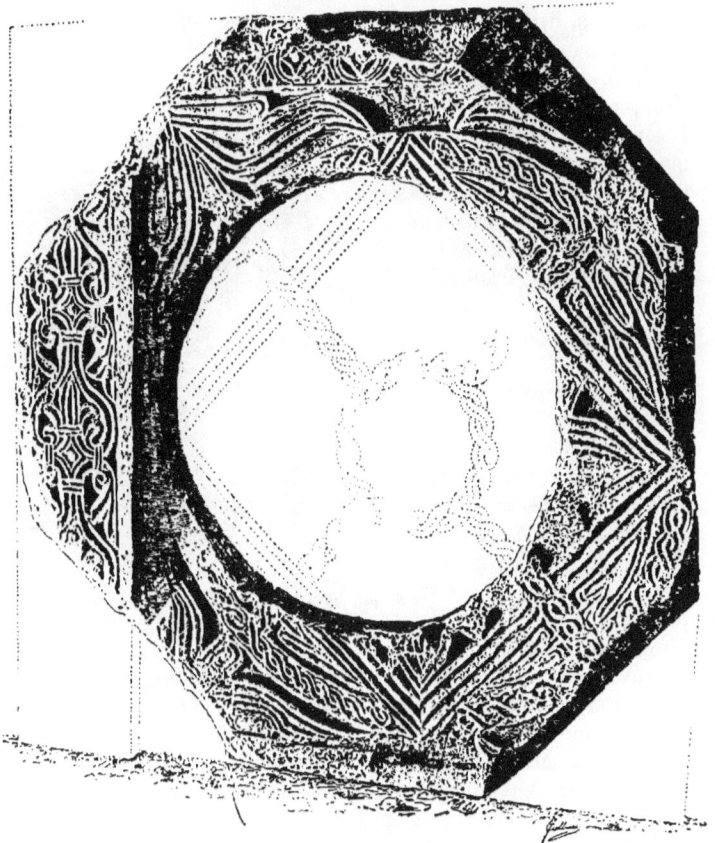

FIG. 42.—Parapet found at S. Augustine at Venice—VIIIth Century.

Torcello; they are for the most part Corinthian, with smooth leaves. One only, much mutilated, shows leaves with intaglio, and much resembles others that we shall see in the museum of Brescia. There is also a fragment of a little pilaster, remains of some chancel, with braided circles containing girandole-stars, roses, or crosses. It is surrounded by a curious band, with little leaves turned face-to-face and curved.

VENICE.—A similar little pilaster I also saw in Signor Dorigo's depôt of marbles; it was strengthened by a graceful band, with leaves which alternated in curvilinear meanders. I also saw there a fragment of a parapet with a band and mixtilinear braidings, and a circle formed of laurel-leaves, enclosing the symbol of the evangelist S. Luke, very similar to that of the baptistery of Cividale.

A considerable fragment of a parapet, in the style of the pilastrini described above, was discovered among the *débris* of the church of S. Augustine; and if Signor Bertoja had not judiciously taken its photograph, we should not know anything about it, because, like an infinity of other Venetian sculptures, it unfortunately passed to foreign parts, and we know not where it has found an asylum. It is admirable for the two elegant bands, with circles and leaves, or the letters SS flowered and interknotted; but above all for the singular decoration of the centre, precious because it teaches us that a similar ornament, with which we shall often meet in Italian works of the ninth century, was inspired by Greek works of the eighth. And, guiding ourselves by the later works above-named, we may infer that the square inscribed in the circle contained in its

FIG. 43.—Window near the Frescada Bridge at Venice—VIIIth Century.

turn a smaller circle, bound with the larger one by braiding and enclosing rosework. Leaves, rough but characteristic of many sculptures of that time, fill up the spaces.

A gracious and interesting Greek work of the eighth century, perhaps brought from *terra firma*, was recently bought in Venice by the Sig. Cav. Guggenheim, who had the happy idea of placing it near his habitation, not far from S. Thomas. It is a little marble window, seventy centimetres high, pierced by various orders of small arches, placed one above the other, or divided by three circular apertures, while lilies and braids enrich its little imposts. But the thing in it that ought specially to hold our attention, is the large arch that terminates it, which is not semicircular but trefoil, and for that reason is the most ancient of this sort that I know in Italy. This shows us once more that only Greeks could have been the authors of these sculptures of the eighth century existing in Italy; because the conceit of the trefoil arch, without doubt of Indian origin and very early date, could only have been introduced by those Greeks who had intimate connections with those distant countries. This example, however, remained unfruitful here, and a mere decorative caprice; and more than four centuries were to pass before that kind of arch, again imported from the East, should become in Italy also a common and organic element of architecture.

The museum of Venice possesses a sculpture of Greek style of the eighth century, brought from *terra firma*; it is part of a curious and elegant archivolt, projecting not by moulding, but from a convexity finely arabesqued with elegant foliage, small leaves, and rampant fillets. We also see a similar archivolt in the museum of Bréscia.

In the same museum of Venice there is a hexagonal baptismal basin, brought, doubtless, from Dalmatia, which remained for ages in a courtyard of the convent of the Redeemer at the Giudecca. The principal side is adorned by a crested cross rich in braidings; and on every side but one it has demi-columns with spiral channellings, with rough capitals supporting a little cornice with spindles, and a large band whereon a long description is engraved. The latter tells us that the basin was caused to be made by a priest named Giovanni, in the time of Duke Wissasclavo. The archaeologists were much puzzled to determine where and when that duke lived, but as the sculptures on that basin were mute, they could not know what time and name to fix on. However, as it shows the style of the seventh century, we can accept as nearest the truth the hypothesis of Kukuljeric of Zagabria (see "Corriere Italiano," Vienna, No. 50, dated 1851), who saw in Wissasclavo a Voiseslavo, a Servian, who lived about 780.

MURANO.— The cities of the lagoons, richer and more prosperous than any other, were not likely to have been the last, even in the eighth century, to invite Greek artists to adorn them with works of art.

FIG. 44.—Baptismal Font at the Museum at Venice— VIIth or VIIIth Century.

Among the most sure testimonies to the presence of a style in a certain country are, without doubt, its tombs, which, owing to their size and to the respect paid to the dead, are not very easy to transport here and there. Now among the various sarcophagi brought to the light through some excavations made in 1867 in the place where the antique cemetery of the cathedral of Murano once existed, one was found, whose front presents bas-reliefs evidently of Greek style of the eighth century. In the centre there is a cross, with a rose flanked by great circles, with elegant and varied rosework, rayed or girandoled, or lilies like those of S. Maria of Cividale. Over it runs a simple twist, only interrupted by the cross. It is kept in the cathedral itself.

Concordia.—In the atrium of the very ancient baptistery of Concordia, among varied works of the ninth century there is

Fig. 45.—Principal Side of a Sarcophagus in the Cathedral of Murano—VIIIth Century.

one of the eighth, a fragment that by its convexity shows itself to have been the front of an ambo. From what remains of it one may divine the elegant and ingenious design of the whole, which was a circle formed by braidings knotted crosswise to the border squared by the same braidings. The circle, perhaps, once enclosed the Lamb and the triangles, which surround it, the symbols of the Evangelists. The only one remaining is that of S. Luke.

Grado.—If the patriarchs of Aquileia desired to avail themselves of Greek artificers to adorn their new residence in the best way that their times permitted, their neighbours, the patriarchs of Grado, would not have liked to be behind them in this respect. And, in fact, in a courtyard, behind the precious cathedral already known to us, there exist, set in a wall enriched with sculptures of various epochs, two considerable fragments of convex parapets, without doubt belonging to an ambo of the eighth century. One would think it must have been an invariable rule in those times that the figure of a cross should afford the sole basis for the decoration of pulpit fronts, for on all those we have seen and are still to see the superficies of each parapet is subdivided into four squares by two bands that cross one another; and thus it is also with the two sides of the ambo of Grado. In both it seems that the upper squares were occupied by the monogram of Christ, made wheel-fashion, formed in the centre by a rosette, rayed or girandoled, and

Fig. 46.—Fragments of an Ambo at the Cathedral of Grado—VIIIth Century.

inscribed in a circle that developes little volutes or knots. The lower compartments of one side were covered by a multitude of little squares; those of the other by a peacock pecking a leaf, between vine-suckers and branches of conventional form, where imitation of similar works of the sixth century is openly displayed.

It is easy to imagine how favours would be heaped upon the squad of Greek artists by the wealthy Lombards and the most conspicuous Italian personages; for these artists, compared with the native ones, must have seemed extremely skilful. The fact that we find traces of their handiwork, not only in the most considerable cities of that time, but also in little towns and boroughs, shows clearly that they were not left in idleness.

VERONA.—Before leaving the "Veneto" let me remember a mutilated capital of simple Corinthian form, existing in Verona, in the apsis of S. Stephen, and bearing on the front a cross placed between A and Ω; and, in the museum of the same city, a fragment of a parapet and the capital of a demi-column. In the first, which, notwithstanding its most incorrect design, shows a certain delicacy of treatment, the interwreathings of little semicircular arches making pointed ones, are notable. In the capital, wherein occurs, as in so many of the same period, the conceit of the cube cut away at the corners, a medallion enclosing a human head (perhaps the least deformed figure that remains to us among these works) attracts our attention; for in it, instead of rough furrows and scratchings, we find an attempt at modelling.

FIG. 47.—Capital at the Museum of Verona —VIIIth Century.

A building, the greater part, if not the whole, of which belongs to this epoch is the little church of SS. Tosca and Teuteria, at Verona, which rises behind the parish church of the Holy Apostles, and was consecrated, as Biancolini affirms,* in 751, by Bishop S. Annone. The present edifice, to which descent is made by eight stairs, shows high antiquity. The plan of it is nearly square; from one of the sides juts out an apsis, while in the middle rise four pilasters supporting full-centred arcades, over which rises a sort of square cupola, covered by cross-vaults and lighted by little windows. Walls, pilasters, and vaults are covered with parget; there is not one cornice, not one bit of sculpture, not even a moulding. The very low floor, the nudity and poverty of the

* Biancolini, "Le Chiese di Verona," 1748.

architecture, and a certain disorder in its organism would induce
us to think that it belonged to the eighth century: but it will
be well to recollect that disorder in construction, rather than
bearing witness to
remote antiquity
and rude ages, is
the fruit of resto-
rations heaped one
on the other in the
same fabric; and,
in fact, this is the
case with our little
church. Certainly
the man who raised
the four pilasters
and curved the
arcades of the
centre must have
had the idea of
a church in the
shape of a Greek
cross with equal
arms. Now why
is the trace of the
perimetral walls,
rectangular instead
of square, and why

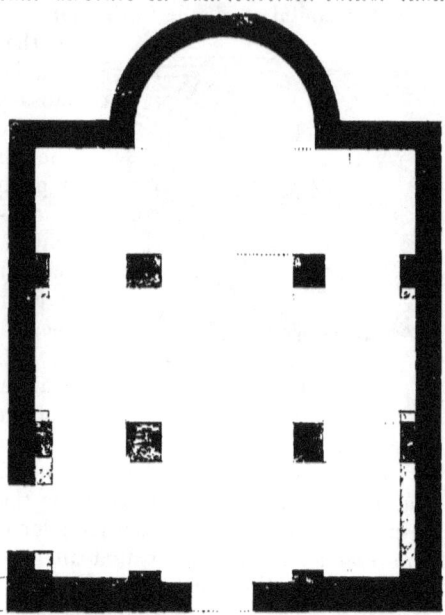

FIG. 48.—Plan of S. Teuteria at Verona —VIIIth and
XIIth Century.

does the end of the apsis enlarge itself much more than
the central arcades, producing a sort of abnormal and embarrassed vault in the space that precedes it, and, therefore,
on the one corresponding to it? Without doubt, because the
perimetral wall and the apsis were built before the erection of
the central pilasters. When this radical transformation occurred
is nearly indicated by the Neo-Byzantine character of the
present edifice, and it is also indicated by what Biancolini
himself says, namely, that after the bodies of the two martyred
saints were found, in 1160, the church was newly conse-

crated by the Bishop Ognibene. Therefore either the restoration gave occasion to the discovery or the discovery occasioned the restoration. The old church of the eighth century was then a simple little basilica divided into three naves by columns or pilasters, reproducing neither more nor less than the old common Latin manner.

VICENZA.—In the museum of Vicenza one may see a florid capital in Greek style of the eighth century (unfortunately very much out of condition), and a fragment of a parapet with part of a cross finely covered by a net and flanked by boughs, leaves, and bunches of grapes.

Another fragment of the same style exists in the ground floor of the Palazzo Orgian. It is the half of a fronton similar to those of S. Maria-in-Valle of Cividale. A good part of the cross in the middle still remains, adorned with braiding and little volutes at the ends of the arms. a wretched lamb bearing a little cross, doves, roses of various kinds, and braids.

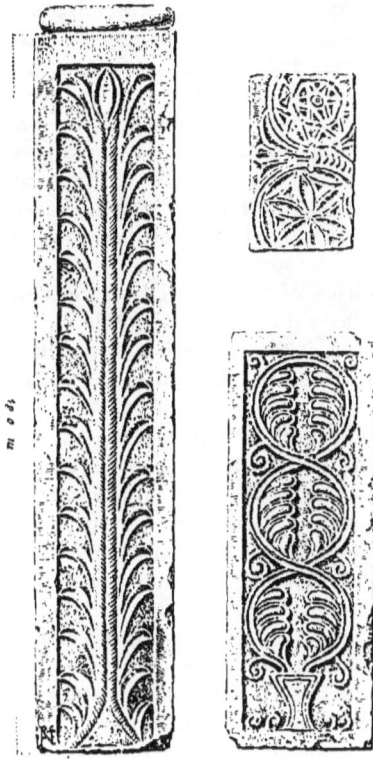

FIG. 49.—Little Pilaster of Monselice and Fragments at the Museum Bocchi at Adria—VIIIth Century.

MONSELICE.—A little pilaster, which must have formed part of the chancel of a presbytery of the eighth century, is preserved in Monselice, near the Municipio. In its superior part we find the remains of the base of the colonnette that served to support the veils of the sanctuary; in its sides it shows the encasements of the parapets; and in front, within a simple square, two twisted cordons that serve as stems for a great many leaves (see Fig. 49).

ADRIA.—In Adria, moreover, in the interesting Museo Bocchi, we recognise our style in a fragment of terracotta with bas-reliefs representing circles, leaves, and stars of various sorts; and again in a low little pilaster adorned with circling braids issuing from a rude vase and enriched with common conventional leaves (palm-leaves, we may suppose), formed of convexities bordered by listels. You may see some traces of these at Cividale and Grado, and it is well to remember them, because we shall see them very much used by Italian artificers in the ninth century.

In the church of the Sepulchre of the same city there is an octagonal baptismal font furnished with a long inscription, where a Bishop Bono is mentioned, who, it seems, lived in the eighth century, but we will not stop to observe it, as it is absolutely bare of decoration.

RAVENNA.—The reader will expect that in our present researches, Ravenna, which, until 752, was the seat of the Greek Esarch, and therefore in continual relations with Byzantium, must demand a long study. Quite the contrary. Perhaps the abundance and the splendour of the sacred monuments, in which that city must have been so rich at that time, caused it not to feel the want of new ones, for no Greek eighth-century work may be seen here except a fragment of parapet with braidings, crosses, and rosettes, existing in the Baptistery Ursiano, and two little bas-reliefs added to the front of a Roman sarcophagus, which are preserved in the museum of the archbishop. The latter consist of a plain cross between two meagre palms and two intertwined circles enclosing two roses.

BAGNACAVALLO.—A few miles from Ravenna and a kilometre from Bagnacavallo there is an ancient basilica dedicated to S. Peter, which we shall have to remember more than once in the following chapters. It possesses considerable remains of the ciborium of an altar, consisting of two headings of arches and of one capital. One of these bears a sculptured inscription,

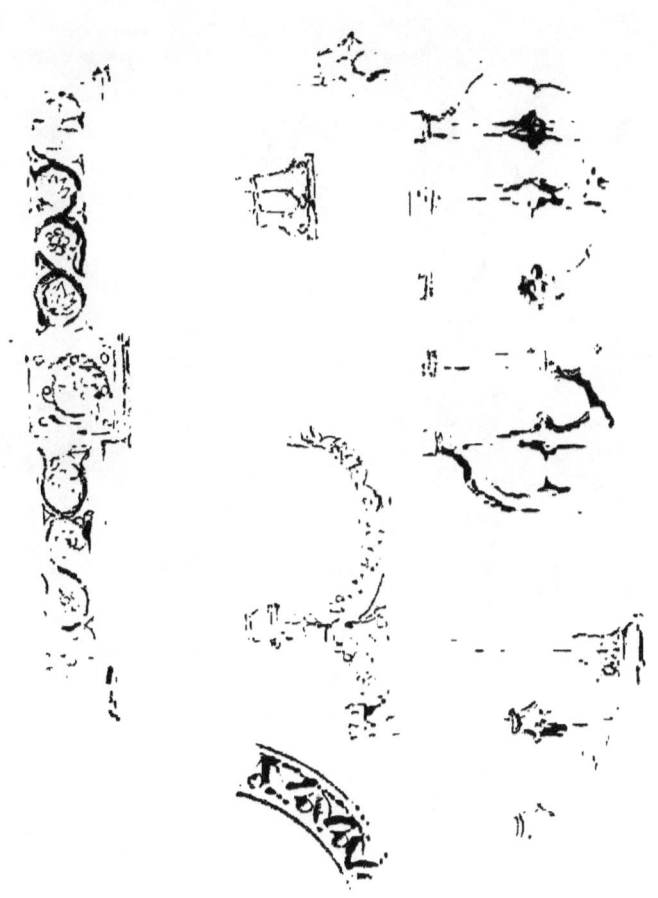

the veils of the sanctuary; in its sides it shows the encasements of the parapets; and in front, within a simple square, two twisted cordons that serve as stems for a great many leaves (see Fig. 49).

ADRIA.—In Adria, moreover, in the interesting Museo Bocchi, we recognise our style in a fragment of terracotta with bas-reliefs representing circles, leaves, and stars of various sorts; and again in a low little pilaster adorned with circling braids issuing from a rude vase and enriched with common conventional leaves (palm-leaves, we may suppose), formed of convexities bordered by listels. You may see some traces of these at Cividale and Grado, and it is well to remember them, because we shall see them very much used by Italian artificers in the ninth century.

In the church of the Sepulchre of the same city there is an octagonal baptismal font furnished with a long inscription, where a Bishop Bono is mentioned, who, it seems, lived in the eighth century, but we will not stop to observe it, as it is absolutely bare of decoration.

RAVENNA.—The reader will expect that in our present researches, Ravenna, which, until 752, was the seat of the Greek Esarch, and therefore in continual relations with Byzantium, must demand a long study. Quite the contrary. Perhaps the abundance and the splendour of the sacred monuments, in which that city must have been so rich at that time, caused it not to feel the want of new ones, for no Greek eighth-century work may be seen here except a fragment of parapet with braidings, crosses, and rosettes, existing in the Baptistery Ursiano, and two little bas-reliefs added to the front of a Roman sarcophagus, which are preserved in the museum of the archbishop. The latter consist of a plain cross between two meagre palms and two intertwined circles enclosing two roses.

BAGNACAVALLO.—A few miles from Ravenna and a kilometre from Bagnacavallo there is an ancient basilica dedicated to S. Peter, which we shall have to remember more than once in the following chapters. It possesses considerable remains of the ciborium of an altar, consisting of two headings of arches and of one capital. One of these bears a sculptured inscription, according to which the ciborium was ordered to be made by a priest Giovanni, under the See of the Bishop Deusdedit. But in those times to what diocese did Bagnacavallo belong? to which of the many bishops of that name, and to what city did the inscription refer? In such obscurity it was natural that those who spoke of the matter, not knowing how to gather from the style of the monument its real epoch, should assign it to the sixth century and a bishop of Voghenza; or the seventh century and the Pope Deusdedit; or the ninth century and a bishop of Faenza; or the ninth century and an archbishop of Ravenna; or the end of the tenth century and a bishop of Imola.

Rohault de Fleury, who better than the rest was able to give an opinion at least approaching the real epoch of these works of the barbarous ages, assigns the ciborium to the ninth century. But Fleury, notwithstanding his patient researches, did not know how to seize the many and conspicuous

FIG. 50.—Arch of Ciborium in the Pieve di Bagnacavallo—VIIIth Century.

characteristics that distinguish the works of the eighth from the ninth centuries, and therefore, as we shall find again and again, he had no scruple in decorating the ninth century with works which belonged to the preceding one. Thus, unawares, he left his work unprovided with monuments of the eighth century, and especially with altar ciboria, so that to make up for the loss as best he might, he sends his reader to the

Fig. 51.—Arch of Ciborium in the Parish Church of Bagnacavallo.—VIIIth Century.

baptistery of Cividale, though that sort of construction of the eighth century is still represented in Italy by many samples, as we have seen and shall see. But, to return to our ciborium, although it had not escaped his observation that none of the dates of bishops of that name (Deusdedit) of the ninth century coincided with the tenor of the epigraph, yet, desiring at any cost that the bishop of Faenza (who ruled between 826 and 830) should be the man alluded to, he sought to justify his predilection by the specious supposition that the inscription refers to gifts gathered in the time of that bishop. But his artifice does not deprive this ciborium of the authentic Greek stamp of the eighth century, and, when we consider that in the series of bishops of Voghenza there is a lacuna from 686 to 772, it is logical to conclude that Bishop Deusdedit belonged to that See and to that interval, and that the village of Bagnacavallo was then subject to him.

In the heading of that inscription a simple braid, followed by a cordon from which spring the usual rampant caulicules limited by a row of beads between two listels, curves so as to form an archivolt. The spaces over the arches are partly occupied by a palm and a rose-tree, in which the stem is remarkable for being represented by a channelled ribbon like those that compose the usual braidings. We shall often see this conventional manner imitated in the following century, and maintained in Italy till the twelfth century, having become a characteristic of Lombard art.

The other heading in the ornamentation of the archivolt copies the preceding one, with the addition of a half-circle of intertwisted vine-branches, enclosing bunches of grapes and leaves. A cross between roses, and lambs, doves, peacocks, fishes, circles, and triangles, complete the rich but barbarous composition.

The only capital that remains of it (now a vase for holy water, poorly ornamented with a timid cordon, rude roses, crosses, and chalices) is worth observation for the ensemble, which reproduces in mass the Byzantine capitals of the sixth century, the form resembling a truncated pyramid turned upside down and rounded underneath.

FERRARA.—If the ciborium of Bagnacavallo has in part filled up the gap in the series of bishops of Voghenza in the eighth century, another work of the same century will serve to the same effect. There are in the courtyard of the university of Ferrara two convex parapets of an ambo derived from Voghenza, furnished with inscriptions in which allusion is made to a bishop named George, without doubt of that city. Here several Georges were brought into the field, but fortunately Fleury this time, perhaps more for the sake of that same gap than with regard to the style of the ambo, halted as we do at the eighth century.

Each side of the ambo is enriched by four squares framed by cordings and bands; the whole covered with vine-branches, lilies, plants, and peacocks. Rude, meagre things you may think them, yet they are expressed with a sort of cleverness and ingenuous grace. The bunches of grapes are notable for being roughly and conventionally surrounded by a listel—a mode which we shall find in favour with Italian sculptors of the ninth century. Besides the ambo one may see in the same courtyard in Ferrara a parapet that, showing the same manner of work, may be presumed to come also from Voghenza. It is certainly work of the eighth century, and among the most uncouth and barbarous that a Greek chisel ever produced. It shows a bare tree with two lions at its foot, then two doves, then two peacocks, and over all two serpents; a composition full of attraction because it is one of the first essays of those bizarre yet obscure representations of animals, which the Byzantines loved to repeat so often in the following centuries, and which reached their apogee with the balustrades and decorative forms of the tenth and eleventh centuries that we shall see in Venice.

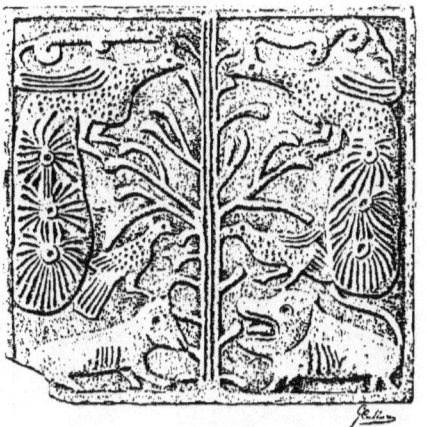

Fig. 52.—Parapet in the Court of the University of Ferrara—VIIIth Century.

MODENA.—Important remains of ambos and parapets of the style of the eighth century are preserved in a courtyard near the cathedral of Modena. Fleury, as usual, held them to be works of the ninth century, but the Greek chisel of the eighth is shown in their smallest details. The curvilinear ambo-parapets are, like their synchronical brothers, corniced and divided by bands into four regular compartments. In one of the sides the cross, formed in the centre, is adorned by goodly circles of leaves, and the border by simple braids. The squares are occupied either by palms with wild acanthus-leaves or by groups of branches. Similar ornaments must probably have embellished the squares of the other ambo-parapet, framed instead by cordings and complicated braidings.

Of a third parapet, which perhaps belonged to the ambo at which the epistle was recited, there remains a fragment with braidings, palms, and legs, perhaps of a peacock.

Bands rich in braids and inscriptions, or fine foliage like those of S. Maria-in-Valle at Cividale, may be seen also among parapets more or less broken up, but noticeable for the novelty and sometimes for the elegance of their decorations. They are arcades of braidings alternated with sticks bearing lilies, and filled up by palms, roses, and roughly-worked birds, great braided and corded circles enclosing a cross richly beaded, and little arches placed one over another like scales. The latter may be compared to certain Roman ones, or several Byzantine ones of the fifth or sixth century, which are gracefully enriched by lilies.

Fig. 53.—Arch of Ciborium over the Place S. Dominic at Bologna—VIIIth Century.

BOLOGNA.—Bologna also preserves some Greek work of the eighth century. The most important is an arch of a ciborium that one sees on the piazza of S. Dominic, applied to the tomb of the Foscherari, and which Fleury, of course, assigns to the ninth century. It is decorated by an elegant archivolt composed of beautiful foliage, like those of Modena and Cividale, among spindles and cordons, a cross on the edge, and a running pattern, that are true and uncorrupted models from the antique. Over the archivolt runs a sort of cornice with spindles, semi-rosettes, lilies, and listels, while the remaining intervals over the arch are occupied by two very coarse peacocks.

At S. Stephen's, in Bologna, where there is a marble basin

* FIG. 54.—Sarcophagus of S. Agricola at S. Stephen of Bologna—XIIth Century.

(catino) with a long inscription — a not very regal gift from King Luitprand to that church, in the contiguous ancient basilica of SS. Peter and Paul, once the cathedral, one may also observe the sarcophagus of a S. Agricola which at first sight recalls the work of the century we are studying. It represents a very barbarian figure of an angel enclosed in a wreath of nondescript leaves and flanked by a stag and a lion amid palms and volatiles in curious and impossible positions. But all this is framed by a reversed gola cut into trilobes in the Roman style, and on three sides by bands rich in ornament which, although savouring slightly of the Byzantine, yet appear so characteristic of the Roman style that we must believe that they, like all the other sculptures of the sarcophagus, belong to the twelfth century in which the church was rebuilt, instead of to the eighth, as Dartein opined, still less to the sixth as was supposed by Fleury. Such are especially those half-leaves projecting alternately from the right and from the left, leaving a zigzag space between them—a motive much used in the centuries succeeding the tenth, especially in painting on glass and on walls.

If I were constrained by valid reasons to assign this motive to the eighth century, from seeing it repeated on the heading of a capital in the same church close by it, I should not, however, draw from it the too rash deduction that Dartein did (followed, as usual, by Selvatico), namely, that the capital ought to be ascribed to the same century. So slight an analogy is not enough to bring us to such conclusions. The sarcophagus, if we accept those few bands of a Roman character, might, through the timidity of its sculpture and the rigidity of its forms, pass even for a work of the eighth century. It certainly does not present any conspicuous sign of novelty; but this criticism does not apply to the capital, in which, even if you despoil it of all its ornaments, there remains a structure that of itself announces a notable change of style. I have neither the courage nor the necessity to invite Dartein to study the Romanic art of the twelfth century, because he knows it perfectly; but I would invite him to reflect a little on the monuments that we have already studied and on many that we are now about to study, because the fact that they had for the most part escaped his researches was the reason that the learned man seems not to have been able to form for himself a just idea of the character of the eighth-century Art, of what those poor

* Fig. 55.—Capital of SS. Peter and Paul, near S. Stephen of Bologna—XIIth Century.

artificers could do, and what they could not do. It is sufficient to throw a rapid glance over the capitals of that century reproduced in this work to persuade oneself that they have not the slightest point of contact with this of SS. Peter and Paul; while those, whose eyes are accustomed to the Lombard style of the twelfth century, will find that this capital, chiefly on account of its broad and low ensemble without sensible projections, bears all the impress of that time.

But perhaps some of my readers, to whom the present question may appear a trifle to be passed over, will think that I treasure up the slightest error of that illustrious writer for the mere vain glory of demonstrating it. It is not true; but, even if it were, my censures could not avail to lessen his great merits and well-acquired fame. Yet I beg the kind reader to believe that the question of that simple capital, though it may appear frivolous, is really of great importance; and this I will now briefly demonstrate.

Without doubt the arguments by which Cordero attempted to persuade us that the old monuments of Romanic style have nothing to do with those that were erected during the Lombard domination were highly valuable; and, in fact, the researches, the discoveries, and the studies of which these pages are the result, confirm his assertion and make us clearly comprehend the difference between the nature of the architecture of the seventh and eighth centuries and that of S. Michael of Pavia and of S. Ambroise of Milan. But if, through too much credulity or lightmindedness, we accept, on the faith of any chronicler or after superficial observations of our own, this or that monument as the fruit of those miserable times, even if it make manifest a character and value much superior to, and radically different from, those of the really authentic monuments of that poor epoch, we shall prepare a nicely greased descent, down which the unwary will continually slide into those rank errors from which the above-praised Cordero, not without toil, endeavoured to rescue them.

And who, in fact, could be astonished if one fine day one of the many sheep that swear *in verba magistri,* finding himself in the church of SS. Peter and Paul, should take the trouble to continue the weak reasoning of Daitein and should say : " This capital is then of the eighth century. Good ; but why not the opposite capital also ? Truly there is some slight difference in the details, but the proportions are the same, the measurements are the same, the style is the same, the chisel is the same. Who can doubt that they are brothers ? " On the contrary, nothing would be more likely than that the sheep, proud of his discovery and continuing his archæological walk through the seven churches, should find new analogies and new comparisons in several other capitals of the same school ; the more so since, in the Herculean labour of swimming against a stream of four centuries, he would find a comforting angel in the guardian of the church, who, prompted by I know not what professor of the city, calls those capitals Byzantine. And if he made a staircase of details to arrive at a whole, he would not be long in discovering that, since those capitals were evidently made for the arches they support, the latter belong to the same epoch. In fact, by force of comparisons and deductions, he would end by persuading himself that there is no obstacle to believing with Agincourt, Hope, and such disciples as remain to them, that the oldest constructions of the Romanic style may very well be attributed to the Lombard era.

And do not think that these breakneck tumbles are confined to my imagination, for there is no matter of study in which they succeed more frequently or hugely, even with wise and judicious people, than in the history of Art ; and among a hundred instances we have a stupendous one in the delirium of P. Gravina about the age of the celebrated mediæval churches of Sicily.

I am not wrong, then, to be severely cautious in attributing this or that monument to the period we are studying, unless we find indisputable historical or artistical proofs.

MILAN.—From my manner of writing, the reader will have seen that I combat the opinion that the Romanic style was cultivated or even originated during the Lombard domination; yet many do not think with me. On the contrary, latterly Dartein, and after him Selvatico, announce triumphantly the discovery of a monument which ought to afford irrefragable proof that Romanic art had already passed its infancy during the reign of Luitprand. The monument consists of the ruins of the church of Aurona in Milan, discovered in 1869 in excavating for the foundations of the new Savings' Bank. Among many fragments they found brackets, little pilasters, friezes, and several capitals of varied forms and dimensions, all richly decorated with ornaments and figures. Those that most attract the eye are two great monoliths, each having the form of four capitals grafted into one another in the form of a cross, and evidently made to crown two balustrades of quadrilobate section —that is to say, two groups of four columns. The idea, the form, and the details obviously show the developed Romanic style, because, from those grouped pilasters, one may imagine the arches which surmounted them, and even the characteristic crosier vaults. But to what time did those ruins belong? I yield the pen for a moment to Selvatico, that he may let us know the origin of that church.

"The most accredited chronicles of Milan relate that one Theodore, archbishop of that city, who died in 739, was continually persecuted by the king of the Lombards, Ariperto, who, being his relative, feared that the pious priest had the deliberate intention of reigning in his stead. The rage of the ferocious king against the good archbishop was carried so far that at last the latter was ousted from the See that he had governed with as much meekness as wisdom. Ariperto treated Tcoderada the mother, and Aurona the sister, of Theodore still worse, for he cut off the nose and the ears of both.

"As soon, however, as death relieved the world of the crowned monster and the sceptre of Italy was given to the benign Luitprand, who (it seems) was brother to the persecuted archbishop, the latter was replaced in his See to the great delight of the Milanese, who appreciated his doctrine and virtue. His unhappy sister rejoined him and founded a sumptuous convent of Benedictines, annexing to it a church.

"When Theodore died, he was, so say Galvano Flamma and other chroniclers, buried in the aforesaid convent."

Such is the story: now for its consequences. One of those two crossed capitals bears carved on its abacus an inscription that says:—

"HIC REQVIESCIT + DOMINVS THEODORVS ARCHEP. QVI INIVSTE FVIT DAMNATVS."

"See," cry Dartein and Selvatico, "here is the lost sepulchre of Theodore, and the narrative of the injustice that he suffered is confirmed. Here, therefore, are the authentic remains of Aurona's church."

Indeed! Have you really found the sepulchre of Theodore? But how can a simple capital be a sepulchre? In what part of it was the sepulchre scooped out, since it is one unbroken mass? And, if the excavation had taken place, could there have been room there for more than a child a few weeks old? It is hard to believe that these natural and spontaneous questions were not put to themselves by these eminent authors. Depend upon it they were put, but rather than abandon their complacency in having at last found what they call the first step of transition from the Barbarous-Latin to the true Lombard style, they sought to deceive themselves and, at any cost, to find their arguments reasonable. But who cannot see that that inscription can be nothing but a simple sign of the existence of the sepulchre of Theodore in that church or under that capital, and that in that *hic* one was meant to understand *in hac ecclesia*, or *in hoc loco?* And if all this allows of no denial, who in the world can maintain that that inscription dates with the capital from the eighth century? Thus the grave and irrefragable argument, on which those writers grounded their conclusions, is reduced to nothing.

Mongeri, for some time at least, was far more prudent than them. He did not allow himself to be deceived by the inscriptions, but opined that those remnants belonged to the time of the rebuilding of the church in 1099 and not to its first erection. However, later on the bad example perverted Mongeri also, for in one of his last publications he presents those capitals as works of the eighth century; but even supposing he had not allowed himself to be borne away on the current, still his judgment would not have been correct; for if it is true that a great part of those sculptures, and specially the two larger capitals, bear the clearest stamp of the Lombard style of the end of the eleventh century, it is no less true that the rest (that is to say some forty pieces of sculpture) are obviously the real remains of the church of the eighth century.

It is among those remnants that may be seen the finest and most elegant decorations that Greek chisels of the eighth century produced in Italy. They for the most part consist in little pilasters or bands that must have belonged to the chancels of the church, richly adorned by spindles, beads, leaves, chalices, lilies of very varied sorts or ivy-branches, sculptured with such grace and freedom that they would not be out of place among our Renaissance decorations.

* Fig. 56.—Abacus of the Church of Aurona, Milan—VIIIth Century.

Let us mention in particular two isolated pillars, about two

* Fig. 57.— Pilasters of the Church of Aurona, Milan—VIIIth Century.

metres thirty-eight centimetres high and twenty-two centimetres broad. They are splendidly arabesqued with little leaves, cordons, gyres, braidings, and elegant roses. Another angular pillar is sculptured with vine-branches, grapes, and leaves. Another and smaller one shows that it had received inserted ornaments of polychrome marbles. Of parapets there remains but one fragment, with part of a little archivolt surmounted by a rose, flanked by a bird's nest with the mother-bird close by. At the side and at the top are remains of inscriptions in relieved letters. Two little mutilated capitals of columns show a not very happy imitation of the Corinthian manner. Two others, on the contrary, which are much larger, in all probability, were abaci of Byzantine style. Similar, though not so high, to those used in the fifth and sixth centuries, they are richly covered with crosses or doves flanked by elegant gyres with grape-bunches and braids.

All these precious sculptures may now be admired in the museum of Brera at Milan, mixed up without order with the Romanic ones of the same church. That these last were frequently imitations of the earlier works was perhaps the reason why they were held to be of the same date; but now that we know how to distinguish the two epochs, it would be well that the directors of that archaeological museum should think of dividing the numerous fragments into two groups rationally arranged.

In the same museum we may see a colonnette in fragments joined to a capital that shows the roughest manner of the eighth century as much as those at the Cividale Museum. Without doubt they are the work of Italian pupils of the Greeks (see Fig. 41).

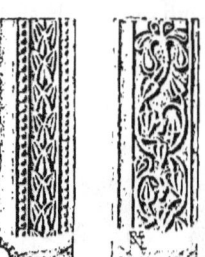

Fig. 58.—Small Pilasters in the Church of Aurona, Milan—VIIIth Century.

The Milanese historian Toire and Castiglioni recorded that the church of S. Vincent-in-Prato at Milan was founded in 780 by Desiderio, the last king of the Lombards. Count Mella, in his studies of basilica, declares that statement to be false, seeing that the Lombard domination ceased in 774. But though one must not accept tradition blindly, it is not to be disposed of summarily without valid reasons. In fact, that date might be the right one if we consider that the grave political circumstance of the fall of the Lombards might have delayed by some years the foundation of that church, for the erection of which Desiderio had perhaps disbursed some money. But to Mella, who at all cost would have it that that basilica belonged to an epoch anterior to the Lombard times, it was of great importance to clear away all obstacles interfering with his theory. We shall show in the following chapter that this church belongs to an epoch somewhat posterior to the Lombards, but we do not deny that it might have had a forerunner, thanks to Desiderio, in a more modest edifice; the less so since we recognise the style of the eighth century in one of the capitals of the naves. It has good proportions and grossly imitates the Corinthian style, showing palm-leaves instead of acanthus; and higher up roses and crosses between meagre caulicules supporting a light abacus. It is much spoiled.

Fig. 59.—Capital of S. Vincent-in-Prato, Milan—VIIIth Century.

BERGAMO.—In the Sozzi Museum in Bergamo one may see three sculptured fragments in the Greek style of the eighth century, of which the largest presents a braid limited by cords and framed by foliage formed of curled vine-twigs.

BRESCIA.—The deep crypt of S. Filastrio in the Rotonda or old cathedral of Brescia, offers us a long series of capitals of every description in a singular chronological progression, for, besides those which are evidently coeval with the construction of the crypt towards the end of the eighth century, several others belonging to older Christian or pagan constructions were added to spare expense. Two of the latter (which were certainly not sculptured for the pilasters that support them, being made for columns, and therefore anterior to the construction of the crypt) plainly show that they belong to that class of simple and meagre Greek capitals of the eighth century, of which we have the prototype at S. George of Valpolicella. They are of rather clumsy form. The leaves around them, though rough, are rendered with sufficient clearness; the corner cuttings are smooth, the volutes not deformed, the abacus of good proportions.

* Fig. 60.—Capital of the Crypt in the Rotunda of Brescia— VIIIth Century.

In the beginning of these pages, I told you how Cordero thought to strengthen his opinions about the continuity of the Latin style in Italy during the whole Lombard period, by indicating a few structures which were proved, according to his notion by irrefragable documents, to have been erected at that time. Now he restricted himself to four examples: the churches of S. Frediano and of S. Michael at Lucca, the Torri Palace at Turin, and the church of S. Saviour at Brescia. The examples are few, but they might have been enough if the supposed irrefragable documents with which Cordero endowed them had not burst like a soap-bubble under a conscientious and disimpassioned examination. We have, in fact, seen above how the two churches of Lucca and the gate of Turin belong to quite another epoch than those of the Lombards; so it only remains to us to see if we can find Cordero in the right at least as regards S. Saviour's of Brescia. Reduced to this point the affair becomes so slight that it is worth our while to spend a little ink about it, for, if Cordero be wrong here also, his whole castle of conjecture tumbles into atoms.

Let us first see what the documents have to say. An ancient ritual of the monastery begins thus: "*Anno ab incarnatione Di CCCCCCCLIII inchoatum fuit monasterium nostrum. . . . Postea consecratum fuit per Dominum Papam cum suis cardinalibus prout invenitur in chronicis satis autenticis in dicto nostro monasterio. . . .*" The historic memoirs and the diplomas assure us that this monastery was founded by the Lombard Desiderio, conjointly with Ausa his wife, before he ascended the throne and therefore during the reign of Astolfo. These notices, as every one may see, have quite the appearance of being authentic, and we ought the more readily to accept them since no contradiction is involved in them.

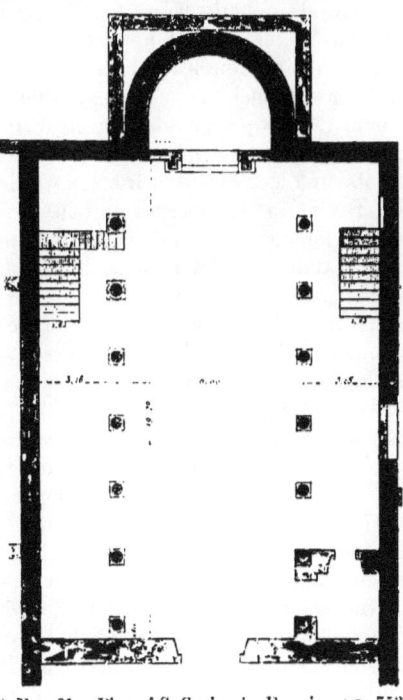

Fig. 61.—Plan of S. Saviour's, Brescia. A.D. 753.

We read, in fact, in Anastasius, that in 753 Pope Stephen III. traversed Lombardy to betake himself to the court of Astolfo. But what gives us something to think about is that in those documents the monastery alone is spoken of and nothing said about the church annexed to it. If before then no church had existed there, it would be reasonable to believe that the word monastery included the church; but, knowing that in the very place where S. Saviour's now stands, the church of SS. Michael and Peter already existed since the sixth century, and that a few Byzantine capitals still remain of it, how can our doubt be called unfounded?

The documents being found, I will not say uncertain, but absolutely negative, it appears that an artistic examination of the monument ought to settle the question; and it does settle it. But if such a doubt had been exposed to Cordero, how would he have been able to clear it away? Would he have known how to separate, in that church, the sculpture belonging to its first construction from those that refer to the rebuilding by Desiderio? I permit myself to doubt it, both because he makes no sign of such dualism (judging all of them to be of the eighth century), and because his studies about the monuments of that age were too imperfect and too confused.

It is only through the medium of the light thrown on the subject by the capitals of Valpolicella, and similar capitals, that, seeing others like them, if not in design certainly in character and chiselling, on some columns in the church of S. Saviour, we can accept Cordero's opinion, and give to the word monastery, used in the document, the widest interpretation.

This church is of primitive basilical form, divided into three naves by two rows of columns, now reduced to six on each side, because an anterior portion of the church was thrown down when the superior part of S. Julia was constructed. The stems of the columns are of various diameters, height, and quality. Among the capitals those which must have served for the pre-existent church are conspicuous, and display the style of the first half of the sixth century. Some of them resemble the Corinthian ones sculptured for the churches erected by Theodoric in Ravenna; others, more ornamented, show the influence of the richest Byzantine manner.

But those that must be ascribed to the time of Desiderio are very poor things. If in the capital of Valpolicella one sees a miserable reminiscence of the Corinthian, in those of S. Saviour such a resemblance is clearly conspicuous. The leaves, however, are hard and smooth, the caulicules meagre, the abacus rigid.

In some of these capitals the central superior leaf is suppressed on every side to give place to a cross.*

Above the capitals some full-curved arches spring immediately. There are no abaci, no piedroits, and no moulding, even if originally they had been ornamented in stucco. Nothing now remains of the superior part of the church, of the windows, and of the roof; but one can well imagine the form of the one and the bare beams of the other from the primitive simplicity of what still exists.

In the end of the central nave there was once a deep apsis of which one still sees the fundamental wall in the crypt below. This crypt is a great subterranean place which extends below the naves for the space of two intercolumns on each side, and is divided into two parts very different from one another in organism and style. One corresponds to the naves, but without at all raising their pavement, and consists of a little forest of columns supporting crosier-vaults; the other corresponds to the apsis, and is high enough to cause the floor above to be raised by several steps. It is formed by brick pilasters supporting arches adorned with stuccoes, and little stone pilasters with capitals. Both serve as the base of a covering of large thin slabs of stone which composed the pavement of the apsis above. Five little windows, made in the higher part of the apsis walls, gave it light.

Fig. 62.—Capital of S. Saviour's Church, Brescia—A.D. 753.

To what age did this crypt belong? Probably to two different epochs. The first part is certainly work of the end of the twelfth century, as one may see from its beautiful and varied capitals, which Cordero first, and afterwards Labus and

---

* Dartein gives us a drawing of one of these capitals with a cross, but wrongly interpreted the mutilated lower part, supposing it to have had only one row of leaves, while, if one carefully examines it, the remains of a lower row are evident.

Garrucci, erroneously attributed to the eighth century. As for the second part, if we observe its organism, we shall see something embarrassed and primitive that suggests, as it were, the first essays of one who found himself before a problem that he knew not how to solve; and if we examine the decorative particulars—that is to say, the capitals and stuccoes—we find them stamped with the character of the Byzantine style of the thirteenth century (see Fig. 64). Must one, then, conclude that this portion of the crypt is contemporaneous with the construction of the church—dating, that is to say, from the middle of the eighth century? Many will refuse to be persuaded that crypts were not in use anterior to the eleventh century; but I do not, because I know that even the eighth century, let alone the ninth, will give us new and more perfect examples of crypts raised higher than the floor of the church and which consequently raised the presbytery floor with them. These I shall therefore prefer to call presbyterial crypts, as did Dall' Acqua Giusti.* Such crypts, as every one knows, became afterwards one of the most salient characteristics of the Romanic churches. They had, in fact, nothing in common with those little subterranean places which, in the ancient Christian basilicas of Rome, opened under the ciborium of the high-altar, and are called *confessions*.

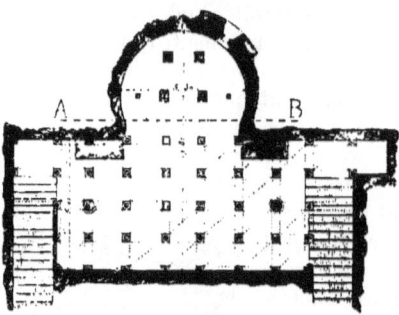

* Fig. 63.—Plan of S. Saviour's Crypt—VIIIth and XIIth Centuries.

But, as every rule has its exception, the *confessions* of the

---

* The Cav. Antonio Dall' Acqua Giusti is Professor of Art History in the Royal Institution of the Fine Arts at Venice; and I, who was his disciple, owe to him much gratitude not only for his teaching, but for awakening in me the warmest love and passion for these studies.

first six centuries sometimes present the elevation and almost
the dimensions of a real presbyterial crypt; and that is noticeable in those low countries in which the marshy soil does not
permit of dry subterraneous places. Thus it was in Ravenna,
where the cathedral and the church of S. Peter Major (now

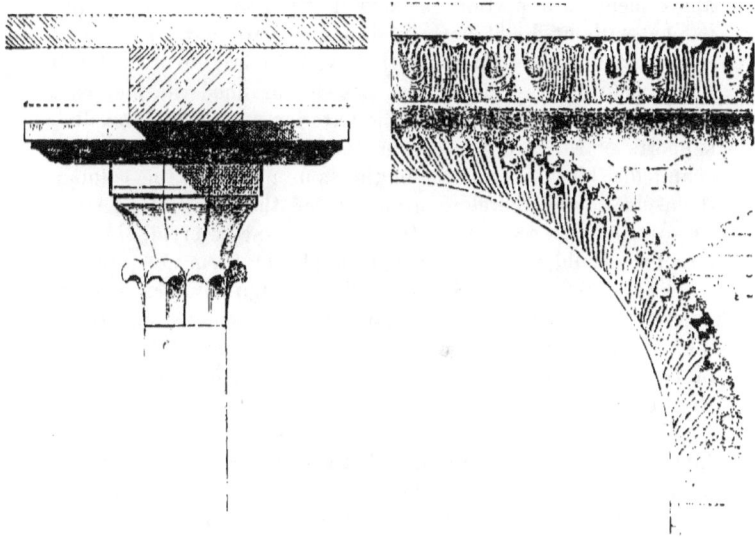

* Fig. 61. —Decorative Details of S. Saviour, Brescia — VIIIth Century.

S. Francis) appear to be provided with crypts corresponding
to the apsides which (by the style of the greater part of the
capitals, and especially of the mosaic pavements that may still
be traced) evince fifth or sixth-century work. These remain
isolated examples, however, and nothing more than unusually
high and ample confessions.

The confessions certainly served as receptacles for the
precious mortal remains of saints and martyrs, and therefore
were only required by churches which possessed such relics.

That S. Saviour of Brescia was one of these we gather from a diploma of Adelchi, son of Desiderio, who recommends himself to the intercession, " *De supra scriptorum corpora qua in ipso sancto cenobio humata quiescunt.*" *

All this seems to me to confirm the opinion that the church possessed a crypt as early as the eighth century, and that the above-mentioned portion remains of it. I say portion, because it must without doubt have been larger than that small space, if it were only for the stairs that were to lead to it. But in all probability it occupied the site of the modern one, as I gather from the fact that, in the anterior crypt, the immediate supports of the two great columns of the nave consisted in channelled blocks of marble of the same nature as the columns themselves, and therefore evidently of the same date ; since, as any one may see, unless they had designed a crypt, the constructors would not have thought of placing them underneath.

The crypt of S. Saviour, which originally was perhaps entirely similar to the apsidal portion that remains, was therefore with every probability the first, or among the first, examples of true presbyterial crypts. Certainly it is the most ancient that I know.

We ought to hold this basilica of Brescia in great consideration, especially when we reflect that several decorative fragments of the eighth century, belonging to the Lombard period, are to be seen there, because if one should ask for a sufficiently preserved construction which represents an idea in itself, and reveals the technique or style of that epoch, this alone can be pointed out. At any rate, it will be difficult to discover another.

If such a church stood in Tuscany or Rome, where the basilical style was always the one preferred by architects, even in the centuries that succeeded the tenth, we might certainly conclude that, during the dominion of the Lombards, the Latin style was still the only one followed in the whole of Italy; but, the church of S. Saviour being situated in that Lombardy which, when the Romanic style prevailed, was the first to banish for ever the old Latin manner, we may logically

* Dartein ; work cited above.

assert, even with this single example, that the basilical system, with very few exceptions, was the only one used in Italy for sacred edifices during this obscure period, specially when we shall see it in the ninth century continued in the same country, and even at Milan, when it is commonly believed to have been in disuse.

But the preciousness of the church of S. Saviour does not end here; it has copiously furnished the contiguous Christian Museum with splendid works of sculpture, remains of the rich accessories, with which Desiderio provided it sumptuously by the hands of the usual Greek artists.

If the sculptures of the church of Aurona are delicate and elegant, those of S. Saviour are not inferior to them. Here also we have squares gracefully covered by geometric ornaments and spindles; colonnettes, some octagonal, some cylindrical, arabesqued like

FIG. 65.—Decorative Details of S. Saviour, Brescia —VIIIth Century.

damask, with ornaments of every kind; capitals of various dimensions, some of them very fine and elegant, others rather gross, but always rich; a square cap-profiled abacus, with intaglio of palm-leaves; several headings of capitals with double brackets to sustain architraves; many horizontal bands which might have been architraves adorned with little arches mounted one over the other and enriched with beads or interwreathing of vine-branches. All these fragments may have belonged to chancels of the choir; but, amid them, the ambo

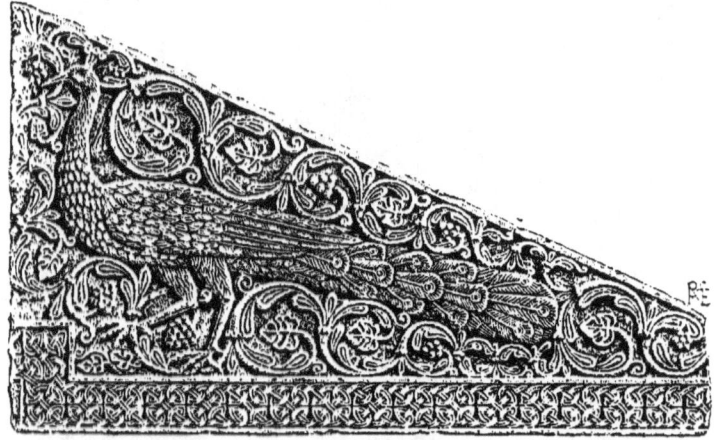

Fig. 66.—Fragment possibly belonging to the Ambo of S. Saviour, Brescia—VIIIth Century.

must have been resplendent with rich elegance. If, among the samples of ambos of the eighth century that we have hitherto seen, we have only found convex parapets of the higher central part, these remains of S. Saviour offer us instead the flanks or parapets of the little staircase that led to the ambo. Such are, according to my judgment, two slabs of marble (one reduced to a little fragment) of the figure of a scalene triangle, framed by a band with complicated and minute rush braidings which enclose, among a profusion of elegant and well-distributed gyres, a superb peacock.

Here we should salute as he deserves the artist who sculptured them, because he is without doubt the best of all who worked during that period in Italy, and certainly not unworthy even to figure among the worthiest artists of the sixth century—if, indeed, the sixth century could produce a peacock of form so elegant, in a field as beautifully ornamented as this of S. Saviour. Its proportions are regular, the movement just and natural, the design very fine, the chisel accurate; and seen among those graceful gyres it looks like a magnificent Oriental carpet. It is the *chef-d'œuvre* of the eighth century.

Several other important remnants are derived from S. Saviour's. Notable for the elegance of its ornaments is a curious and pretty

Fig. 67.—Other Details of S. Saviour, Brescia— VIIIth Century.

Fig. 68.—Little Window of S. Saviour, Brescia— VIIIth Century.

little convex archivolt, very like those we saw in the museum
at Venice; a slab of marble with a beaded cross amongst
roses, palms, and tresses, and lastly a very important stone
hollowed by two little arches supported by colonnettes, with
archivolts, capitals, and headings rich in ornaments and having
a band below with large and curious caps. It was most
probably the base of the altar turned towards the people, and
the two little windows, furnished with an iron grating, and
communicating with the crypt, probably rendered visible the
tombs of the saints deposited there, exactly as on certain
confessions of churches in Rome.

PAVIA.—As we find these Greek artificers working in cities
of minor importance, and sometimes even in villages, it is easy

FIG. 69.—Tomb of Theodota, Pavia—VIIIth Century.

to imagine how much more they must have worked in the
capital of the Lombard kingdom, Pavia; but of the many works
that they doubtless left there very few remain to be recorded,
and they are some fronts of sarcophagi, more or less orna-

mented, existing in the courtyard of the Malaspina Palace. Those that enclose the ashes of Teodota (that victim of the brutality of King Caniberto, who it appears died a nun in 720) * take precedence of all others.

Here the connection with the sculptures of Cividale comes out most vividly. An elegant band with intertwined circles, alternately large and small, and filled up with rose-work, or leaves and bunches of grapes of a certain fineness and originality, forms a frame to the representations on the sides of the sarcophagus. In the one we see two roughly carved peacocks drinking at a vase, among roses, lilies, and braidings; in the other two winged lions of less barbarous design, with bodies that terminate in dragons' tails, placed beside a fantastic tree, very like those we saw sculptured on the parapet of Sigualdo in the baptistery of Cividale. The most notable difference is in the two heads issuing from the vine-branches. They are lions' heads at Cividale, but here griffins; but at any rate either animal or the other is reproduced on both monuments. One of the sides of the sarcophagus shows, enclosed in a contour of gyres, a lamb bearing the cross. Besides these

Fig. 70.— Exterior Wall of S. Maria delle Caccie, Pavia—VIIIth Century.

remains and the above-indicated stones, ornamented in some parts, one sees under the same portico a band and a fragment, perhaps a bit of a parapet, decorated with circles, roses, and crosses.

* Muratori, "Annali d'Italia."

If the seventh century has not bequeathed to us any edifice in Pavia, almost the same must be said of the eighth century, because time and circumstances did not spare even one. I said *almost*, however, because if not an entire edifice, at least a portion remains to us, and of one not devoid of interest. It is a lateral wall in terracotta, of the church of S. Maria, *foris portam*, now *delle caccie*, a basilica whose foundation is, by the greater part of the historians of Pavia, attributed to the Princess Epifania, daughter of King Ratchis (744-749). Dartein made this wall known to the public, but it was held of little account because, when confronted with the remains of the church of Aurona, it could not show any progress towards Lombard architecture. I, on the contrary, value it much, exactly because, while showing no introduction of new forms, it once more confirms what our researches have hitherto demonstrated, at the same time that, manifesting a return to the Byzantine forms of the sixth century, it acknowledges the hand of Greek artificers. Such are the blind arches of the lateral naves supported by bands which frame externally the windows of the lateral naves, corresponding to the internal arcades, as in the cathedral of Grado, in S. Apollinaris beyond the walls of Ravenna, and in so many churches of that city and of Greece that belong to the sixth or to the fifth century.

Fig. 71.—Fragment of Parget found at Libarna—VIIIth Century.

LIBARNA.—A trace of the Greek style of the eighth century is also found in the little colony of Libarna, on the Apennines, north of Genoa. It is a fragment of parget with stucco bas-reliefs, already noted by Cordero, who assigned it to the third century. Its spirals connect it specially with the fragments of Bergamo, and its crosses with those of Torcello and Ravenna.

ALBENGA.—Within the very old baptistery of Albenga (known through a little monograph by the much-lamented Commendatore Edoardo Arborio Mella di Vercelli), by the two sides of the large rectangular niche, at the end of which was the original entrance, now blocked up. one sees two tombs on the ground disposed under arches like the ground-arches of the catacombs. They are decorated by slabs of marble

Fig. 72.—Tomb at the Baptistery of Albenga—Fragments of VIIIth Century.

sculptured with ornamental bas-reliefs, which to the above-praised Mella appeared to be of Roman manner, but which I must class among the Greek works of the eighth century.

The variety and multiplicity of the pieces, and the fact that they are not adapted to the dimensions of the sepulchres or to the forms of the ground-arches, clearly show that we have here a fragmentary work, made up from remains of a presbyterial balustrade, of a ciborium, of windows, and other works of the eighth century.

The most considerable piece is a rectangular parapet framed with cordons and the usual braided withes, adorned by circles linked together and divided by lilies and crosses, filled in with large roses of various kinds, or by bunches of grapes and leaves.

Mixtilinear braidings are noticeable on the other slabs, as well as certain decorations of interwoven SS that remind one of those at Cividale. The mouth of the tomb is closed on one side by a fragment which has on it a beaded Greek cross, on a pole flanked by rayed or girandoled roses, and enclosed between cordons and braids. On the other side is a bit of an arched slab with a cross formed of simple braidings, and bored into circular holes, which show it to have belonged to a window.

The arch of the tomb on the left, the only ornamented one, shows an archivolt, perhaps of a ciborium, with rampant caulicules, large roses and spirals, and below a semicircular lunette, which seems to be made for the archivolt, and which is the only thing of this sort and of this style that I have met with hitherto. It is a band with little spirals, and its field is adorned by a palm among unconnected decorations of withes and mixtilinear braids.

OSIMO.—There is much analogy between the band that frames the fronts of the sarcophagus of Teodota at Pavia and that framing the epitaph on the tomb of a bishop of Osimo, which runs thus: "IHIC REQVIESCIT IN PACE— VITALIANVS SERVVS XPI EPC." We know that this Vitalianus was at the Roman council in 743, and it appears that he died during the pontificate of Adrian I. (772-795). On this band we see a vase with handles, from which issue vine-branches with grapes, leaves, and withes. Above there is a Greek cross in a circle, and here and there rosettes.

PERUGIA.—An extremely remarkable monument of the eighth century is in the celebrated museum of Perugia. It is an altar with its ciborium in a complete and well-preserved state. It comes from a church of S. Prospero, and is formed of four columns bearing as many arches, crowned by an eight-sided roof that ends in a pine-shaped flower. Rohault de Fleury, as usual, erroneously judged this work to be fruit of the ninth century.

FIG. 73.—Capital at the Museum of Perugia— VIIIth Century.

The altar is absolutely without decorations ; but, by way of compensation, the archivolts of the ciborium are variously and profusely arabesqued with very elegant ornaments, braids, palm-leaves, roses, wild acanthus, among stars, doves, peacocks, fans, and other caprices. These archivolts, without doubt, merit a place among the most beautiful things that the Greek artificers of the eighth century have given to Italy.

Where, however, their chisel fails considerably is in the capitals of the columns, which are here, as is almost always the case, defective. It would seem that these poor artists, who were often skilful in finely decorating a plain surface, lost all their cunning and showed all their inefficiency when it was necessary to model in full relief.

In the same museum there is a little capital of this epoch, much coarser than those of the ciborium, with very hard palm-leaves, which are scarcely better than the worst that we have seen in Upper Italy.

SPOLETO.—Spoleto was a city that was held in high consideration at this epoch, and retained its prosperity for a long time, because the Lombards had made it the capital of one of their duchies. I therefore visited it in the hope of finding some work that might aid me in my present study ; and, in fact, I found there two sculptures that appear to belong to the eighth century.

One consists of a rectangular slab of marble used as material in the construction of the belfry of the cathedral, together with many other Roman or mediæval sculptures. It is subdivided by braids and spindles into four squares, occupied below with palms similar to those of the ambo of Modena, and above by large roses and groups of lilies, as at Cividale, Murano, and other places.

The other sculpture (derived from the church of the Apostles) is kept in the atrium of the Pinacoteca Comunale, and is decorated with three small arches, supported by little pilasters, composing one of the most barbarous bits of architecture that have ever been seen. There are no bases, no capitals, but mere superposed steps, pyramidal in form below and inverted above; arches falsely poised, with no *membrature*, but simple listels awkwardly enriched with little circles, squares, meanders, teeth of saws, and especially by innumerable little drilled holes.

The human figures and the animals carved on this stone present fewer imperfections, and, though very barbarous, are, however, less so than the horrible ones of Cividale. Of the three arches only two retain images of saints, dressed in togæ and long tunics, and whose heads are surrounded with concave aureoles in strong relief. As at Cividale, some of the features are traced on a flat surface about two centimetres higher than their background, outlined by furrows in the folds of the drapery and extremities, and by a depression of some millimetres.

Fig. 74.—Balustrade existing in the Belfry of the Cathedral of Spoleto—VIIIth Century.

There is an ingenuous attempt at truth in the drapery, which looks ridiculous, and a certain pretence of indicating the nude which it covers One would think the author was a painter, or

Fig. 75.—Bas-relief at the Pinacoteca Comunale, Spoleto—VIIIth Century.

rather that he was trying with his decrepit and dying art to copy the forms of some picture or mosaic of Byzantine style.*

* Far more than for the sake of those wretched works of the eighth century Spoleto ought to be known to architects and Art-historians for having a Christian

NARNI.—In the environs of Narni, in a church at S. Oreste, is an old altar chiefly formed of fragments of parapets of the eighth century. It exhibits braidings both curvilinear and mixtilinear; rather rugged spirals of leaves; a Greek cross with caulicules and plaits between four roses; a frieze of little arches filled with crosses, lilies, or palms: but what most attracts the attention is an elegant wheel enclosing a square and connected by means of plaits with a smaller interior circle; it resembles that broken wheel, which, as we have seen, was discovered amongst the ruins of S. Augustine at Venice.

ROME.—At Rome, as at Ravenna and at Pavia, I could find very few Greek works of the eighth century, and even those are not of a striking character. Nevertheless Selvatico, after studying the baptistery of Cividale, observed that the same rugged style appeared in numerous works of sculpture scattered here and there among the Roman basilicas; but he had considered the execution more than the style, and therefore, in spite of Rohault de Fleury's assertion to the contrary, he

monument of the highest importance, the façade of the very old basilica of S. Saviour, now the church of the Campo-Santo. It dates from the sixth century, and is entirely preserved with the exception of the portico, which was perhaps added afterwards, and part of the fittings. The style of the three doors and the three windows is decadent Romanic, but is not without majesty and elegance. To reassure the doubtful and convince the unbelieving the friezes of the three doors bear a cross in the centre, from which is developed a rich decoration of spirals, flowers, and rosettes. It is, in fact, a construction of such value to the historian of Romanic-Christian architecture that not even Rome or the East can show another like it. And yet, though situated on the side of a hill exposed to the gaze of everybody, I blush to say that the first to discover its unknown but immense importance was a foreigner—Hübsch! But I am still more ashamed to confess that from 1871—in which year De Rossi, in his "Bullettino," spoke of the wonderful discovery—to this present day, no professor, none of our own writers on Art-history, has said one word about this unique monument. That fact implies that in Italy little is printed, less is read, and nothing is studied.

Those who have not the opportunity to go to Spoleto and admire the precious monument, should at least look at it as delineated in the work of Hübsch, or in that of Mothes, or in the "Bullettino" already cited, where important information about the excavations made in that church may also be found. But the reader must not believe, with De Rossi, that various other doors and façades of churches at or near Spoleto are coeval with S. Saviour's; because, with the sole exception of a frieze on the tympan of the temple of Clitumnus, they are neither more nor less than works in imitation of those of the thirteenth century. I know that the learned archæologist has already repented his error.

Fig. 76.—Capital in the Fieramosca Palace, Capua—VIIIth Century.

Fig. 77.—Capital in the Museum at Capua—VIIIth Century.

assigned to the eighth century works that belong to the ninth, and which we shall soon examine.

In the Christian museum of the Lateran, at the foot of the great staircase, I found a frieze with spirals, withes and dry leaves, animals and fantastic monsters of rugged forms. In the midst of the staircase that leads to the lapidary galleries, there is a rectangular slab, with a great Latin cross on it adorned by braids, which from their fineness and the fact that there is a bead in every row, in the manner frequently characteristic of the Greeks in the eighth century, seems to me to be a Greek work of that time. Six other little crosses of various dimensions, some enriched like the larger one by very minute braids, others in low relief and smooth, occupy the lateral spaces between inscriptions in the Armenian language. The Latin inscription at the foot of the cross was without doubt added in the twelfth century. Such are the very few works in Rome which may with some probability be attributed to Greek chisels of the eighth century.

CAPUA.—In the courtyard of the Fieramosca Palace in Capua two capitals of medium size and curious forms are to be seen. Instead of leaves, there are curved bands, or very projecting caulicules, half way up. They are curled in the centre and meet one another at the angles, detached from the bell of the capital. Higher up, other caulicules and roses support the abacus. It seems that, what was to those artificers the insuperable difficulty of carving leaves in relief, made them resort to these strange combinations. But there are pretty boughs carved in slight relief on the smooth sides of the bell; and cords, braids, or triangles on the caulicules.

Two other slim, rugged, but not inelegant capitals are exhibited in the museum of Capua. They are clearly related to the more simple ones of Istria or Venetia.

The same museum also contains the least barbarous figure that remains to us of the Greek eighth-century work in Italy. It represents an angel, whose feet are naked, with a concave aureole, and clad in a tunic with a toga richly adorned by gems and pearls. The right hand holds a wand. The proportions are free, as in the other figures, but the pose is rigid, the

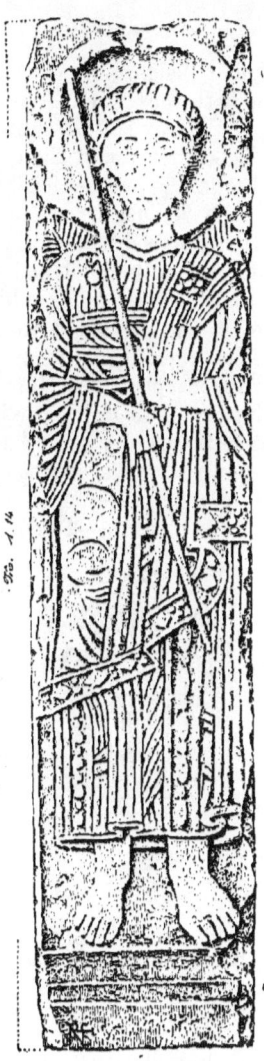

FIG. 78.—Bas-relief in the Museum at Capua — VIIIth Century.

relief insignificant, the folds crudely traced. As a whole it is a barbarous work.

S. ANGELO-IN-FORMIS.—Three kilometers from Capua, on the side of Mount Tifata, rises the old basilica of S. Angelo-in-Formis, famous especially for its antique pictures, and important to us because it contains a Greek work of the eighth century. It is the pedestal of the holy-water vase, and on two sides is covered with florid and elegant decorations, slightly departing from the style we have hitherto seen, but so strongly reminiscent of it that we ought to class it with the rest. On one of the sides there is a great vase with handles, from which rises a vigorous plant that throws out leaves, flowers, and fruit of all kinds. Two doves perch on the vase and peck. On the other side is carved a great bush of wild acanthus, from which arise spirals in which bunches of grapes are mingled with roses, laurel-leaves, and little birds.

BENEVENTO.—I would not omit visiting Benevento, once the celebrated capital of a Lombard duchy; but my researches only resulted in the discovery of a little capital now employed in the picturesque church of S. Sophia. It has something of the bizarre elegance of those of Capua, and recalls, at the same time, certain motives of its brother capitals in High Italy.

FIG. 79.—Capital in the Cloister of S. Sophia at Benevento—VIIIth Century.

With this capital, I terminate the series of all the Greek works of the eighth century that I was able to discover or become acquainted with in Italy*—a series that might not only be increased but doubled by more patient, extended, and prolonged researches, since our peninsula is still a country for the most part unexplored by the studious, and may therefore still furnish Art-history with new and pleasant surprises. Never-

---

* I have thought it best to exclude from this series all Greek works of the same period in wood-sculpture, stone-sculpture, or goldsmiths' work existing in Italy, which were executed in Greece or imported from that country after the eighth century.

theless, it seems to me that the number of monuments pointed out by me in this chapter are more than sufficient to demonstrate the rapid diffusion of the Byzantine-Barbarian style of the eighth century through every region of Italy, and the common characteristics of its physiognomy as displayed from one end of the country to the other. Indeed, if the limits imposed on me by my programme did not forbid it, I could demonstrate that those Greek artificers who, through desire of gain or persecutions or wars, were impelled to leave their own country and seek our shores (even to the extreme west of the Ligurian Riviera), did not stop at the Alps but crossed them and passed into France. It is certain that we can easily recognise the work of their chisels in the very beautiful sarcophagi of the crypt of S. Paul at Jouarre, enclosing the ashes of S. Téchilde and S. Aguibert; in the fragments of another sarcophagus existing in the church of the Minimes at Venasque, where Boëce, bishop of Carpentras, was deposited; in remains of parapets visible in the museum of Arles; in several friezes inserted in an altar of the cloister of S. Saviour's at Aix, in Provence, and in many other places. In all these sculptures, there is not one motive that does not find a perfect counterpart in the works in Italy that we have now been studying, and therefore they ought to be attributed to the eighth century and not to the ninth, as Fleury has done.

Nevertheless, I have reason to believe that Italy is richer than other countries in this manner of work, and perhaps not only richer than France, but even than Greece itself, in which the revolutions of the eighth century, and especially those of later ages, certainly could not have been propitious to Art production and preservation. The remains in Italy suffice to afford us a perfect idea of the ensemble of a church of the eighth century. We have examples of doors and porches, altars and ciboria, confessionals and windows, presbyterial chancels and ambos, fonts and baptismal ciboria, vases for holy water, and tombs. And in all these accessories we often find numerous types, and invariably a variety of forms and details. Take, for example, a progression of capitals of the old

Ionic and Corinthian form to those basket-shaped and cubiform with cut corners. We pass from the simplest and unadorned to the richest and most delicate; from smooth columns to arabesqued ones; from square to octagonal pilasters; from uncouth ornaments to the most delicate. But what is most surprising is the prodigious and admirable variety and originality of ornamentation, coupled with a grace which is entirely Greek, ever evident though often rough. One may say that those artificers, in compensation for the lost perfection of their art, sought to abound in fancy and in richness.

CHAPTER III.

ITALIAN ARCHITECTURE

FROM THE END OF THE VIIIth TO THE XIth CENTURY.

ITALIAN-BYZANTINE STYLE.

I HAVE said before, that the most eloquent proof that the monuments we have hitherto studied are works of emigrant artists consists in their sudden appearance and disappearance in the brief time of little more than half a century, leaving Italian art almost in the same barbarous state in which they found it. It must not, however, be believed that this visit of the Greeks to Italy was of no educational value to the natives. It was, on the contrary, of the highest value to them. And though they never arrived at that perception of grace innate in the Greeks, and several centuries had to pass before they attained to the production of capitals equal in worth to those of the baptistery of Cividale, or peacocks similar to those of S. Saviour's of Brescia, yet the example given by the Greek works availed, at least, to awaken in our artists the love of richness, profusion, and variety of decoration; and thus in their new works the rigid poverty of ornament that made the old deformities the more noticeable and disagreeable, at any rate, disappeared.

They studied, then, to imitate the Greek sculptures, but not in such a servile manner as to preclude a conspicuous difference between the works of the two schools. It is true that, far from emulating the Greeks in fecundity of fancy, they did not know how to augment the large measure of ornamental motives inherited from them, but, on the contrary, reduced those motives to so limited a number that they sank into a monotony which their masters had very cleverly contrived to avoid; but, with all that, their works are distinguished by a certain breadth of composition and touch that may be derived from their very roughness, but that to most spectators probably answers better to the description of architectonic feeling and thought than do the Greek minutiæ.

They were prudent in almost always avoiding representations of the human figure, and using even those of animals with the greatest parsimony, as their inexperienced chisels could only produce monstrosities in that genre. Among ornaments they abandoned the confronted SS's and the tied and flowered ones, the champignons, the corridietro, the ivy, the thorny acanthus, the little columns, and the little arabesqued pillars. They rarely made use of the spindles, the interwoven arches, the vine-branches, and it is curious to see how, out of the two ways employed by the Greeks in representing bunches of grapes, our men showed predilection for the most clumsy and conventional way, namely, that of enclosing the grapes in a listel shaped like a heart. Palms, crosses, rayed and girandoled roses, leafy spirals, beads, rampant caulicules, were frequently reproduced; but the decorations preferred by them were the curvilinear and the mixtilinear braidings, which they applied and developed so freely that we must consider these braidings as the dominant note of the ornamental sculpture of this period. In them they had discovered a free, facile, and appropriate element of decoration, which might assume a certain variety and richness without exacting too much from the mind or the chisel of the artificer, in whom a little ingenuity and diligence would be sufficient. And most heartily they gave themselves up to this, being fortunate in their ability to attain to those intricate combinations that force the spectator to follow their capricious labyrinths with curiosity, while they almost craze those who try to copy them.

Some have ascribed this genre of ornament to Arab influence, being aware that it forms the base of decoration in Mahomedan buildings. But, if we reflect that the Arabs did not, as far as we know, possess any special architecture of their own in the eighth century,* and that that bizarre fashion, after-

* It is usual to point out the Mosque of Omar at Jerusalem, founded in 682, as the most ancient example of pointed arches organically used, and as the oldest example of the Mahomedan style; but this judgment is absolutely erroneous.

wards brought to the highest perfection, of adorning with varied and most ingenious interweaving or braiding (almost always rectilinear) only began to manifest itself in the East towards the eleventh century, one is induced reasonably to conclude that Arab art of the eighth century could not have influenced Italian art in the least. Besides, we who know where this style of braiding came from, and how much more antique it is than Mahomedanism itself, may firmly maintain that the Mahomedans learned it from the Byzantines, just as they had learnt constructive organism; from the Sassanide Persians their cupolas and their fantastic *flora*, and from the Buddhists and Hindoos the inflected, the trefoil, and the horseshoe arch.

In the seventh century and in the beginning of the eighth, before the fresh influence of Greek art, we do not find a true style existing in Italy, nor do the miserable works of that time appear to be everywhere of the same character. But towards the end of the eighth, and in the following century, things were very different; because those modes of ornamentation that are seen in Rome, appear also in the Neapolitan province, in the Marches, in Umbria, in Tuscany, at Ravenna, in Lombardy, in Venetia, and even in Istria and Dalmatia where the old traditions have either disappeared or been momentarily forgotten. This uniformity can only be explained by admitting that this new style originated and developed in only one region of Italy whence it was spread through the peninsula and even elsewhere through the medium of its artists. What country, then, was the cradle of this new style? Apparently that which offers the most numerous examples of it: but such a deduction, though reasonable theoretically, does not hold practically in the present case, because the works executed by that system have nearly all vanished, and the fact that more of them exist in one country than in another may be the effect of independent causes; not to mention that the country now regarded as poorest in a certain

All that remains of seventh-century work in the Mosque is clearly of Byzantine style, and all that differs from it, as (for example) the external wall, the interior row of pointed arches with the corners alternately sharpened, and the cupola, must belong to a restoration effected in the ninth century (see Voguë, " Le Temple de Jerusalem ").

class of remains may, by accurate research or accidental discovery during a restoration or an excavation, be regarded to-morrow as the richest in the peninsula.

Therefore we must seek the support of a more valid argument which, in my opinion, can only lie in the greater longevity of that style in one country than in another, for, like a plant, the style must have taken deeper root in its native soil than in the foreign ground where it had been transplanted. And, coming at once to the application, we soon see that, while that style entirely disappeared in Rome to make room for the Neo-Latin, in the south for the Arab-Sicilian, in Tuscany for the Latin-Lombard, and in Venetia for the Neo-Byzantine; in Lombardy, on the contrary, it developed itself more amply and was gradually transformed into the Lombard or Romanic style in which, among other features, it especially maintained, till the twelfth century, the character of the complicated braidings.

In Lombardy, then, which history itself exhibits to us as the most active theatre of the arts in Italy towards the eleventh century, that new system of decoration, which is a reflection of the Greek modes, imported in the eighth century, must have begun. This conjecture becomes still more probable when we consider that, as Lombardy was the most vital centre of the Lombard kingdom, the work of the Byzantine artificers must have been most active there in the eighth century, and therefore it was easy for Italians to form themselves in their school.

And now let us take another turn in Italy to seek for monuments and remnants of this Italian-Byzantine style, which represents the first faint dawning of the resurrection of Art.

ROME.—Rome, in which we could only find a few remains of Greek sculpture of the eighth century, offers us, in compensation, numerous remnants of the works of Lombard artists dating from the end of that century and the following centuries, and even some entire edifices.

The pontificates of Adrian I. (772-795) and of Leo III. (795-816) signalise a period of great constructive, if not artistic, activity These two pontiffs, freed by the French arms from every menace of the Lombards, and finding themselves, through the donations of Pepin the Little and Charlemagne, lords of wide and fertile domains, at once began to make the Christian monuments of the eternal city experience the beneficent results of their new power.

There was not a church in Rome but was richly adorned by one of those two popes with Tyrian and Alexandrian figured stuffs, or endowed with ciboria, chancels, lamps, statues, vases, &c., all worked in silver or in the purest gold, and often covered with gems—fabulous treasures! On the other hand, they restored decaying churches and totally rebuilt the ruined ones. But, though the gold of the popes sufficed to complete such magnificent works, the number of Roman workmen was insufficient; and there remain to us letters of Adrian I., in which, among other things, he asks Charlemagne for workmen (*magistros*). That does not mean that he asked for artists from France, but from those regions of Italy that, through the fall of the Lombards, had passed into Charlemagne's power; and the monuments permit of our believing that those artists must have been either Lombards or the famous Comacini, who, in that time, must have enjoyed the fame of being the best artists in the peninsula.

The most remarkable monument of the time of Adrian I. that remains in Rome is, without doubt, the church of S. Maria-in-Cosmedin. Anastasius (Anastasio), the librarian, says that Adrian found this church of small dimensions *sub ruinis positam . . . maximum monumentum de tiburtino tufo super eam dependens*. And as this colossal ruin impeded the enlargement of the church which the pontiff was deliberating, they demolished it by force of hand and fire. Then, the place having been cleared of the *débris*, Adrian built *a fundamentis* the new spacious basilica, *tres absides in ea constituens*.

And, pausing for awhile at this last expression, how is it that the antique documents, probably read by Anastasius, make no mention of this church? Evidently because it must have been new; and, in fact, before this epoch there was no sign of it, nor does there exist in Italy any church, anterior to this epoch, which presents the same arrangement of the ends of the naves. Was this novelty—which was so popular as to become soon quite common—a spontaneous birth of Italy, or was it imported by the Greeks in the eighth century? If one by one we examine all the churches of the fifth and the sixth centuries in Constantinople and Thessalonica, or those of Italy erected in the same centuries under the immediate influence of Byzantine taste, we perceive but one apsis alone. But if we pause instead to look at those erected contemporaneously in Central Syria, grand ruins of which still remain, we shall find in the church of Soueideh, assigned by Vogüé to the fifth century, that the two cells or chapels, lateral to the apsis, curve interiorly in the form of niches, and that, in the great basilica of S. Simon Stylite at Kalat Sem'an, constructed in the year 500, the bottom of the little naves is built, both inside and outside, in semicircular form. This is, perhaps, the oldest example that we have of the basilica with three apsides; but it may also be the only one remaining of many others of the same epoch which were destroyed, and which were not without influence even in the adjacent land of Greece. And, though we

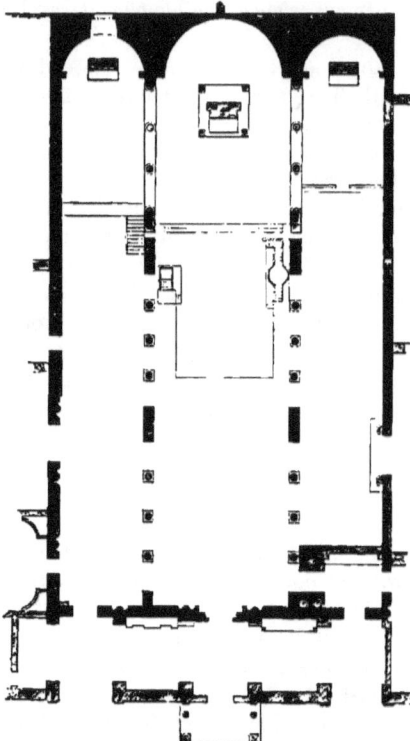

Fig. 80.—Plan of the Church of S. Maria-in-Cosmedin, Rome—A.D. 772-795.

cannot tell (from ignorance of any still-existing church of the seventh to the ninth century in that region) whether the custom had taken root there in that period, yet, seeing it constantly followed in all churches from the end of the ninth century and later, we suspect that (even before then) it had begun to be adopted. At any rate, it is very reasonable to believe that the use of the apsis came to Italy from the East.

The church of S. Maria-in-Cosmedin is therefore the most ancient example remaining to us in Italy, and perhaps the first that was seen in Rome. In fact, the church, as built by Adrian I., is substantially the same that we see to-day, if we except some transformations in the colonnades of the presbytery, in the portico of the façade, and those few, but magnificent, embellishments which were made in the thirteenth century—that is to say, the ciborium, the ambos, the pavement, and the belfry.* Its extension is nearly determined by certain remains of those grand ruins that Adrian caused to be thrown down; and they consist of several great Corinthian columns, which connect the facial wall, and part of the wall of one side, with a thick wall which forms the opposite angle. To preserve this wall no external projection was given to the three apsides.

After the apsides, the most salient particular of our church consists in the supports of the naves, which are formed of groups of three columns, separated by oblong pilasters that have all the appearance of portions of wall. Some have supposed that they were old arcades built later to consolidate the edifice; but this idea does not hold water when we consider that their dimensions do not correspond with those of the other arcades, and that every group of columns presents different dimensions in the intervals. Those pilasters are therefore originals, and were,

Between the writers who judged the fine mediæval belfries of Rome to be of the sixth or seventh century and those who declared them to be all posterior to the year 1000 Mothes intervened as conciliator, asserting that both parties were at once right and wrong, because, according to his opinion, in all those towers the lower half, with its great blind arches, belonged to the sixth or following century, and the superior part, pierced by little arches supported by columns, to the twelfth or thirteenth. But the good German was here again deceived. With all my research and study in Rome, I could not find a single belfry older than the eleventh century.

without doubt, put there to render the construction more solid and to secure more firmly the thick wall above, whose weight had bruised the slight and badly proportioned columns.

These columns are, as usual, of various marble and different proportions, some of them channelled, some plain. They have various bases and very various capitals, the greater part Corinthian or ancient composite ones, of which some may have served in the first church of the sixth century. As we saw in the first chapter, that Byzantine composite certainly belonged to it. There are, however, five that, either wholly or in part, belong to the time of Adrian. They are rough, but not bad, imitations of Romanic composite, with hard, smooth foliage and utterly unadorned volutes and champignon. They recall the simplest modes used by Greek artists in Upper Italy of the same century, and show the first footsteps of the renaissance of Italian art. Every capital is charged with a large heavy squared plinth, which, like those of S. Agnes-beyond-the-Walls and of S. George at Velabro, has lost every trace of the Byzantine character. I said elsewhere that this church contains a crypt in the form of a little basilica with three naves, in which I have pointed out traces of the style of the eighth century, visible in the capitals of its columns, which are identical with the rude composites of the upper naves.

Fig. 81.—Capital of S. Maria-in-Cosmedin, Rome — A.D. 772-795.

Three other sculptures appear to have belonged to this precious church of Adrian I.; they are two rough Ionic capitals of the existing porch, and an undoubted fragment of an architrave, in the vestibule. It is decorated by rough little arcades in bas-relief,* only interrupted by a square hole for inserting an

---

* It is curious that Crescimbeni (op. cited), far from seeing in these arcades a mere motive of decoration, as is the fact, supposed them to represent a portico or aqueduct restored by Adrian.

iron bar, meant to sustain a lamp or a curtain. It is certainly
the work of Lombard chisels, and of the style that I prefer to

Fig. 82.—Fragment of Architrave of S. Maria-in-Cosmedin, Rome—A.D. 772-795.

call Italian-Byzantine. The incised inscription assures us that
it is of the period of Adrian I. :—

" *de don* IS DI ET SCE DI GENETRICIS MAriae
*temporibu*S DONI ADRIANI PAPE EGO GREGORIVS NO . . . "

Although the old basilica of S. Saba on the Aventine does
not appear in the long catalogue of the churches restored by
Adrian I., given by Anastasius, yet I permit myself to suppose
that it was reconstructed in that period and to consider those
colonnades of the naves as its remains. But I am led to this
conclusion not only by the fragmentary mixture of marbles and
capitals, but by the barbarous execution of some of them which
were without doubt sculptured expressly for the edifice.

As long as the pagan ruins offered capitals sufficiently well
preserved to be used anew, we have seen that the Christian
architects of Rome gathered them with care and arranged them
as best they might in their churches. But when those ruins
had, in falling, buried under their *débris* all works of art, or so
crushed and spoilt them as to render them useless, or (more
probable still) when the mine was exhausted of capitals, whose
dimensions could be fitted to edifices of a medium size, such
as were the basilicas of that time, the new constructors and
restorers were forced to supply work from contemporary chisels.
It must have proved a harsh necessity to them. Accustomed,

as they were, to search comfortably amongst ancient ruins for what was wanted in order to build and adorn their churches, they had neglected the necessary training of mind and hand, without which no success in Art can be attained.

Now these unskilful stoneworkers of the eighth century, before replacing some deteriorated capitals in S. Saba, tried to imitate the Ionic forms, but in the most disgraceful way possible, scarcely rough-hewing the marble, not caring to hint at the champignons, the volutes, and the cushions, by intaglio or even with furrows; so that those capitals have rather the appearance of rude masses hardly squared, just as they came from the quarries, than of finished works of sculpture. These capitals are really so barbarous that I should be tempted to assign to them the period of the beginning of the eighth century, if their visible relationship with those of S. Maria-in-Cosmedin, and the presence in S. Saba of rugged sculptures of Italian-Byzantine style, did not persuade me to believe them to be of the time of Adrian I. They may, however, be classed among the oldest works of that style in Rome, and they possibly date back much further than S. Maria-in-Cosmedin.

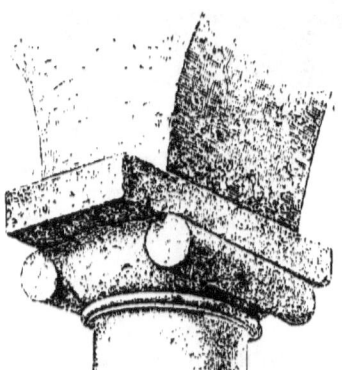

Fig. 83.—Capital of the Church of S. Saba, Rome—End of the VIIIth Century.

Fig. 84.—Capital of the Portico of S. Laurence-in-Lucina, Rome—A.D. 772-795.

The Italian-Byzantine sculptures of S. Saba are two fragments of a parapet fitted into the pavement of the left nave, sculptured with squares formed of knotted osiers, filled up with grapes, leaves, little palms and roses. A small pilaster, with rough rounds of leaves, after the Byzantine style, now serves for a staircase to one of the doors that forms a passage from the neighbouring monastery to the kitchen garden; and, built into the north wall of the same one sees two long friezes in the same style with gyres of vine-branches enclosing rugged animals.

Fig. 85.—Mouth of the Well in the Lateran Cloister, Rome—End of the VIIIth Century.

According to Anastasius, the church of S. Laurence-in-Lucina was also rebuilt by Adrian I., and six columns and two antæ still remain of the old external portico. The capitals of these last imitate in their ensemble the Corinthian forms; and, although the leaves are rough and plain, like those of S. Maria-in-Cosmedin, yet they are in vigorous, full, and almost exaggerated relief. The capitals of the six columns, on the contrary, are Ionic, and, though rugged, compare to great advantage with those of S. Saba. They present a sculptured champignon, and the volutes are ornamented with many spirals; here at least the bit of intaglio mitigates the roughness of the chiselling.

We read in Anastasius that Adrian I., among many other secular constructions, restored and embellished the antique Patriarchal residence near S. John Lateran, that is to say the Papal residence of that time. In the centre of the lovely cloister of Vassalletto, by the side of the basilica, an antique well, attributed by several to the end of the ninth, and even the tenth century, is to be seen; but, observing the extreme roughness of the work, I should deem it to be of the time of Adrian. It is of cylindrical form, and sculptured on the outside with bas-reliefs divided into two zones by a plait of rushes. In the lower zone, crosses are alternated with palms; in the higher one meagre arches adorned by rampant leaves, and beneath the little arches are placed little trees, crosses, or birds pecking at grapes.

To the same period, and to the same chisels, I incline to attribute two fragments of parapets that exist in the cloister itself; one of them adorned with braidings, the other by a great circle enclosing a species of cross formed by knotted plaits and adorned on the sides by various sorts of leaves, which are unfortunately very roughly done. It is a rough reproduction of the central part of the parapet of S. Augustine at Venice or that of S. Oreste near Narni, Greek works of the first half of the eighth century.

Ciampini did not err in asserting that under the reign of Charlemagne *bonæ artes aliqualiter cœperunt revirescere;* the fine arts—here we speak only of architecture and decorative sculpture—really then began slowly to revive. But I cannot bring forward the monument that Ciampini indicates as the architectonic model of that time and the proof of the amendment of Art. He refers to the church of SS. Vincent and Anastasius, "with the three fountains," beyond the walls of Rome—a church that, built originally by Honorius I., seems to have been totally restored by Leo III.

But the present church cannot boast of such high antiquity.

That prostyle, with architraved Ionic columns, those cornices
chiefly of terracotta, those windows like loopholes, those long
bands of masonry at the sides, and the plan of the church,

* Fig. 86.—Archivolt of the Ciborium discovered at Porto, Rome.—A.D. 795-816.

which forms a cross at its upper end, are all characteristic of
the churches of Neo-Latin style, erected after the eleventh
century. And I think Kugler touched the mark in assigning it
to the beginning of the thirteenth century, before 1221, in which
year it was the object of a consecration.

To see some remains of sculpture of the time of Leo III.
you have only to go to the Lateran Museum, in which are
deposited, among various capitals, the remains of an altar-
ciborium, discovered a few years ago among the ruins of an old
basilica of Porto—a city once situated by the sea at the mouth
of the Tiber, near the famous Port of Trajan. Several of those
capitals have all the physiognomy of rough Ionic capitals or
composites, such as Italian artificers of the eighth century could
produce One may also find there the whole arched front of a
ciborium bearing the following inscription:—

" + SALBO BEATISSIMO DOMN LEONE TERTII
PAPAE STEPHANVS INDIGNVS EPISC FECIT."

This precious inscription follows the curve of the archivolt while the mixtilinear lateral triangles are adorned by roses, lilies, and the usual ingenious braidings of osiers, characteristic of the Italian-Byzantine style.

To Pope Paschal (Pasquale) I. (817-824) we owe the most important constructions of the ninth century preserved in Rome.

One of these is the basilica of S. Praxeda on the Esquiline, which he rebuilt from the foundations. The precious Byzantine mosaics with which he adorned the apsis and the triumphal arch are still resplendent there, and this fact sufficed to make many writers imagine that the entire basilica was of the same period, and with its naves (interrupted after every third column by arches supported by strong pilasters) marked a preliminary step towards the Lombard style of churches. But these pilasters and arches, like all the higher part of the church, together with its cornices, its belfry, and the external atrium, according to my judgment, should be referred to a restoration made in the twelfth or following century. The style of every detail proves this, and it is confirmed by the equal distance between the axes of the columns between them and between the columns and the pilasters, while it differs in the intervals on account of the size of the latter. That shows clearly that the pilasters have replaced the antique columns, and, therefore, that the church in the ninth century was like all its Italian sisters, of basilical form. It was not, however, one of the most simple, for it had a transversal or cruciform nave or transept, which was the case with only a very few of the oldest and largest basilicas in the city. Very probably Paschal only reconstructed the church on its old foundations; and, therefore, we may not regard its fine plan as a conception of Paschal's time. It presents a certain singularity at the point of junction of the minor naves with the transversal ones. This singularity consists in the double inter-columns, and the columns attached to the balustrades which serve as antæ.

It is too true that awkward modern restorers have spoiled the interior of this basilica, covering the walls with insignificant and vulgar paintings, transforming the demi-columns into antæ and renewing the capitals of the naves in uncouth style. Some ancient ones remain, however, and they belong to those very demi-columns, afterwards made into antæ, named above, which they could not altogether hide. They are antique Roman-Corinthian ones with the exception of one which manifests the style of the ninth century, and, in its relative perfection of mediocrity, bears testimony to the good progress made in Rome by the Italian - Byzantine style. Indeed this column so surpasses its contemporaries that, if we did not see other and similar authentic examples of this style in other constructions of Paschal's time, we should have difficulty in assigning

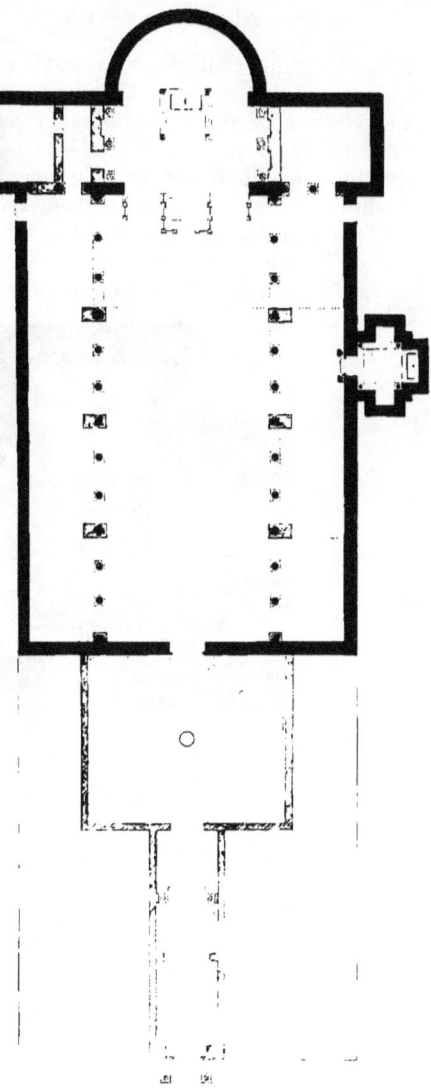

Fig. 87.— Plan of the Church of S. Praxeda, Rome— A.D. 817-824.

it to the ninth century, or at least it would make us suspect the intervention of some Greek artist. It is, without doubt, an imitation of those Corinthian capitals of Byzantine style, with large, rough leaves, which were frequently used in Ravenna in the oldest of Theodoric's constructions (see S Apollinaris), and which also abound in Venice.

Another little capital, and not at all an ugly one, of the ninth century is to be seen in S. Praxeda, at the end of the left lateral nave. It possibly belonged to an altar-ciborium. It affects the

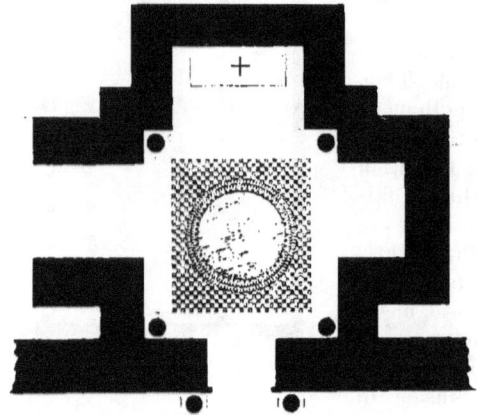

Fig. 88.—Plan of the Chapel of S. Zenone at S. Praxeda, Rome— A.D. 817-824.

composite manner, and shows only one row of leaves resembling those of the palm.

But the most remarkable relic of the ninth century contained

> The presence of Greek artists seems, however, confirmed by the mosaics of the basilica. Like those which were executed in or out of Rome from the sixth to the ninth century, they are, according to my judgment, of Greek workmanship. This opinion agrees with what Leone Ostiense says—namely, that when Desiderio, abbot of Monte Cassino, founded in 1066 a species of school of mosaic work under the direction of Greek masters, he revived this art in Italy, after it had been five hundred years extinct. Cicognara ("Storia della Scultura"), and Gerspach ("Le Mosaïque"), starting with the preconceived idea that such mosaic work as existed in Italy at that period was the work of Italian artists, treated Leone as an exaggerator. I, on the contrary, believe that he was right.

in S. Praxeda is the precious little chapel of S. Zenone, also a work of Pope Paschal, as a synchronical inscription attests. We reach it by a rectangular door, whose posts are enriched with plaitings of osiers in accordance with the Italian-Byzantine style. Two columns of precious marble, but of unequal diameter, rise beside it on rich and disproportioned antique bases, and support those Ionic capitals of Byzantine workmanship of the sixth century, of which I spoke in Chapter I. They are crowned by plinths of medium height roughly sculptured in zigzag by the same rude artificer of the door-posts. An extra-rich and enormous cornice, taken from an antique pagan edifice, runs above the columns, thus giving an air of classical gravity to the decorative ensemble of this door. The top and the sides of that fragment of cornice were not allowed to remain unadorned, but received an intaglio of circles and leaves, or such finish as Italian-Byzantine chisels could give. Over this door there is an arched window framed by a double row of mosaic medallions enclosing barbarous effigies of saints.

FIG. 89.—Base of Column in the Chapel of S. Zenone, Rome—A.D. 817–824.

The interior of the chapel consists of a square space. On three of the sides there are three rectangular niches; it is covered in by a cross-vault and adorned at the angles by four Corinthian columns that support useless cornices which are devoid of ornament. The bases and socles are works of different periods. One is very rich and splendid, being a *chef-d'œuvre* of Roman art; others, on the contrary, present the Byzantine style of the sixth century, while for the most part the fronts of the socles are enriched by bas-reliefs of the ninth century, representing vine-branches issuing from vases.

The pavement of the chapel is also worthy of special observation. It is formed of white marble, porphyry, and serpentine. It is among the most ancient examples of pavements of *opus sectile*, in which they abandoned the old system of minute mosaic called *opus vermiculatum*, and adopted that of little pieces of marble cut into various geometrical forms, so as to obtain elegant designs. This new system—probably imported from the Greeks in the eighth century—developed slowly but surely in Italy during the ninth and tenth centuries, and in the end succeeded in almost entirely supplanting the old fashion. It triumphed most in the Roman and Sicilian basilicas.

In this chapel of S. Zenone which, by reason of its modest proportions, could easily be covered in by vaults, even by the inexpert constructors of the ninth century, there is a powerful Byzantine inspiration increased by the magic splendour of contemporary mosaics, by which it was completely reclothed, and which gained for it the too poetical name of the "Garden of Paradise."

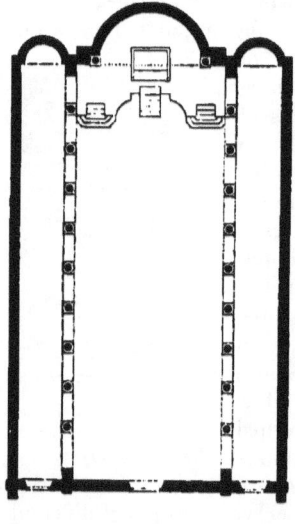

Fig. 90.—Plan of the Church of S. Maria-in-Domnica, Rome — A.D. 817-824.

Paschal I., who erected S. Praxeda, also reconstructed the churches of S. Cecilia-in-Trastevere, and S. Maria-in-Domnica on the Cœlius. Of the former the apsis remains, adorned by mosaics of that time, and a portion of the original pavement of the tribune, in which we discern the same decorative motives, the same manner, and the same marbles which exist in the pavement of the chapel of S. Zenone.

The church of S. Maria-in-Domnica, or "della Navicella," may be said to be almost the same as that which Paschal I. constructed, and therefore the best preserved of those of the ninth century which remain in Rome. It has three naves divided by eighteen columns supporting arches, and terminating in three apsides. The centre nave still shows, in its upper extremity, the important mosaics of Paschal. The colonnades are, as usual, of fragmentary materials, with capitals for the most part of antique Corinthian style. Only five are works of the ninth century, and seem almost to be brothers of those of S. Praxeda, differing from the latter merely in the lower row of leaves, to which an intaglio has been given that, later on, became common to many Neo-Latin works. These columns, which are far from being ugly, and the care with which the arches have been imposed on them, without the help of heavy abaci, show us, when we remember the barbarous constructions of S. Maria-in-Cosmedin, and of S. Saba, a considerable progress in Italian-Byzantine art during the ninth century at Rome.

Fig. 91.—Capital of S. Maria-in-Domnica, Rome—A.D. 817-824.

According to the testimony of Anastasius and Ugonius, the pontiff Eugene II. (824-827) executed many works in S. Sabina on the Aventine. Till the second half of the sixteenth century, the marble chancels which he made were still existing, and probably several fragments of Italian-Byzantine sculpture, visible in the internal atrium of the basilica, are remains of them. They consist of two slabs of parapet, adorned by crosses with roses and palms at their sides, and closed-in by little arches supported

Fig. 92.—Parapet of the Church of S. Sabina, Rome—A.D. 824-827.

by pillars. There is also another enriched by many little squares framed in braids, and having, in the first zone, doves; in the second, peacocks; in the third, vine-leaves; in the fourth, the usual badly-sculptured heart-shaped bunches of grapes. It reminds one both of the ambos of Ravenna and the gates of the old chancel of S. Maria-in-Valle at Cividale.

After Paschal I., the Pope of the ninth century, whose name lives best in his works, is Gregory IV. (A.D. 827).

He rebuilt the church of S. Mark, of which the apsis with its mosaics still remains. Every other part has been repeatedly remade and transformed in the centuries that preceded the eleventh. Only one sculpture of the style of the ninth century, very probably a remnant of Gregory's work, is preserved in the portico of the church. It is a fragment of a parapet covered with osier-circles knotted together, and enclosing rayed or girandoled roses.

To Gregory IV. we also owe the most considerable remains of Italian-Byzantine sculpture that exist in Rome. Anastasius, the librarian, states in his writings that that pontiff built against the apsis of the basilica of S. Maria-in-Trastevere a high tribune, on which the altar, that till then had been too low, was placed, and that he also constructed the presbytery. Well, the grand works of restoration, undertaken by Pius IX. in 1865, have given rise to the discovery, under the existing pavement of that basilica, of the beginning of the ancient apsis, which curved in the place wherein the triumphal arch is now situated, and, before it, of the vestiges of Gregory's tribune with the steps that led to the altar, besides a great number of sculptured marbles, which must have composed the *rugæ* or chancels of the above-mentioned presbytery * and which were found turned upside down and used as a pavement.

There are nearly twenty almost entire parapets. I am inclined to think that two of them date from the end of the eighth century, or at least that they issue from a different hand than the others. I am induced to believe this by the great carelessness of the design and the in-

* De Rossi, " Bullettino d'Archeologia Cristiana," anno 1866.

elegance of the composition. In the one we see an ingenious interweaving of curved and right lines; in the other, two palm-branches and two crosses surmounted by two peacocks drinking from a vase between serpents, bunches of grapes and

Fig. 93*a*.—Parapet of S. Maria of Trastevere, Rome—A.D. 827.

roses—a wretched work that seems to have come out of the same workshop as the well of the Lateran Museum.

One cannot say the same of the other parapets, for though their chiselling is not much better, yet they show a diligence in the tracing of the various ornaments that often approaches to elegance. Here all those loose compositions of animals, crosses, and palms, which the Greeks delighted in, are banished because they exacted too much skill of the artist. Geometrical decorations, and especially complicated braidings of circles and right lines, are preferred. In the study of these designs it seems those artists exercised all their diligence and experienced an extraordinary pleasure. The drawing serves much better than a minute description to give the reader an idea of those parapets, each one of which differs from the other. We shall find them almost all reproduced here and there in Italy in the works of the ninth and the following century.

Besides these parapets, the portico of S. Maria-in-Trastevere shows us two archivolts of a little ciborium, adorned in the same Italian-Byzantine style, and without doubt contemporaries of the former. They are decorated with bands and

Fig. 93b.—Parapet of S. Maria of Trastevere, Rome—A.D. 827.

braids, spirals with cruciform leaves, lilies, peacocks, and caulicules.

Certain fragments of parapets within the church of S. George at Velabro, or under the fine external portico, present the same character and must also be referred to the time of the pontificate of Gregory IV., who, as we read in Anastasius, rebuilt the apsis from the foundations. Especially worthy of remark are certain interwoven circles, small and great, formed by bands which are also

Fig. 93c.—Other Parapets of S. Maria of Trastevere—A.D. 827.

interwoven. One may also see there fragments of pilasters, the posts of a little door adorned with Byzantine spirals, a capital of a pilaster with plain, hard leaves, and finally a little bracket-formed abacus, adorned with foliage—several copies of which are scattered among the ruins of the Roman Forum close by, and in the Lateran Museum.

Sergius II. (844–847), the successor of Gregory IV., caused the Lateran basilica to be entirely rebuilt, and to this period a parapet covered with ingenious and carefully wrought curvilinear interweavings, which exists in the neighbouring cloister, may be assigned.

There are so many works of the Italian-Byzantine style in Rome that if I described them in detail I should fill up the whole chapter with them, and tire my reader. Hitherto I have only mentioned those whose age seemed to me to be authenticated either by historical notices or synchronical inscriptions. With regard to the rest, I will only pause before the most remarkable works, and content myself with a rapid glance at the others.

Important sculptures of the Italian-Byzantine style were brought to light at S. Clement's, on the Cœlius, on the occasion of the fortunate discovery of the subterranean church. They consist of two parapets, one with Byzantine spirals, the other with mixtilinear braidings, and a convex stone, on which is sculptured a Greek cross with four rude palms placed diagonally between its arms. In the pavement of the square portico of the basilica, along the right-hand colonnade, is another fragment of parapet of the same kind. Further on is a capital, which is very precious because it exhibits in its lower part the style of those of S. Praxeda and of S. Maria-in-Domnica, and in its upper part nothing but rude caulicules, such as are common in Italian-Byzantine works, and thus confirms the age which I have attributed to the former.

But the most important thing in this style which S. Clement has to show us, is the door between the street and the quadriportico, because it is the only complete one that Rome possesses, and one of the very few remaining in Italy. The two doorposts, each formed of three pieces, are covered with varied braidings, and so is the architrave which they support. This door must have been taken from the inferior church when, after

Fig. 91.—Details of the Door of S. Clement on the Cœlius, Rome—IXth Century.

the horrible incendiarism of Roberto Guiscardo, the present church and porch were constructed.

In the neighbouring basilica of the SS. Quattro Coronati there is a fragment of a parapet of Italian-Byzantine style, adorned by knotted squares roughly carved. It is built into the left wall of the second courtyard. In the atrium of the church of the Holy Apostles are two Italian-Byzantine parapets, of the coarsest style. On one of them are two little arches enclosing two braided crosses, among palms and bunches of grapes. On the other is a trunk from which issues a series of spirals symmetrically distributed, and, like certain ones of S. Maria-in-Trastevere, they are a gross imitation of those of S. Maria-in-Valle, of Cividale, or of the ciborium of Bologna. Among the spirals there are birds chiselled in the most primitive fashion.

On the terrace above the atrium of the basilica of S. Maria Maggiore, among the fine mosaics that adorn the old façade, are two little round quadrilobed windows whose lights are cut out of slabs of marble covered with ornaments in the Italian-Byzantine style. Fleury, who has noticed them, took them for parapets; but I, after a careful examination, recognised in them four archivolts of a ciborium, adorned with braids, cords, lilies, spindles, and curled cauliculos.

At S. Agnes-beyond-the-Walls, along the great staircase, fragments of the coarsest Italian-Byzantine style are also to be seen. The most considerable presents an arcade of braiding supported by coarse pillars, in the upper part of which is a curved cross, and, in the lower part, a rude rosette inscribed in a circle formed of several ribbons knotted at equal distances. Vine-leaves and grapes fill up the gaps.

From this epoch until the eleventh century the Roman Forum must have been encircled by a thick ring of churches in the formation of which the old temples and the spacious basilicas were very serviceable. It is certain that the extensive excavations effected in our times in the very heart of the grandest empire that ever existed, have brought to light a considerable number of Italian-Byzantine sculptures, which, without doubt, once formed part of neighbouring churches. Fragments of parapets, pilasters, capitals, abaci, crosses, &c., now rest alongside of the marvellous splendours of ancient pagan Art to demonstrate by a strong and singular contrast the most profound decadence of Christian art.

Among the most noteworthy pieces are two marbles adorned with

FIG. 95.— Parapet of S. Agnes-beyond-the-Walls, Rome — End of the VIIIth Century.

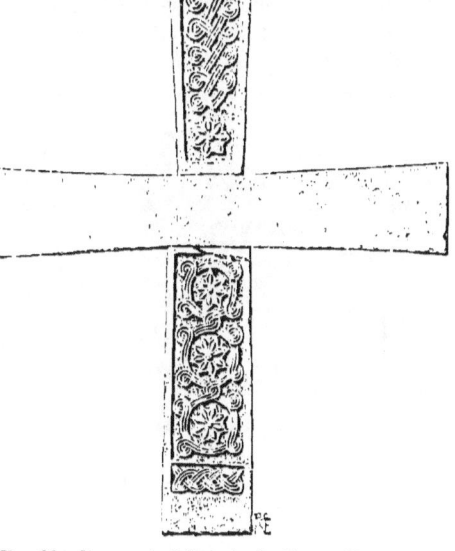

FIG. 96.—Fragment of Cross in the Roman Forum—IXth Century.

braids, which were disinterred from the church of SS. Cosmas and Damian. At first sight one would suppose them to be pilasters, but on observing their form, lightly splayed at the extremities, one sees immediately that, together with a horizontal piece now lost, they must have composed a large cross, perhaps one of those that, in the Middle Ages, were placed on the top of certain isolated columns in front of churches, in squares, or on crossways. Several are to be seen in Bologna, in S. Petronia, and in the museum.

Another remarkable Italian-Byzantine sculpture in the Roman Forum is a parapet on which is sculptured the usual composition of a cross flanked by palms and roses, enclosed in an arcade, an old symbolic representation in which is suggested our Lord Jesus dying on the cross, with His mother Mary on one side and the beloved disciple on the other, above whom are the sun and the moon. This composition of the Roman Forum is among the richest preserved in Italy.

Remnants of Italian-Byzantine style are to be found even on the Palatine, near the sumptuous palace of the Cæsars, and even among the colossal ruins of the thermæ of Caracalla. In the Lateran Museum, besides those already cited, there are several others, the most noteworthy of which is a parapet placed in the middle of the great staircase that leads to the lapidary galleries. It is rich in knot-works that compose a cross enclosed in a circle among doves and roses and other plants.

Fig. 97.—Mouth of a Well at the Office of the Minister of Agriculture, Rome—End of the VIIIth Century.

The cloister-well at the Lateran is not the only one preserved in Rome. There are three others equally cylindrical, sculptured in the same Italian-Byzantine style. One of these is seen in front of the church of S. John at the Latin

Gate, enriched by spirals in the Byzantine manner, and with an inscription which mentions a certain Stephen as author of the sculptures; it is the only sculptor's name that monuments of this style have preserved for us.

In the vestibule of the Artistic Industrial Museum, and at the entrance of the office of the Agricultural, Industrial, and Commercial Ministry, the other two wells are preserved. The fundamental idea of their decoration is in each case the same—that is to say, a row of five little arcades supported by coarse little pillars and crowned by rampant caulicules. But in the first, which is very rich, the usual crosses are inscribed between roses and palms; in the other, on the contrary, are only rude and simple palms.

The reader must not believe that I assign to the ninth century all these undated Roman works because they show the Italian-Byzantine style. Many of them may belong to the tenth century, for the same manner of ornamentation (and in Rome, one must add, of architecture) in use during the ninth century was common also in the tenth in every part of Italy, excepting the islands of the Venetian lagoons.

One basilica of Rome founded in A.D. 900, and therefore appertaining more to the tenth than the ninth century, is that of S. Maria-in-Aracœli. There still remain of this epoch the three vast naves divided by columns bearing semicircular arcades. Stems and capitals show the most grotesque confusion of picked-up marbles. Some of rough Ionic form hint at the time in which the church was built. Fragments of fasces and parapets of Italian-Byzantine style may be seen in the interior of the ambo on the right side, and present the usual spirals or else little arches holding crosses, roses, &c. Three interesting stems of columns, of unequal dimensions, that must have belonged to ciboria, were discovered during the recent demolition of the old convent of Aracœli. They are striped one-third up vertically by large channellings filled up by batons, and the other two-thirds are striped spirally by Doric channellings. That these elegant stems should be attributed to the Italian-Byzantine style, is confirmed by other ciboria of Ravenna authentically of the ninth century, which are similarly adorned. Nothing Byzantine is revealed in them: they are absolutely Roman in character; for—strange circumstance!—while the pagan Greeks never omitted to channel their columns (no matter of what dimensions they might be), the Christian Greeks, on the contrary, kept them invariably smooth

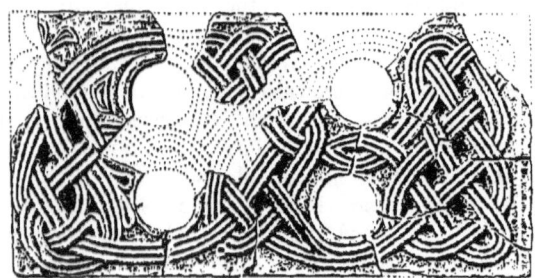

Fig. 98.—Bas-relief from the Cloister of S. Laurence-beyond-the-Walls, Rome—A.D. 1024–1033.

in order to enjoy all the beauty of veined or many-hued marble. On the other hand, the Romans cared but little to channel columns of rough stone, but took much pains to channel those of white marble, in order to moderate their dazzling whiteness with reposeful shadow. At the end of the empire the Roman architects of the decadence sought after bizarre channellings, which they often preferred gyrated or cut into various lengths, or fashioned into batons and gules rather than shell-patterns.* One would say that the stems of these Italian-Byzantine ciboria were copied from some Roman model of the third or fourth century.

The Italian-Byzantine style must have been dominant in Rome during the tenth, and even part of the eleventh century; and of this I have proofs. In the melancholy and picturesque cloister of S. Laurence-beyond-the-Walls, where there are two spiral door-posts of Italian-Byzantine style and other frag-

* A beautiful Roman stem divided into three ringed zones and channelled, in part vertically, in part spirally, may be found in the ancient crypt of S. Maria-in-Organo at Verona.

ments of parapets of the same style, with the usual arcades and crosses—works that may be referred to the ninth or tenth century—there are also several very rudimentary stucco bas-reliefs, covered with crosses and palms, or with strange ruffled braidings, partly flowered, in which a certain tendency toward the Lombard style is revealed. They were executed between 1024 and 1033, during the pontificate of Pope John XIX., as one learns from the following inscription: " TEMPORIB(us) DOMIOHI XVIIII PAPÆ."

Fig. 99.—Fragment of Parapet in the Museum of Capua—IXth Century.

Capua.—It was natural that the Italian-Byzantine style, which had penetrated Rome at such an early period and reigned there for more than two centuries, should have reached further south and taken root even in the Neapolitan Provinces until the time when the Neo-Byzantine, Arab, Tuscan, and Lombard styles supplanted it. I have not been able to travel much in that region; nevertheless, the few monuments I have come across prove to me that the Italian-Byzantine art has been there, and that many examples of it must still remain. Capua alone offers me traces of it in the museum, and in an entire church, which without doubt belongs to the tenth or the second half of the preceding century.

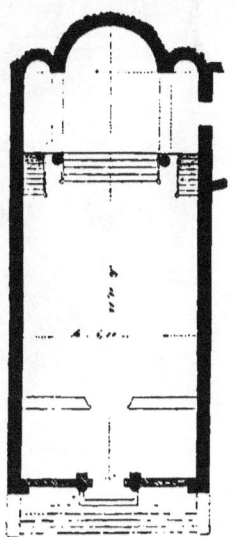

Fig. 100.—Plan of the Church of S. Michael, Capua—Xth Century (?).

In the museum a fragment of a parapet with concentric circles knotted together may be seen, and the ribbons, as we saw at S. George-in-Velabro, in Rome, are covered with smaller braidings. Roses lilies, and other smaller circles enrich the composition somewhat awkwardly.

At a short distance from the museum there rises a little church, dedicated to Prince S. Michael (as the people call him) —a church no longer used for divine service, because of its very bad condition. It has only one nave, terminated by a little presbytery raised by several steps, bounded on the front by two isolated columns bearing semicircular arches, and at the back by an apsis flanked by two great niches. Under the presbytery a crypt opens, made on a similar plan. It is covered by vaults, supported in the centre by a single column. Originally the church must have had an external portico sustained by two columns, which are now encased in a modern wall, for they wished to prolong it at the expense of the atrium.

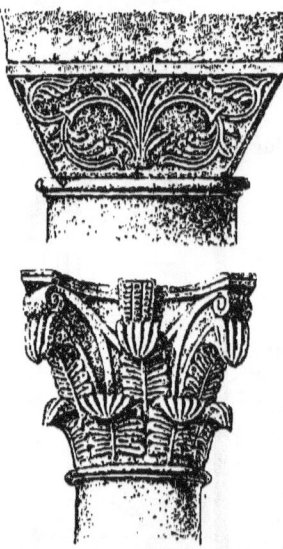

FIG. 101.—Capitals from S. Michael, Capua—Xth Century (?).

The raised choir, the presence of a crypt, and the signs of three apsides, prevent us from thinking that this church might have an earlier date than the middle of the eighth century ; and since we know that Capua was founded in A.D. 856, we may reasonably doubt that its origin can be later than this date. But if we wish to establish the date with sufficient precision, we have the decorative details, and specially certain capitals of the columns. We will not look at those of the presbytery, as they are old Corinthians, but we must pause before the column in the crypt and the two columns of the façade. The first has something of the form of a Byzantine abacus, but it agrees badly with the round column that bears it, while it appears made for the vaults which it sustains. Its sides are adorned with ornamental bas-reliefs, with leafage and palm-spirals in the Italian-Byzantine style. The capitals of the façade are of Corinthian form, but of that rude Corinthian which the sculptors of the ninth or tenth century produced. The leaves are not of acanthus, but palm-leaves; their curls are roughly and conventionally striated, like those of the Greek capitals of the eighth century of S. George of Valpolicella, or the museum of Capua itself. Rough, stiff caulicules and a miserable abacus complete it. These capitals, and especially their leaves, show much analogy with similar works of Northern Italy, which belong, as we see, to the second half of the tenth century; and therefore I should be led to assign the same date to this precious church of S. Michael of Capua.

TOSCANELLA.—Returning towards the north we must halt at Toscanella, which, in the church of S. Maria Major, offers us several Italian-Byzantine sculptures, that certainly must have figured in an older church than the present one, which is a fine basilica of Lombard style of the twelfth century. Towards the end of the central nave, on the left, rises a grand ambo, sustained by four arcades planted upon columns. Fleury took the whole thing for a work of the ninth century, and offered it as an example of ambos of that time; but he was evidently in error, because that work, as a whole, and in many characteristic details, is a fruit of the twelfth century. This we recognise, first, in the form of the ambo, which is entirely Romanic, and therefore later than the year 1000; secondly by its capitals, its intermediate cornice, and in particular by that little angular figure surmounted by an eagle supporting the reading-desk. Fleury's error finds, however, some justification in the fact that the ambo is composed for the most part of sculptures that are really in the style of the ninth century. Such are the higher parapets, which must originally have belonged to a choir. The arcades below must certainly have formed part of an antique ciborium (perhaps that of the high altar), which is now replaced by a much larger one.

It is needless to say that here also everything is covered

by rich decorative sculpture, representing the usual mixtilinear braidings, ingenious combinations, spirals, crosses, roses, and rampant caulicules; in fact, all those details that we lately observed on the Italian-Byzantine monuments of Rome.

Various other fragments in the same style are dispersed among the churches, principally in the form of altar decorations.

ORVIETO.—The museum of Orvieto encloses an ornamental parapet in the Italian-Byzantine style, covered with circles of intertwined withes, and enclosing crosses, bunches of grapes, twin caulicules, tresses, volatiles, and other caprices.

SPOLETO.—I also saw a fragment of a parapet, sculptured in interwreathed circles, in the usual Italian-Byzantine style, set in the front of the belfry of the cathedral of Spoleto, where I had already found a Greek bas-relief of the eighth century.

ANCONA.—The Italian-Byzantine style also appears on two fragments of parapets adorned with braidings, existing in the old crypt of the cathedral of Ancona, and on another fragment outside the church on the north-west side.

two arcades supported by pilasters enclosing two large crosses among palms, braids and birds. Little braidings wind round the arches, descend on the pillars, run along the arms of the crosses, and it is curious to see how they change below and are transformed into palms (see Fig. 102).

Fleury says that between Rome and the shores of the Adriatic there was, in the tenth century, a great affinity of style, chiefly explained by the pontifical dominion over the Marche and the Esarcato. He does not, however, show clearly whether he means to say that Rome in the ninth century exercised artistic influence over the Adriatic coasts, or *vice versa*. But, whichever it be, I believe that not only Rome, but the western shores of the Adriatic, submitted to the direct and exclusive influence of Lombardy from the first half of the eighth century till beyond the eleventh.

Nor can I accept what Fleury adds, namely, that sculptural decoration in Tuscany had a different character in the ninth century from that of the surrounding regions. It is an absolutely gratuitous assertion, since he did not attempt to prove it; nor could he, I believe, have done so. What motives, in fact, could have caused such isolation in Art in Tuscany? Towards the eleventh century she took so little part in political events and commerce, and was held in such small account, that there could be no reason for her development of an original Art much superior to that cultivated in the rest of Italy. It seems that Fleury could not find monuments of the eleventh century in Tuscany, like those in Rome and elsewhere, and, without doubt, founded his conjecture on their absence. I, on the contrary, deduce therefrom that the unpropitious conditions of that region did not favour the constructive activity and large employment of Italian-Byzantine art, of which Rome and many other Italian regions could boast. In spite of everything, I firmly believe that if there was any Art in the ninth and tenth centuries in Tuscany, it could only be the Italian-Byzantine one, and of this I can offer a proof.

PISA.—In the external walls of the largest apses of the cathedral of Pisa four bands, adorned by ornamental bas-reliefs in Italian-Byzantine style, are built. On them appear the accustomed curvilinear or mixtilinear braidings, more or less complicated, knotted circles, and rosettes of various kinds.

Ciampini, D'Agincourt, Cordero, and several others, who pointed out the church of the Three Fountains, near Rome, as the proof of progress in the arts towards the end of the eighth century, did not fail to guide the student to the church of the Holy Apostles of Florence, to gaze on something much better in the shape of that graceful basilica, which, according to tradition, was founded by Charlemagne himself. Vasari had already said so in the preface of his "Lives," adding that this church shows that, in Tuscany, "some good artificers had remained or reappeared, and that it is such a one that Brunelleschi did not disdain to use it for a model when he built the church of the Holy Spirit and that of S. Laurence." That Brunelleschi was inspired by the church I can well believe ; but I cannot admit that the present edifice is the same as that which arose in the time of Charlemagne. Certainly no one doubts that S. Miniato al Monte is a work of the eleventh century ; well, let all the most minute details of the church of the Holy Apostles be confronted with the analagous ones of S. Miniato, and one must without hesitation conclude that the two graceful edifices belong to the same epoch. I have paused before this error of Vasari, not because I regard myself as the first to demonstrate it, but only in the hope of convincing, once for all, several doubting minds.

RAVENNA.—I reconduct the reader to Ravenna among the tombs of the precious basilica of S. Apollinaris-beyond-the-Walls, where there was a grievous example of the monstrosities produced by the miserable Barbarous-Latin art of the beginning of the eighth century, before it felt the beneficent effects of the second Byzantine influence.

The sarcophagus of a certain John, archbishop of the city (I believe him to have been the ninth of this name), who died A.D. 784, is rough and mean, but not without importance, since it presents some characteristics of the Italian-Byzantine style, and therefore serves to prove how early this style had penetrated into Ravenna and how quickly it was diffused through the various regions of Italy. One recognises the Italian-Byzantine chisel in those crosses with their curled extremities, after the Greek fashion, and in that horizontal band of the arched covercle formed by simple interweavings of withes. The arch, however, must have belonged first to some pagan tomb; this is chiefly shown by the reversed moulding that frames the front, which, although very simple, attests a hand so skilful that we cannot believe it to be the same that sculptured the crosses and the inscriptions.

Another sarcophagus of the same church, where lies the Archbishop Gratiosus, who died in 788, presents a greater profusion of crosses, but the same idea and the same chisel.

Fig. 103.—Sarcophagus of the Archbishop Gratiosus in S. Apollinaris, near Ravenna - A.D. 788.

Of the same time must be the front of a sarcophagus existing in the museum of the archiepiscopal palace which contained the bodies of the consorts Gregory and Maria. The inscription is framed in braids and flanked by two crosses with curved extremities.

We must now return to S. Apollinaris-in-Classe to see

the most important (because almost intact) monument of the Italian-Byzantine style of the ninth century that remains to us in Italy. It is the ciborium of the altar of S. Elucadius, which, according to an inscription, a priest called Pietro caused to be sculptured during the See of the Archbishop Valerius (A.D. 806-816). It must originally have been isolated in a spacious place, and only after many centuries have been transported to the angle of the left nave where we now find it, having lost the bases of its columns and received a crowning cornice which does not form part of it and which it might have dispensed with.

Rohault de Fleury is not of this opinion. According to him the ciborium has always occupied its present place; but, to convince one's self of the contrary, one need only look at the internal sides of the two arcades against the walls all covered with bas-reliefs like the external ones, and with the vertical bands half hidden by the superposition of the marble slabs. This awkward arrangement is the result of turning those arches towards the inside of the ciborium that they might remain visible instead of being hidden against the walls of the nave.

The ciborium is formed by four columns supporting as many monolithic archivolts, whose space is somewhat less than a semicircle. One-third of the columns is striated vertically, the other two-thirds spirally, exactly like those found near the church of Aracœli in Rome and without doubt by the same artificers. Though Rome lent no helping hand to show us Italian-Byzantine capitals that had departed from the Corinthian or Ionic modes, the ciborium offers us four which, in their ensemble, remind us much more of the Byzantine basket forms than of Roman ones. They present various decorations of roses, crosses, caulicules, and leaves of wild acanthus and of palm.

The four arches are varied like the capitals that support them. On the front side curves a graceful and complicated band of mixtilinear braidings of excellent effect, and in the over-arches wave two branches of the vine, rich in leaves, and

Fig. 104.—Ciborium of S. Elucadius in S. Apollinaris, near Ravenna—A.D. 806-816.

the usual bunches of grapes surrounded by a listel. Interwoven bands, more or less complex, compose the other archivolts, in whose over-arches we see braids, or rudely-carved peacocks drinking from a vase, or doves at the sides of a cross between four rayed or girandoled rosettes. One pretty conceit is a band formed by a branch with spirals, each of which forms itself into a cross.

In the same church of S. Apollinaris there is also a sarcophagus already known to us (see Fig. 3), which appears to be work of the latter part of the sixth century or of the first half of the seventh (of the covercle this may be said positively), but in the ninth or tenth century, perhaps in order to make it ready for another body, this sarcophagus must needs be enriched in front by two coarse little pilasters with leafage, and at the sides by small twin arches enclosing spirals with little pilasters and archivolts decorated with bead-work. What most attracts us in it is the form of the little arches, which, instead of being semicircular, are what are called horseshoe arches. It is not necessary to see here a caprice of the sculptor, but rather a far-off Arab influence, and the oldest example of such an influence that I have found in Italy.

FIG. 105.—Side of a Sarcophagus in S. Apollinaris, near Ravenna—VIth and IXth Centuries.

Before leaving the basilica, I will mention an important

work in the Italian-Byzantine style; it is an arch that perhaps crowned a little ciborium and now serves as an ornament to the door of the belfry. It is the oldest example of a cusped archivolt, and is, moreover, ornamented with rampant caulicules; it is the prototype of those adornments over ciboria or doors, that in the Lombard style at first, and then in the Gothic, were much employed and obtained a great success. Several other fragments of sculpture in Italian-Byzantine style—abaci of capitals, pilasters, pierced parapets, archivolts.

FIG. 106.—Cusped Archivolt in S. Apollinaris, near Ravenna—IXth Century.

&c.—are to be seen in the churches or in the palaces of Ravenna. Columns similar to those of the ciborium of S. Eleucadius stand in the atrium of the basilica of the Holy Spirit, and most probably sustained a ciborium, of the arcades of which two fragments remain in the sacristy of the said church. They show an elegant band with knotted branches from which droop palm-leaves. Italian-Byzantine fragments are to be found in the Ursiano Baptistery, in the Rasponi Palace, in the Classe Museum, and on the belfry of S. John-the-Evangelist. A sarcophagus named "delle treccie" (the braided), because adorned with bands of that characteristic decoration, may be seen in the vault of Braccioforte, near the tomb of Dante.

BUDRIO.—In the museum of Bologna is a reproduction in plaster of a great stational marble cross existing in Budrio, and, like that of S. Petronio, hoisted on to the stem of a column. Its principal façade bears the following inscription: "+ INDI NO RENOVA CRVX TEMPORIBV DOM VITALE EPSC." Bologna's only bishop of that name held his See from A.D. 789 till 814. Therefore that cross must have been carved in that time, and, in fact, its finely arabesqued decorations have all the impress of the Italian-Byzantine style.

VERONA.—Canobio, in his story of Verona (Book V.), wrote that "in A.D. 780, in which time Bishop Lothaire lived, the church of S. Maria Matricolare was not very large," and that the said bishop "rebuilt it with the help of Bertrada, who was the wife of Pepin and the mother of Charlemagne, and also of the wife of Desiderio and of Charlemagne; which church in better form was afterwards chosen by Bishop Ratoldo (A.D. 802-840) for the cathedral." This precious notice caused all the historians and archaeologists who wrote about Verona during various centuries to suppose that the modern cathedral in its most antique parts—that is to say, the external walls, the apsis, the doors, &c.—was the same church that Lothaire rebuilt, and that was perhaps finished by Ratoldo, who chose it for a cathedral. Critics some years ago demonstrated the absurdity of that opinion, declaring that to the twelfth century belonged what was for so long believed to be of the eighth or ninth. In confirmation of this, and to convert the obstinate, came a happy discovery made in 1884 in consequence of certain excavations in the picturesque Lombard cloister near the cathedral. At about two metres' depth large pieces of a vermiculated mosaic pavement, beautifully worked in geometrical combinations and with leafage, fruits, animals, and inscriptions, were found; and, with the mosaic, a marble column, which was easily placed on its own intact base and crowned with its own capital. Other remnants were found, corresponding to this belt of mosaic, in the neighbouring church of S. Helena and in a magazine close by. To what sort of edifice and to what time could these relics belong? The dimensions and subdivisions of the pavement, the nature of the antique inscriptions (where the names of the faithful who contributed to the work are chronicled), and the position of the column, persuade us that it belonged to a church. And if we look at the style and technique of the said pavement, we must recognise it as similar to and therefore synchronical with those of Parengo, Pola, Grado, which everyone knows belong to the sixth century. This being considered, it is only reasonable to conjecture that these are the remains of the ancient, and by no means large, church of S. Maria Matricolare; and for me the conjecture becomes certainty when I lift my eyes to the capital of the column, which is, without doubt, work of the eighth century, and of that Lothaire who, according to the truthful statement of Canobio, restored the church in 780.

It is a capital in the Corinthian manner, with hard, smooth leaves, meagre caulicules, and a very stiff abacus. Take note of the ribbon which curves under the central caulicules. This capital, as the reader can see, has much analogy with the Greek ones of S. Saviour's-in-Brescia, and, without doubt, like those of the same time in S. Maria-in-Cosmedin of Rome, is one of the first essays in Italian-Byzantine art.

Fig. 107.—Capital from the old cathedral of Verona—A.D. 780.

Guided by this capital we can find in Verona several others, which considerably enrich our catalogue.

In the little neighbouring church of S. John-in-Fonte, an old baptistery of the cathedral, of the twelfth century, in the form of a little basilica with three naves, one may see, among synchronical capitals of the sixth century, two very similar to that found in the cloister and evidently of the same epoch.

In the church of S. Stephen, in that apsis where we have already found a mutilated capital of Byzantine-Barbarian style, and in the adjoining crypt, we may see not less than thirty capitals of average dimensions so much resembling, both in design and sculpture, those of S. Maria Matricolare and the baptistery, that it is useless to describe them. This proves that the church of S. Stephen must, towards the end of the eighth century, have undergone a thorough restoration, but does not prove that the apsis and crypt, in which those capitals were employed, were of that date. The fact that several of them were mutilated so that, being shortened, they might better adapt themselves to the columns to which they were assigned, is opposed to that idea. As to the apsis, we shall see, towards the end of this chapter, what epoch suits it; and as for the crypt, we may from this moment declare it to be of the twelfth century—that is to say, of the same epoch as the greater part of the present church. I rely principally on the resemblance between certain of its capitals, really chiselled for the vaults that they support, and the analogous capitals of the crypt of S. John-in-Valle, a church indubitably of the twelfth century.

But S. John-in-Valle is of much more ancient origin; and though its crypt cannot claim an earlier date than the twelfth century, four of its capitals are evidently much older, presenting the Italian-Byzantine style. In the stiffness of certain leaves, and the ensemble of their form, they repeat those of S. Stephen; but the caulicules, the central leaf, and the abacus, show a notable improvement. I assign them, therefore, to the ninth century rather than the end of the eighth.

A curious capital of a pilaster existing in the crypt of S. Maria-in-Organo, must be nearly contemporary with them. It is a rough Corinthian one with stiff leaves, but presenting the strange originality of four parallelopipeds, planted on the reverses of the angular leaves and rising to sustain the volutes of the abacus.

Four more of the same style as the last, but less simple and more in accordance with the general character of ninth-century capitals, may be seen supporting a sarcophagus in the crypt of S. Zeno-the-Major. They incline to the Corinthian style, have smooth, stiff leaves, but between the caulicules show a palm, or a rosette, or a channelled convexity like those so much used in the Greek capitals of the eighth century. These columns, which, perhaps, supported a ciborium, are the only sculptures that remind us of the basilica of S. Zeno erected, according to tradition, by Pepin, and finished or restored by Otho I. in the tenth century.

VILLANOVA.—The ancient and precious church of S. Peter of Villanova in the Veronese domains, between S. Bonifacio and Soave, offers us in its naves and crypt of the twelfth century several capitals of columns, so similar in design and chiselling to those of S. Stephen and the other churches that we saw at Verona, that we must assign them to the same time and the same workmen.

FIG. 108 Parapet of S. Peter's of Villanova —End of the VIIIth Century.

This church also offers us a rare thing in Veronese churches, an entire and well-preserved *pluteo* of the same epoch which we find inserted in the back of the high altar. It is adorned above by a frieze and little arches; below by a cross between bunches of grapes and roses, with a peacock on each side at the foot, and higher up interwoven rushes. The inelegant incorrectness of the design, the roughness of the chisel, and the want of connection in the composition, that seems to imitate the Greek manner, persuade us to attribute this *pluteo* rather to the end of the eighth century than to the ninth, and the style of the capitals confirms this opinion.

PADUA.—I only found two miserable fragments of Italian-Byzantine style in Padua with rudely-made animals or crosses, &c., existing in the public museum. The deplorable conditions of the city in the eighth and ninth centuries were certainly not propitious to the prosperity of the Arts; and here perhaps is the cause of the almost total absence of buildings and sculptures of that period. Such was not the idea of Dartein, who affirms that he recognised a notable monument of the ninth century in the famous apsis of the church of S. Sophia of Padua, which for him is only a portion of a rotunda constructed in the time of Charlemagne. This conjecture appears to me a mistake, as I shall try to prove later on.

TREVISO.—In the vast crypt of the cathedral of Treviso, constructed in 1140, in Venetian-Byzantine style, we find nine capitals of columns that, by their style, acknowledged the ninth century. They show two rows of leaves: the lower ones of wild acanthus broadly chiselled and not of barbarous form, the upper ones a sort of palm alternated with caulicules.

The museum of Treviso also possesses works of Italian-Byzantine style. The most important is the cylindrical mouth of a well, like those of Rome, but perhaps derived from Venice. It is decorated with interwoven bands, flowered spirals, little arches enclosing circles, geometrical combinations, large roses, or certain fan-shaped ornaments of original and not inelegant forms. There are also two fragments of a pilaster, with cross and ornaments and two short demi-columns, said to have come from an old building in Mogliano, provided with curious capitals, with designs in zigzag, and concave chamferings in part filled up with large tongue-shaped leaves.

FIG. 109.—Capital of the Crypt of the Cathedral of Treviso—IXth Century.

CIVIDALE.—At Cividale also, inside and outside of the cathedral, there are remains of Italian-Byzantine sculpture. The most remarkable piece is a *pluteo*, that lies near the baptistery of Callisto, and seems to invite immediate comparison between eighth-century works and those of which it is a specimen, that is to say, ninth-century ones. It is covered with rectangles, formed by the usual withes woven together, and enclosing braids or little birds or leaves, or a cross with curved extremities.

The Italian-Byzantine style was not tardy in reaching

the Venetian lagoons, but made an even pompous display of its productions there, of which many still remain. But, while in several other Italian regions it could reign without dispute, here, on the contrary, it was confronted by a powerful rival, the Byzantine-Barbarian style returning by Venetian boats to invade this corner of Italy. On account of the special conditions of ninth-century Art in maritime Venice, I have deemed it convenient to devote a separate chapter (the next) to the subject.

In the meantime, let me note that the Italian-Byzantine style did not halt at Timavo, but continued its road along the coasts of Istria and Dalmatia, adorning those cities with monuments, that have in part survived. These I will indicate to the reader.

TRIESTE.—Among a few remains of Italian-Byzantine works of the eighth century, the Vinckelmann Museum possesses several Italian-Byzantine sculptures of the ninth century. They are fragments of parapets covered with cruciferous spirals; a bit of a little pilaster adorned with interwoven rushes; various friezes sculptured with little arches and half-roses, or with braids and caulicules; and lastly a little column of a chancel with its capital formed of rough leaves and plain volutes.

MUGGIA VECCHIA.—The church of S. Maria is a basilica with only one apsis and three naves divided by nude pilasters in lieu of columns. The extreme poverty of the forms, the barbarous disorder of the construction, and the absence of any sign of an attempt at organic novelties, would induce one to assign this church to one of the barbarous ages that we are now studying. This seems in part confirmed by the chancels of the presbytery, which are without doubt Italian-Byzantine of the ninth or tenth century. Pilasters and *plutei* are adorned by large fasces sculptured with interweavings of rushes, in the manner then common.

PARENZO.—In an angle of the quadriportico of the famous sixth-century cathedral, amongst many sculptures of various periods there collected, is a marble chair without a back, but only flanked by two elbow-rests, high and strangely profiled. The front of them is adorned with a braid of withes and two crosses, and the sides with lilies, caulicules, and cordons. It therefore acknowledges the ninth century.

POLA.—The same century has left remarkable works in Pola.

The cathedral of this city must have been built in the sixth century, and have resembled the basilica of Parenzo and those of Ravenna. This appears clearly from certain Byzantine capitals of its naves, certain remains of mosaic pavement with inscriptions relating to donors, found, during the last repairs, together with several parapets, some with geometrical perforations, some sculptured in bas-relief representing the monogram of Jesus Christ among ribbons and crosses, or between peacocks, or vine-branches issuing from a vase, or doves with little olive-branches, or lambs by the side of the cross.*

This church presented in its hinder part one particular worth notice. Beyond the apsis it had a rectangular place divided in three parts, communicating with one another by means of arcades supported by columns. This appendix to the naves of the basilica seems to have been destined for the reception of the relics of the saints, and atoned in some degree for the lack of a confessional. Its plane was certainly somewhat lower than the basilica, and there was no access to it from the back of the lateral naves.

In the present church, which rises on the same foundations as the ancient one, the apsis has vanished, nothing remaining of it but the triumphal arch of Roman style supported by two isolated columns; and what, in the basilica of the sixth century, was the chapel of the relics, has therefore resulted in a veritable prolongation of the naves and the new presbytery. When did the present church arise? Outside, set in the lateral wall, one sees a slab of marble in the form of a frontispiece, bearing in the midst of it an inscription flanked by two peacocks (not very barbarous work), and surmounted by a monogram and two

* It is curious that some of these parapets, similar though they are to those of S. Clement of Rome and many other churches of the sixth century, were not taken by Pulgher of Trieste to be anything else than the fronts of conjugal tombs. (See "Relazione ed Illustrazione di alcuni cimeli ritrovati negli scavi del Duomo di Pola," in the "Atti e Memorie della Societa Istriana di Archeologia e Storia Patria," 1884.)

doves. The style of these sculptures is Italian-Byzantine of the ninth century, and this is confirmed by the inscription, which says: "AN · INCARNAT · DNI · DCCCLVII · IND · V · REGE · LVDOWICO · IMP · AVG · IN · ITALIA · HANDEGIS · HVIVS · AECCAE · ELEC · DIE · PENTE · CONS · EPS · SED · AN · V." Trusting to this inscription, D'Agincourt, followed by Cordero, attributed the existing basilica to Bishop Andegiso, with the date of 857; but Kandler* declared this conjecture to be erroneous, observing that the edifice, whose naves are divided by acute arches, cannot date earlier than the fourteenth century. But although he asserts that there does not remain in the cathedral one bit of ornament of the ninth century, he still agrees with D'Agincourt in admitting that the inscription records the building of the church in 857. Lastly, Cleva,† while he demonstrates that the inscription, being nothing else than the sepulchral stone of Andegiso, has nothing to do with the cathedral, rejects Kandler's opinion, following it only in affirming that " in the cathedral there are neither capitals, nor friezes, nor inscriptions which may be with certainty referred to the ninth century." Now, this negation of the presence of sculptures of the ninth century is an error which, if pardonable in Kandler, in whose time the cathedral showed only two capitals of the columns of the triumphal arch and a third much smaller, mutilated and turned upside down, now reduced to the humble office of bearing a pole, is by no means pardonable in the present time, since, owing to the lowering of the floor of the presbytery executed in 1884, several capitals and a long series of sculpture, which to intelligent eyes immediately proclaim themselves of ninth-century work, and not of the sixth as Pulgher judged, have been brought to light. The capitals are those of the columns which divide the old chapel of the relics, sculptured, like those of the triumphal arch, in that rude Corinthian style with plain leaves and hard caulicules which we saw dominant in the Italian-Byzantine constructions of Rome and Verona. The other sculptures are

* Kandler, " Istria," 1847.
† D. Jean Chan. Cleva, " Notizie storiche del Duomo di Pola," inserted in the " Atti e Memorie," &c., 1884.

numerous fragments of archivolts, parapets, friezes, and little pilasters reunited to a colonnette—remnants, without doubt, of some barrier belonging to a precinct of chapel or choir; and a very uncouth winged lion holding a book, the symbol of S. Mark. Here the style is indeed Italian-Byzantine; for here are crosses, roses, palms, rampant caulicules, and, above all, the characteristic interweaving of withes.

Now, all these sculptures evidently prove that the apsis and the chapel behind, if not the entire basilica, were radically restored in the ninth century. Nor would it be too rash to attribute such restoration to that Andegiso who received honourable sepulture in the cathedral itself, of which the fronton still remains, sculptured in all probability by those same artificers who worked inside the church.

Besides the cathedral, Pola could have shown the studious a remarkable monument in its ancient baptistery if it had not been destroyed by Austrian vandalism. Kandler, who was in time to see it, has preserved its description. It rose in front of the façade of the cathedral and at some distance, which makes one suppose that it was put in communication with the basilica by a quadriportico. It had the form of a Greek cross, whose central space was determined by three arcades on each side supported by columns, which in some way separated it from the wings. Over the arches rose a square building illuminated by a few windows and, like the wings, covered with a simple wooden roof. The columns were of precious marbles, but had deteriorated; the bases were Attic, and the capitals after Corinthian fashion, with rude leaves marked only by lines without any intaglio. This description betokens such a simplicity of form and rough poverty of details as to make us suspect that the basilica belonged to the ninth century, and that its capitals were brethren of the very rough ones of the cathedral. And the suspicion almost becomes a certainty when we consider the remains of the cover of the baptismal font, of which Kandler writes that it was hexagonal and formed by archivolts of marble sustained by columns. One of these archivolts, for the most part well preserved, presents, according to the same writer, a monogram with the letters A and E; but from what remains of it one sees that there were three letters. A N E. Kandler. who had no idea of the style of the ninth century. judged that the monogram referred to *Antonius episcopus*. whose See was in the first half of the sixth century: but he is evidently in error. because the archivolts in the beautiful complicated and ingenious interweavings. with which they are entirely covered, acknowledge the ninth century. The monogram must. therefore. refer to a bishop of that period. perhaps the already mentioned Andegiso—the only name that occurs in the vast gap existing in the series of Polan bishops of the ninth century.

Fig. 110.—Fragment of Baptismal Fonts at Pola - IXth Century.

Among the Italian-Byzantine remains once appertaining to the cathedral and baptistery of Pola. there are also two middle-sized columns. with united capitals. said to have come from the celebrated suburban abbey of S. Maria of Canneto, which has now been destroyed. These capitals attract attention by the strangeness of their forms. which, in their ensemble, very roughly reproduce the Corinthian style, but in detail are adorned by certain incisions like caulicules and certain very original X's. They seem to have served for some ciborium of the ninth century. To the same church belonged a stone on which is sculptured the common representation of an arcade supported by rude columns. which enclose a cross between two palms: this shows ninth-century work.

The museum of Pola placed within and around the famous temple of Augustus is also rich in sculptures of Itálian-Byzantine style. There are capitals of columns of various dimensions and of varied merit, which, however, invariably recall the Corinthian style: some with hard and unadorned leaves and with barbarous zigzag caulicules; others well-proportioned and carefully sculptured, with a row of elegant leaves, unfortunately much dilapidated, and having the volutes of the caulicules separated by certain vertical cordons detached from the quick. Besides these capitals there are numerous fragments of fasces, with simple braidings, inscriptions, and caulicules, among which is an angular one with the shell below prettily ornamented by checkwork in relief; and finally a square parapet adorned by circles woven with right lines, and by doves, very similar to one existing in the baptistery of Concordia, and therefore probably by the same author.

The fine work of Jackson,* recently published, permits us to know several other specimens of our style, scattered through the various cities of Dalmatia.

Ossero.—In the church of Ossero there is an old episcopal cattedra, or seat, wrought in marble, the armpieces of which belong to parapets of Italian-Byzantine style, sculptured with large and small interwoven circles, enriched by paterae and roses.

Arbe.—The cathedral of Arbe possesses a ciborium of Italian-Byzantine style, which is, perhaps, the best preserved one remaining to us. It is a little hexagonal chapel, formed by six columns that sustain the same number of archivolts, and covered by a dodecahedral roof capped by a graceful pineapple. From what I am able to judge through the drawings I have seen—since my *de visu* researches did not extend beyond Pola—the capitals of the columns seem to me Byzantine of the sixth century, and the cornice that runs round the under-side of the roof modern; but the roof and the archivolts have all the character of the Italian-Byzantine work of the ninth century. They are variously enriched by fasces with braids of curved and mixed lines and by circles alternating with squares enclosing roses, lilies, or symbolic animals.

Nona.—The little church of S. Crose at Nona shows a door-

* "The Dalmatia, Istria, and Quarnero."

head of our style, with two zones of ornaments, leafy spirals below, and above interwoven circles containing rosettes.

NOVEGRADI.—A parapet of Italian-Byzantine style is here preserved, covered with knotted circles, occupied by doves pecking at grapes or little leaves.

ZARA.—Near the cathedral of Zara rises the church of S. Donato, an annular rotunda, with galleries and three apsides, which historians, guided by an inscription, considered, or at least conjectured, to be of the ninth century. I, however, do not believe this, because its architecture seems to me inspired more probably by the Neo-Byzantine style after the tenth century. Nevertheless, in certain of its decorative details, most likely belonging to its first construction, we must recognise the Italian-Byzantine style of the ninth century. The most noteworthy is an archivolt made of laces, and gracefully adorned with rampant caulicules.

A fragment of a parapet of the same style may be seen in the museum of Zara, and presents a portion of a circle, which ought to hold a quadruped. On the side is a peacock, and around a band of leaves and trefoil.

SPALATRO.—In the baptistery of Spalatro are several sculptures that show the style of the ninth or tenth century. Among these is a parapet adorned by a great circle formed of simple plaits and enclosing a pentagonal star among roses and roughly-chiselled birds. Of importance is also a barbarous but graphic bas-relief, which represents a king on his throne with the cross in his right hand, a man's figure standing on his right, and another prostrate in the act of supplication. A braided band finishes the stone and, still better, marks its style and period.

RAGUSA.—At S. Stephen of Ragusa there exists a parapet of Italian-Byzantine style, on the front of which are sculptured two small arches containing crosses, palms, and lilies.

CATTARO.—The Italian artificers of the ninth century found their way even as far as Cattaro, a city at the extremity of Dalmatia, and left works of their chisel. Very remarkable is the arch of a ciborium still seen over the door of the sacristy of the cathedral of that city. The fillet of the archivolt, with braids of mixed lines framed by two spindles, is elegant, and so is the cornice adorned by a zone of lilies and, on the summit, by little interwreathed semicircular arches. Roughly carved animals and more simple fasces complete the decoration of the heading.

Fig. 111. Arch of the Ciborium of the Cathedral of Cattaro—IXth Century.

And now we will carry our researches into Lombardy, where problems difficult of solution and of paramount importance will meet us.

BRESCIA.—The most ancient works of the Italian-Byzantine style in Lombardy are to be found in the old rotunda of Brescia, or Winter Cathedral, dedicated to the Virgin. In the chronicle of a certain Rodolfo, notary of the eleventh century, we read that towards the close of the eighth century Raymond, Count of Brescia, founded an important church in this city: "*Raimo comes Brixiae, quum audiret quam bonae recordationis essent nomina ducum Marquardi et Frodoardi, quorum unus inceperat adificare a fundamentis, et filius perfecerat grandem et celeberrimam civitatis basilicam, et cui munera ad adiutorium rex Grimoaldus etiam contulerat, ipse cepit fundare similem basilicam, . . . sed non compleverit.*" This church, built by Raymond, according to the united opinion of the historians, is the vast rotunda that rises by the side of the cathedral.

It is composed of a circular enclosure covered by a cupola, supported by piedroits and arcades, surrounded by a little concentric nave covered with crosier vaults. Over the entrance and close to the drum of the cupola there was a square tower, which fell later on, and of which the traces still remain. The pillars

The recent work of restoration has given rise to the discovery, in the massive lateral walls of the entrance, of the little staircase which led to the belfry.

and internal arcades are massive and plain, and the external walls that correspond to the lateral naves are equally unadorned. The cupola, on the contrary, is adorned by slender projections alternated with deep niches, gradually widening, and is crowned with friezes of bricks in zigzag and by a pretty cornice with pensile arches. Now, can we accept this rotunda as a fruit of the eighth century, as Dartein did with many others? Certainly not; because although, for the most part, rude and unadorned, it shows too fine a design and too much constructive art to be put on an equality in strength of execution and character of conception with the Italian-Byzantine art of the eighth and ninth centuries. It is true that the rotunda of Aix la Chapelle arose towards the end of the eighth century, and is by no means inferior in organic worth to the Brescian Rotunda, but it is also true that the church of Charlemagne, showing in its details the pure Byzantine and not the Italian style of that epoch, must be reputed the work of Greek architects, and therefore of artificers much more able than our own. And if the organic ensemble of the rotunda of Brescia shows us forms that were not visible in the Italian-Byzantine monuments, the same may also be said of its decorative details on the exterior of the cupola, which display the Lombard style of the twelfth century.

But, without losing breath by attempting to demonstrate with words that the rotunda cannot have been built earlier than the eleventh century, here are the facts which prove it and settle the questions. In the present restoration of the church, one of the pillars supporting the cupola was found to be in great part composed of antique fragments adopted as simple material of construction, and among these appeared a tombstone dated DCCCXCVII. The rotunda is, then, at least posterior to the ninth century, and I firmly believe it to be posterior to the tenth. If we try to search for the circumstances that caused the rebuilding of the old basilica of Count Raymond, it is easy and reasonable to recognise them in the terrible conflagration that, in 1097, devastated nearly all the city.

* Muratori, "Annali d'Italia."

But was Raymond's church a rotunda like the present one? and has nothing been left of it? There is no document to lead us to suspect that the eighth-century church had a circular form; nothing to support the opinion of Dartein, who, in order to explain in some way the presence of such a vast and grand construction in a century so unfortunate for the Arts, imagined that the base must have belonged to a pre-existent rotunda. The church of the eighth century was very probably of basilical form, like all its contemporaries in Italy. The only information we have about it treats of the existence therein of a subterranean place or confessional. It is the same chronicler, Rodolfo, who writes: "*In huius Comitis (Villeradi) etiam tempore Rampertus episcopus de Ecclesia Sancti Andreae portavit corpus sancti Philastrii intra civitatem in confessione majoris ecclesiae sanctae Dei Genetricis.*" The same event is also recorded in a sermon of 838, written and pronounced by the same Bishop Rampertus. Well, the rotunda of Brescia still has a crypt with every appearance of being that constructed towards the end of the eighth century. This seems to be the only residue of the basilica of Count Raymond. Let us observe it.

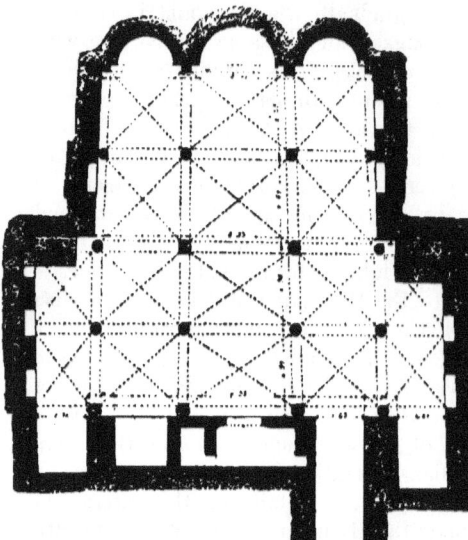

* Fig. 112.—Plan of the Crypt of the Rotunda of Brescia—End of the VIIIth Century.

It is an entirely subterranean chamber, quite deprived of light, of irregular form; divided into five, then into three little naves, by isolated columns supporting intercrossed arcades.

The three central naves terminate in three large niches, which seem to indicate three apsides which then began to be used—a fact that leads us to conjecture that they existed also in the basilica above, which has now disappeared. If Brescia showed us in S. Saviour's a first attempt at a presbyterial crypt; in this rotunda we find a first finished example. Several of its capitals belonged to antique pagan constructions; others, as we saw in the preceding chapter, date from the first half of the eighth century, and are of Byzantine-Barbarian style; and, lastly, some show by their style, their chiselling, and their dimensions, that they were the work of the time in which the crypt was constructed, and that they were made on purpose for the crypt. Such are those rough Corinthians with caulicules and double volutes and double range of leaves, which in their ensemble still recall the Byzantine manner of the previous half-century, and seem even to be an offspring of the same art that sculptured many of the flowered capitals of S. Saviour's in the hands of a less skilful Italian disciple.

FIG. 113. Capital of the Crypt of the Rotunda of Brescia—End of the VIIIth Century.

Brescia can still show two fragments of sarcophagi of Italian-Byzantine style, in her Christian Museum, with remains of inscriptions and crosses and interbraided withes.

COMO.—The wise restoration, executed a few years ago in the church of S. Abbondio of Como, originated the discovery of a large number of marble slabs sculptured in the Italian-Byzantine style which, like those of S. Maria-in-Trastevere at

Rome, had been turned upside down and condemned to serve for pavements in the present church. Boito, in his fine monograph on S. Abbondio,* alluding to those stones, says that there are too many of them to allow us to suppose that only the choir and the sanctuary were surrounded by them; and, seeking thereupon for another place for them, he finds none better than the superior galleries of the ancient church which, it appears, arose in the fifth century and gave place to the present cathedral.

* Fig. 114.—Parapets of the old Church of S. Abbondio (IXth Century).

Boito thus indirectly, but expressly, attributes them to the fifth century. Dartein is not of this opinion, but instead judges, somewhat grotesquely, that they may be the produce of the sixth, seventh, or eighth century,† as if Art could remain stationary for the long course of three hundred years. Selvatico, on the other hand, comes out of the dilemma with an oratorical subterfuge, declaring that those fragments are sculptured " in that barbarous Latin style, without special type, to which writers

* " Architettura del Medio Evo in Italia."
† Page 316 of work before mentioned.

on Art and architects give the name of Byzantine, in order not to expose their ignorance of its origin." * Mothes assigned them to the eighth century; Rohault de Fleury to the ninth. I have chosen to quote these examples of judgments regarding a single monument, just to show what confusion reigns, even among the persons most versed in these studies, when they refer to the art of those obscure ages. The reader, however, will already have understood that among all these authors the last only, namely Fleury, hit the mark, since those sculptures have all the characteristics of the works of the ninth century.

They are for the most part parapets, little pilasters, and friezes of the old choir, all covered with rich ornamentation in bas-relief of the Byzantine style, reproducing perfectly all those motives which works of the same kind and epoch show to us in Rome and other cities in and out of Italy. Where these sculptures of S. Abbondio exhibit more advanced study than is revealed by the others, is in the braiding, the ribbons of which are interwoven with turnings and knotting so ingeniously complicated as not to be surpassed. Here one finds already formed that sort of interweaving, invariably curvilinear, which afterwards prevailed for ages in edifices of the Lombard style.

Fig. 115. — Altar-front of the old Church of S. Abbondio—IXth Century.

MILAN.—We may say that we are arrived happily with our researches up to this point, because all the really authentic monuments that we have met with either second the order of general decadence or common progress, nor have we found any obstacle in our road which we found it impossible to overthrow.

* " Le arti del disegno in Italia," page 271.

Therefore we may affirm that we have seen Italian art in the centuries which we have glanced over manifested in a particular manner in each country, and yet uniting in common characteristics. But what does all that signify if we now fall in with a monument that threatens to throw us quite into confusion? This is the celebrated church of S. Ambroise of Milan.

Under the right lateral nave, not far from the entrance-door, there lies against the wall a plain stone arch, over which a long metrical inscription says that it encloses the remains of the Archbishop Ansperto (868–881); it exalts the rare virtues of the deceased, and among other enterprises of his it records that "*atria vicinus struxit et ante fores,*" which, according to the common interpretation, would mean that he constructed the neighbouring atria, that is to say, the present passages of the quadriportico of the basilica and the doors of the latter. These passages are formed by a series of ample and majestic arcades, supported by mixtilinear pillars, on which are planted the cross-vaults that cover them. The capitals present flattened forms and superficial planes carved with a rich bizarre profusion of meanders, leaves, and fantastic animals. The over-arches are cut from slender columns which run up to a pretty cornice with

* Fig. 116.—Epitaph of Ansperto, Archbishop of Milan.

pensile arches; the whited stone alternates with the brick. In this atrium one must acknowledge that the Lombard or Romanic architecture is manifestly in full flower.

But let us see the logical consequences of its date. It is placed against the façade of the basilica, but not so intimately connected with it as to prevent our suspecting that it was added to it after the façade and the internal naves were already completed. In fact, whoever mounts to the ceilings of the lateral porticoes of the atrium sees, at the back of them, the continuation of the cornice with the little pensile arches of the lower stage of the façade covered by the porticoes themselves. This fact proves indisputably that the latter are of later date. Nor could the interval of time between one and the other construction have been brief, to judge by the greater accuracy and progress exhibited by the sculptor of the atrium in comparison with those of the church. One must conclude that not less than half a century separates the one from the other. If, then, the atrium was built shortly after the middle of the ninth century, it follows that the naves and the façade must have belonged either to the beginning of the same century or the end of the eighth.

Guided by such reasoning, Dartein thought he did not wander far from the truth in attributing the rebuilding of the three internal naves and the façade to that Archbishop Angilberto (824-850) who had already enriched the high altar of the church with the famous and very precious altar-front, and who, according to tradition, adorned the semi-basin of the apsis with the still existing mosaic. As the apsides, with a small portion of the adjoining naves, show themselves both by their style and their low level of construction to be much earlier than the rest of the church, Dartein baptised them work of the eighth century. Selvatico, as usual, followed him, and with them went almost all those who have written, read, or talked of S. Ambroise; for such, indeed, was practically the view of Ferrario D'Agincourt and Hope before Dartein. Almost all have acknowledged that, even some of the most angry enemies of the presumed antiquity of the Lombard style; and no one had dared to write the contrary for fear of being accused of temerity or rashness*; in fact, by a truly strange circumstance, this epitaph of a line, or rather the vulgar interpretation of it, was always an authority before which everyone thought fit to to bow. It is solely on that account that people continue to attribute the birth and development of Lombard architecture to the Lombard domination. For the sake of consistency alone did Dartein boldly attribute to the eighth century the capital of SS. Peter and Paul of Bologna, the ruins of the church of Aurona, at Milan, and the whole of the Rotunda, at Brescia. These examples were naturally what were needed to corroborate the assertion of the epitaph. But for me, who have had to despoil myself of all this baggage of auxiliary examples, who by the conscientious researches which I made before taking up my pen, am able to prove that Italian art until the ninth century was still in its infancy, this epitaph becomes an inevitable rock against which my frail skiff threatens to dash itself to pieces. In fact, the basilica of S. Ambroise is not an edifice of the Byzantine style, or the Indian, or the Arab, that one may be allowed to suppose it to be an importation of foreign artists like the baptistery of Cividale. It offers, on the contrary, a style which, while preserving the Roman and Byzantine elements, presents them transformed and overlaid with characteristics foreign to either, so as to form a new style. These forms do not look like the timid attempts of an art in process of formation, but, on the contrary, like free and masculine specimens of an already perfect art; so much so, indeed, that S. Ambroise may be considered as the most representative type of Lombard architecture. Now, we know that a complete system of architecture cannot be suddenly evolved at birth, like chickens from eggshells; for no artist, howsoever great he may be, will be capable, at any period, of inventing a new and

---

* The few writers who refused to believe that S. Ambroise dates from the ninth century are, as far as I can recall them, the four following: Cordero, whose work has been cited; Kugler, "Storia dell' Arte"; R. von Eitelberger, "Die Kirche des heiligen Ambrosius zu Mailand," Stuttgart, 1860; and the celebrated Viollet-le-Duc, "Dictionnaire de l'Architecture française au Moyen-âge," vol. ix. page 243, note. Their opinions have, however, been but feebly echoed, for they have supplied no evidence in support of them, and such reasons as they adduce do not bear examination

complete method of construction. The foregoing applies even more strongly to Lombard architecture. Having been born in the midst of profound barbarism it could not expand without great difficulty, and its numerous qualities, especially the organic ones, must have been the fruit of careful but slow observations made in the course of time; and for this art to arrive, during the former half of the ninth century, to the height of S. Ambroise, would it not be necessary for it to have been already vigorous in the eighth century, or at least to have been born in the beginning of the seventh? And, if this was truly the case, what might have grown from all the examples which we have erstwhile seen, if it were not the inexplicable extravagances of a retarded art?

Such are the fatal consequences of this epitaph. But before permitting my boat to dash itself to pieces against this perfidious rock, it will at least be conceded that I may examine the nature of the obstacle, and assure myself if it be really so solid that it may not be shaken by wise reasoning, and by the researches which we have already made and those which we propose to make. Let us begin by reviewing this line of the epitaph, to see if the reading and the version generally adopted be open to criticism: "ATRIA VICINAS STRVXIT ET ANTE FORES." Though no writer who has studied S. Ambroise has given a literal translation of this verse, all have clearly believed that *vicinas* relates to *atria*, and especially those like Selvatico, Romussi, and Malvezzi,† who have concluded that even its doors were the work of Ansperto. But is that the most reasonable and grammatically just interpretation? I do not think so. Above all, can this *ante fores* be seriously translated by *front doors*? And would it not, on the contrary, be more reasonable to translate literally: *before the doors*? In the second place, how can this feminine *vicinas* agree with *atria*, which is neuter? It may be replied that it is not necessary to cavil at faults of grammar, because, in those barbarous centuries, they flowed from every pen like so many graces. Well, let us grant it for an instant, and erase this

* Milano ne' suoi Monumenti, 1875.   † Le glorie dell' Arte lombarda, 1882.

importunate S; but what have we done? We shall have relieved the verse of a pretended error and have saddled it with another not less gross; for, in erasing this S, we alter the metrical quantity of the verse, which, being a pentameter, exacts that the last syllable of the first hemistich be long, as the *uas* of *ricinas* is, in fact; whilst the *ua* of *ricina*, according to the rules of prosody, would be short. Is it then legitimate to suppose that the author of the epigraph wished to sacrifice grammatical propriety to the exigencies of verse? This supposition might be admitted if the rest of this long epigraph contained several other solecisms; but as we fail to find any, it seems logical to suppose that there none in the verse in question. That being settled, it becomes evident that *ricinas* can only relate to *fores*. Overcoming, then, the strange sensation which this complicated construction produces on our delicate ear—familiar though it be to this language, especially when it is adapted to the rules of prosody—it will be necessary to read this line as follows: *Et struxit atria ante ricinas fores.* The epitaph does not, then, attribute the doors to Ansperto, but merely names them in order to indicate the place occupied by the vestibules which he had constructed, and adds the word *ricinas* to indicate that the basilica itself was referred to, in which the defunct Archbishop was buried.

But if the vestibules or porticos constructed by Ansperto preceded the doors of the basilica, it follows that they must have surrounded the court, not only of the three anterior sides, but also and especially the fourth along the wall of the church; that is to say, that which immediately precedes the doors of the naves. Now, in examining the present vestibules of S. Ambroise, I do not find that they correspond to these additions, for the three anterior wings evidently belong to an epoch very different from that of the wing of the fond; and the worst is that the latter seems to be several decades older than the three others. The three anterior wings, attributed up to that time to Ansperto, would not precede the doors, but more exactly the façade of the church. This one objection would suffice, in my opinion, to arouse a suspicion in all reasonable minds that the atria of

Ansperto were very different to the existing atria, and bore a resemblance to those ancient square porticos, with pillars, of the primitive Christian basilicas, which extended without interruption right round the court-yard, and consequently along the side of the church. This wing—and it was a veritable defect of these same basilicas—never presented an ingenious agreement with the façade of the church, as in the existing church of S. Ambroise, but seemed detached from it in order to follow the porticos, or presented the wretched aspect of an appendage in bad taste.

But it will speedily be objected that I endeavour to maintain my ground, not by serious arguments, but by the subtleties of a literal interpretation. I therefore put my sophistry on one side for an instant, but at the same time I defy my opponents to prove to me by any solid reasoning that the vestibules of the present S. Ambroise are indeed those of Ansperto. Dartein alone among them all rises to object that it is impossible to suppose that the existing atria are a reconstruction of those of Ansperto, for though they exhibit art more advanced than that of the church, it is not sufficiently advanced art to warrant the belief that they belong to a period later than the year one thousand. Now, he continues, it would be unlikely that the porticos of Ansperto were at the end of one hundred years in such a state of decay that the rebuilding of them was absolutely necessary, more especially as no historian has informed us that during the tenth century the church suffered from disaster.[*]

These reasons, as anyone may see, have very little foundation: first, it would have been neither unique nor very strange if this edifice had only lasted a single century, for, whether the structures of the Lombard and Carlovingian ages wanted solidity, or whether the artistic and economic conditions became really better in certain countries in the tenth century, but more commonly in the eleventh and twelfth, the mania, not only for building, but for replacing churches and monasteries, amounted almost to frenzy. An old chronicler of the time [†] informs us that

[*] Work quoted, p. 73.
[†] Glaber Raoul, a French chronicler of the eleventh century, "Vie de saint-Guillaume."

this was done even with monuments which, being in perfect
condition, were in need of nothing. In the second place,
leaving on one side the question of construction, to come to the
essential, which is the artistic question, what arguments can
Dartein advance in order to demonstrate to me that in the ninth
and tenth centuries Lombard architecture had made such
progress as to be able to produce the atria of S. Ambroise? No
one can be satisfied with mere words, facts are wanted; that is
to say, documents authentic as the ciboria of Valpolicella, of
Ravenna, of Porto are authentic; the baptistery of Cividale,
the altar of Ratchis, the tomb of Theodosius—monuments, in a
word, the age of which is affirmed not by a chronicler, nor by a
lapidary inscription out of its place, nor by popular tradition, but
by an inscription graven upon the very stone of the monument,
which presents the unequivocal characters of contemporaneity.

What reply will Dartein make to these exactions? Will he
fix the age of the vestibule after that of the church? I do not
think so, for he will see that in this case the last cannot be
established without the support of the first; that is to say, if the
existing atrium cannot be that of Ansperto, how can he reasonably suppose, and have a profound conviction, that the interior
naves are the work of Angilbert? Will he think to find an
excuse in the Lombard ruins of the church of Aurona? That
would be useless trouble, for we have seen that they declare
themselves to belong to the close of the eleventh century. If,
however, he persists in believing that they were executed during
the first half of the eighth century, because they betray an art
adult and no way inferior to that of the atria of S. Ambroise, how
far must he go back to discover the infancy of the Lombard style?
To the time of the invasion of Alboin perhaps. And if, after the
first decade of the eighth century, Lombard art had attained
such progress, how could this progress be all at once arrested,
and remain stationary and immovable up to the eleventh
century? And why, notwithstanding its numerous attributes,
should it remain shut up in Milan like the worm in its cocoon
during more than three hundred years, ignored by the other
towns of Italy, in which no trace of it is found? Could it be

that these last were sufficiently tainted with their gross and effete art to prefer it to a new art ten times superior, and to reject the latter with a persistence at once tenacious, incomprehensible, and thrice-secular? If I am answered that monuments of entirely Lombard style raised in Italy before the eleventh century may have all disappeared, or partly subsist without affording possibilities of recognition, "Why, then," I should rejoin, "have the weakest structures survived while the strongest have crumbled away? Or could our ancestors have been sufficiently *bizarre* and wanting in taste to endeavour to preserve only those works which least merited conservation, and to inscribe on these only the names of their master-builders and artists, and their respective dates?"

I do not believe that Dartein or his disciples, destitute as they are of the necessary evidence, can oppose a word to these logical objections. It seems to me that they have undermined three-quarters of the base, large in appearance but hollow in reality, of the redoubted rock. I will now furnish a last and decisive refutation.

If, in the ninth century, Lombard architecture flourished at Milan, it would be impossible that there could be any room at the same time for another, greatly inferior and still barbaric, which I am accustomed to call Italian-Byzantine, and of which we have seen numerous and authentic traces all over Italy, as far even as Como —that is to say, almost up to the gates of Milan. Two schools, different and even opposite in character, may indeed subsist simultaneously in a country provided that they attain the same degree of worth, but never

FIG. 117.—Fragments of Doorpost in the chief entrance of S. Ambroise, Milan—IXth Century.

when one is infinitely inferior to the other. Men may have different tastes, but never perverted enough to blind them to the point of not rejecting with all their heart that which is ugly when they can obtain at the same price that which is really beautiful. Nevertheless, if there came to be discovered in Milan some fragments of the Italian-Byzantine style to attest the presence there of this style in the ninth century, the question would be at last decided in favour of my opinion. Now these fragments exist, and it is not I that have extracted them from the bowels of the earth, nor who have discovered them in some hidden corner of the city, but they have been, from the ninth century down to our own days, constantly under the eyes and under the hand of all the world, in a place much frequented, much studied, even in the basilica of S. Ambroise!

I will speak further on of the various fragments existing in the church. I am here only concerned with those that are found in the vestibule. There are two which are set in the wall beside the architrave of the little door to the right. They present numerous squares formed of simply twined bands decorated either with rayed girandole rosettes, vine branches or grape clusters, or crosses at the bent extremities. The other fragments—there are six of them—form, placed one upon the other, the jambs of the principal door; they are covered with very complicated intertwinings similar to those of S. Abbondio of Como; one only presents, in twenty-four rectangular squares bound together, lilies and roses of different shapes, crosses, grapes, animals, and even a human figure (a grotesque Hercules with his club preparing to attack the Nemean lion), the first that appears of the ninth century. These marbles cannot be of the same period as the door; first, they present themselves in several superposed pieces of which two are mutilated; and next, their sculptures represent an art still in its infancy, much inferior, and therefore anterior, to that not only of the atria, but also of the façade and of the interior naves.

These examples appear to me almost sufficient to confound Dartein and his school. However, to prove irrefragably that from the time of Ansperto no architecture was in vogue in

Milan except the Italian-Byzantine architecture common then throughout the peninsula, I will draw attention to the best monuments that one can choose, viz.: the three edifices constructed by the above-mentioned Ansperto. Let us return to our famous epitaph, and read the verse which follows that which we have discussed: "TVM SANCTO SATYRO TEMPLVMQVE DOMVMQVE DICAVIT."

It was dedicated, that is to say, or constructed, with a church and a house, to the memory of S. Satyrus. Ancient historians write (the rest of the epitaph partially confirms them) that Ansperto arranged, from the year 879, that his houses and gardens should serve for the construction of a church (TEMPLVM) and a hospital (DOMVM), which was one of the first to be erected in Italy. Now if, before this date, there existed in this place merely some houses and gardens, it is reasonable to believe that everything which one finds there that is not posterior to the ninth century dates back to the work of Ansperto. Such is the ancient little church known ordinarily by the name of the Chapel of the Deposition. As it shows in its ensemble and in its details a style decidedly anterior to that of the atria of S. Ambroise, it was natural that Dartein should judge it to be anterior to the century of Ansperto, and exclude it for this reason from the circle of his studies. For my own part, guided by the touchstone of the monuments we have hitherto studied, I am convinced that it is truly the work of the famous Archbishop. I shall demonstrate this point later on, for I wish to keep as far as possible to the chronological order of my researches.

The two other synchronical edifices to which I alluded are the church and the baptistery of the village of Alliate, to the north of Monza, edifices which Milanese historians declare to have been constructed by the Archbishop Ansperto. This detail appears entirely to have escaped Dartein, for he does not mention it, and commits himself to the opinion — entirely opposed to that relating to S. Satyrus—that these constructions of Alliate are posterior to the year 1000. I am certainly not too prone to put my faith in vague popular traditions, still less to believe in the assumed antiquity of as many monuments, but on this occasion I must subscribe to the tradition and the assumption, for having visited these edifices, I found that they entirely conformed to the manner of construction and ornamentation in use in Italy (and especially in Lombardy) in the ninth century, and I have noted with the greatest satisfaction unequivocal points of resemblance to the synchronical sculptures of S. Satyrus, as I shall prove later on.

Such are the proofs which I adduce to demonstrate that the present atria of S. Ambroise are not those of Ansperto, proofs that appear to me sufficient to settle a question so important in the history of Italian architecture. This rock apparently so formidable, sinks, entirely undermined by logic and by facts, if the metaphor be permitted me, into the ocean of errors, dragging with it all the card-castles erected on its base. And, in truth, the municipality of Milan was in too great a hurry to put this stone (which will have to be removed) on the exterior of the quadriportico: "ANSPERTO DA BIASSONO — ARCIVESCOVO DI MILANO—DAL DCCCLXVIII AL DCCCLXXXI ERESSE QVEST' ATRIO."

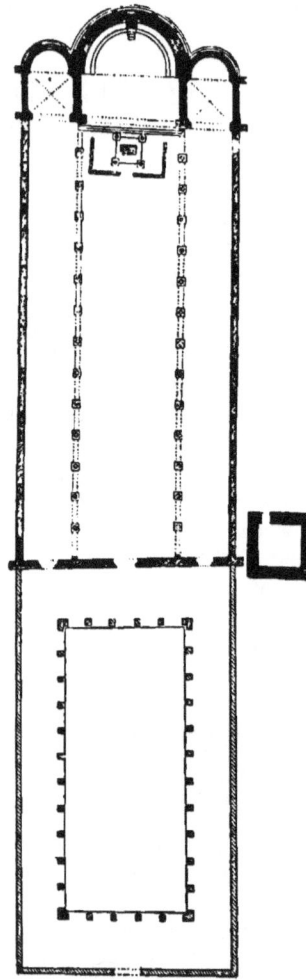

Fig. 118.—Plan of S. Ambroise of Milan as it was in the IXth Century.

And now that we have succeeded in breaking these chains, the strongest perhaps of all those which will impede our progress, let us continue tranquilly on our road, trusting in that light which our patient and careful researches have hitherto yielded us.

We have seen that the pre-judgment by which the atria of S. Ambroise would be the work of Ansperto had induced Dartein to attribute the three naves to Angilbert, although he was totally unprovided with documents, and though he was consequently obliged to put the three apsides of the fond nearly as far back as the middle of the eighth century, because they were evidently constructed considerably before the naves. Now we, who have shaken off the yoke of the epitaph, which insisted on our pre-dating the monuments, let us see what epoch best agrees with these three apsides.

Before all, the fact that they are three instead of one prevents one even from suspecting that they can date back to a very remote age, for, as we have seen above, the three apsides of S. Maria-in-Cosmedin, at Rome, built by Adrian I. (772–795), are in all probability the first example of this sort seen in the Eternal City, and certainly one of the most ancient in Italy. However, there are other considerations from which we infer that those of S. Ambroise cannot claim more remote antiquity than those of Rome. The three apsides do not bend exactly where the arcades of the naves finish, but between the one and the other we find some yards of wall evidently of the same period, for they are on the same plan and bound organically and artistically to the apsides. They serve for foundation to an open arch over the central nave, and to two cross-bars over those at the side. Now, as M. Boito so judiciously observes in speaking of S. Abbondio of Como— in " The Christian Basilicas of the First Seven Centuries"—the apsis is always bent (with rare exceptions), either in the wall of the base of the transversal nave or in the place where the colonnades of the naves abut; but it is never made to project from the perimeter of the church beyond its natural half-circle, and it never appears to have been extended into the interior, I shall venture to say, by lateral walls or by an arch, as in S. Ambroise. This extension begins to appear about the eleventh century, especially in the churches used by monks, who, being obliged to pass a large part of the day and night over their psalmody in the church, found the need of a place less exposed to the air and less accessible to the gaze of public curiosity than were the open railings of the ancient basilicas. And this invention, of the monks perhaps, was later on regarded as so convenient, that during the eleventh century it was extended equally to churches in which the secular clergy officiated, and finished by becoming common even in the greatest cathedrals, insomuch that it became one of the characteristic features, not only of the Roman churches, but even of all those constructed since the commencement of the eleventh century down to our own days. This custom became even a want, insomuch that, as it appeared inconvenient to the clergy to officiate in churches arranged after the ancient manner, the regrettable step of altering them was too often taken, now by changing the interior, and now by destroying the apsis to replace it by a choir. That is exactly what we have to deplore in our own times in connection with the basilica of S. John-Lateran in Rome.

Now we know that the Archbishop of Milan, Peter, entrusted the care of the basilica of S. Ambroise to a group of monks in 784, who installed themselves in an adjoining house that became later on a sumptuous monastery. Herein is found the probable justification of the abnormal lengthening of the apsis, which was certainly one of the earliest examples of such an innovation.* It is precisely because it is one of the first that it shows itself rather timid, if one compares it to the very deep choirs customary after the ninth century—see that of S. Abbondio, Como—extended without doubt in proportion to the always increasing number of monks. It is not, however, to be supposed that the monks of S. Ambroise undertook the important work of demolishing the ancient apsis in order to construct three by lengthening

* We shall see in the next chapter that the most ancient known example of a similar extension is found in the abbatial church of S. Hilary, in the midst of the lagoons of Venice.

the church, as soon as they arrived: first, because the confirmation of their new possession was only granted to them five years later; and next, because the Archbishop, having reserved to himself the property of the basilica, with the right of accomplishing the most solemn ceremonies therein, such as the coronation of kings, it was to him alone, and not to the caprice of the religionists, that the right belonged of putting his hand to works of restoration, as we have in effect seen done by Ansperto for the ancient atrium of the same church. To what epoch, then, and to which of the Archbishops, should we attribute the lengthening of the basilica ? In view of the absolute dearth of authentic documents let us try to bring our minds to a conclusive examination, and to an always profitable comparison, of the monuments.

From the fact that Ansperto had reconstructed the quadriportico of our basilica, one may reasonably conclude that by this work he had intended to continue and finish the entire restoration, and, possibly, the reconstruction of the church which his predecessor had already undertaken but left unfinished. It is not, in fact, reasonable to think that he undertook to renew the least important, and at that time scarcely accessory, part of

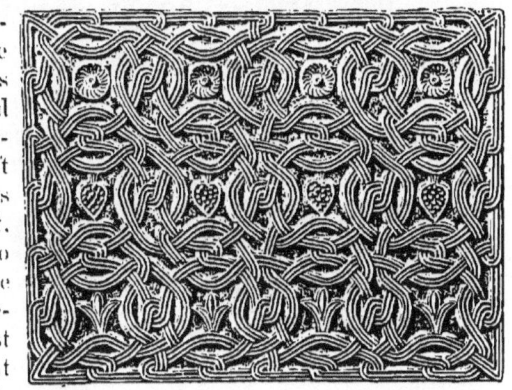

Fig. 119.—Parapet of S. Ambroise of Milan — IXth Century.

the edifice. The fragments of sculptures which we have seen in the atrium ; others of the same kind which to-day compose the altar of the very ancient chapel of S. Satyrus in the basilica (and amongst them, especially, a beautiful parapet covered with ingenious and elegant lacework of rushes with roses, lilies, and grapes) : ' the episcopal seat which rises in the fond of the apsis, and which the people believe to be truly that on which S. Ambroise was seated, but which, on the contrary, by the two roughly wrought lions which form its arms and by the tresses below them, betrays a work of the ninth century (see Fig. 120); the four capitals of the columns of the ciborium of the high-altar, which reveal the same chisel and the same epoch (see Fig. 122), are so many eloquent witnesses that the basilica must have submitted during this century to radical innovations. And in support of this assertion, and at the same time to assure ourselves that the three chapels and the present apsides are the only intact remains of this rebuilding, we are so fortunate as to

Fig. 120.—Archbishop's Chair in S. Ambroise of Milan—IXth Century.

meet with the church of Alliate (see Fig. 128), with its three chapels and its apsides — perfectly identical in their ensemble and leading characteristics with those of S. Ambroise. Simple basilical forms, as the excavations of 1869 have proved, must have characterised its three naves, separated by thirteen columns on each side.†

In seeking, then, for the Archbishop to whom the merit of this great restoration might be attributed, we are stopped,

---

* All the stones which compose this altar are not of the ninth century. Several are modern, imitating the Byzantine style. It is easy to tell that from the colour of the marble and the unsuccessful resemblance of the sculptures.

† Apropos of this, see the recent publication of Landriani, entitled, " La Basilica di S. Ambrogio prima della sua trasformazione in chiesa a volte," wherein the author has reproduced some of the superannuated errors which I have here refuted.

in spite of ourselves, by the illustrious name of Angilbert (824–859), for legend, tradition, and an important monument have rendered it for ever inseparable from our basilica. Legend surrounds him with marvellous prodigies presumed to have occurred in the church itself, and tradition attributes to him the mosaic of the demi-basin of the apsis—a mosaic which certainly could not be a work of to-day. But all that, though the fruit of imagination, tends, notwithstanding, to show us that Angilbert must have had a considerable share in the history of this church, since he has thus survived in the memory of the people. In 835 he had made them a gift so magnificent that they certainly could not forget it. This gift is the celebrated and very precious front of the high-altar,* the pearl of the basilica.

And one may reasonably be induced to see, to some extent, in this altar-front the work which Angilbert desired to form the worthy crown of his labours of restoring or entirely rebuilding the basilica.

* This altar-front, executed in plates of gold and silver enriched by enamels, pearls, gems, and bas-reliefs, is a magnificent piece of goldsmiths' work, truly admirable for its epoch. And after having seen and admired it as it deserves, we must needs conclude, first, that goldsmiths' work in those days, perhaps because it was the art most encouraged, was the only art that never fell into total barbarism ; in the second place, that this altar-front must certainly have been the work of no ordinary artist; and lastly, that it must have come from a Greek workshop, because Greece only, and rarely, could, in those times, produce works of such importance. In fact, the style of the figures and the ornaments is Greek, as one can especially discern in certain paintings on silk that form the internal lining of the back part, and represent ornaments of Byzantine taste, and a chase with a man on horseback, where among various animals and plants we see a dog biting a stag, quite similar in attitude to certain Byzantine sculptures of this ninth or following century, which we shall hereafter see. According to some judgments the artist's un-Greek name, VVOLVINVS, would contradict this, but all know how little one should rely on the evidence of names, from which, especially if isolated, deductions should either be made with the utmost reserve and caution, or altogether avoided. Italian writers consider him an Italian, and only admit that he had learned art in Greece. Some French writers, on the contrary, would have him to be of Northern origin, induced thereto by the double VV with which the name, that they always translate *Wolvino*, begins. But I think they cannot have thoroughly examined the inscriptions on the *paliotto* itself, where the two V's are not coupled and united, as is commonly supposed, but separated one from the other as much as the remaining letters. Now, as in the Latin alphabet V serves also for U, I think that the second V should be pronounced U like the last V of the termination; and, therefore, not *Wolvinus* but *Vuolvinus* should be read.

ORIGINS OF LOMBARD ARCHITECTURE.

These conclusions are not without importance for us, for the great apsis of the basilica of S. Ambroise, instead of presenting, as at the back, a naked wall, shows us a decoration which comes very opportunely to shed light upon our researches. It was not desired that the gap which, in apsides covered exteriorly with rectangular vandykes, is formed between the inside half-basin and the exterior wall should be hidden or useless in that of S. Ambroise; but that it should serve to form a series of deeply vaulted niches on a rectangular plan which, turning under the cornice very near one another, should form a coronal frieze of certain and agreeable effect.

FIG. 121.—Details of the Heading of the Apsis and the Presbytery in S. Ambroise of Milan—IXth Century.

Each little vault is sustained by small pillars, and has for archivolt a second little concentric arch, slightly larger, which projects the thickness of a brick, and at the place where its jamb occurs generally rests upon a small console jutting from the little pilaster which separates them. The niches are, by three and three, separated by long and thin vertical projections which sustain the small archivolts to which they correspond, and descend to the ground, thus cutting the wall into five spaces, in three of which windows—large, arched, and simple—are pierced. The extremity of the cornice merely presents a brick tower jutting at the angle between two horizontal layers of the same nature. This little cornice also crowns the two walls corresponding to the arched roof of the choir; but in place of being supported by superadded niches, it is sustained by a series of small bas-relief arches in double rank, each resting on two small superposed consoles, and supported only at the extremity by thin vertical projections.

Here, then, is a case of great importance, for this is certainly one of the most ancient monuments preserved, wherein are exhibited several elements truly characteristic of Romanic architecture which is posterior to it, and of the ogival style at the same time. Such are principally the cornices with pensile arches and long vertical projections; one and the other of these elements, and very often both of them, are seen constantly in all edifices constructed after the tenth century in Italy and elsewhere under the powerful influence of the Lombard school. But may we, nevertheless, believe that this agreeable and happy species of cornice is an entirely original invention of the Lombard artists of the ninth century? Truly it is not seldom that an inventor, after having discovered something that is new for him, for his country, or for his epoch, finds presently to his great chagrin that he has been forestalled. Conscience recognises the merit of his discovery, but apart from it, who will believe him? It may be thus in the case under our consideration. This excellent conception may very well have had its germ in the minds of the Lombard or Comasque builders of the ninth century, knowing no other example of this sort; but who can lead us to believe that was so while we are aware that, on the contrary, more than three centuries before them there were not only in the East, but even in Italy, identical works which may have been great teachers to them? It is certain that several churches built, either towards the end of the fifth century or that following it, in Central Syria, presented ranks of decorative bas-relief arches placed for the most part underneath the cornices, and often on the outside of the apsides. Sometimes their pendant foot is below, curvilinear; another is supported by a small console in slight relief, and fairly often the small arches are hollowed shell-wise. We have among many others an example of this in the great basilica of S. Simeon Stylite at Kalat Sem'an. But without going thus far, there are the parish church of Bagnacavallo, and S. Victor of Ravenna, churches of the sixth century, ornamented exteriorly under the extremity of the side cornices with small brick arches which are alternately pensile and supported by a vertical projection. There are even some churches of the first half of the fifth century, such as the baptistery of S. Ursa and S. Peter-Major (now S. Francis), all at Ravenna, decorated with this characteristic cornice, which, especially in the last of these churches, presenting numerous and quite small arcades, hanging by four and four, supported by a vertical projection, has altogether the Lombard character.* Now these examples, reproduced nearly in an identical manner on the tribune of S. Ambroise, lead us to think with reason of the remainder that they might have struck the Lombard artists of the ninth century who saw them at Ravenna. Here I find it well to venture an idea which is my own—that is, that Romanic architecture perhaps owes its development, and a portion of its attributes, to the profit doubtless drawn by the Lombard artists from their frequent journeys across Italy and beyond it, enabling them to see and study ancient Christian and pagan monuments. We have already noted the presence of these Lombard artists by the aid of those numerous *débris* of Italian-Byzantine art which are found scattered about the peninsula and on the other side of the Timavo.

The arched niches which are placed under the cornice of the apsis of S. Ambroise also merit special attention. As for the small pendant arches, they have no point of comparison with buildings anterior to the ninth century, and one may on that account even believe them invented by the Lombard builders.

---

* Hübsch has the merit of having put in evidence this singular cornice of S. Francis of Ravenna. I have been able personally to convince myself *de visu* of its high antiquity. There only remains, however, a very short portion on the southern side towards the apsis. The only difference that one can remark between these small pensile arcades of the fifth and sixth centuries and the Lombards of the ninth to the thirteenth is, that the first have a very large foot, and the second, on the contrary, a very small one resting on a little console very free in form.

who perhaps received some vague inspiration from the little holes which were often pierced nearly in the same place with a view to airing the ceilings. But however that may be, it is certain that these niches became one of the special attributes of the Lombard apsides of the ninth and tenth centuries, as we shall see further on; and they did not stop there, but reappeared in more graceful form wrought on the baptistery of Novaro, on that of Arsago, on the Rotunda of Brescia, on the apsis of S. Nazaro of Milan, and towards the twelfth century they developed little by little so fully that, the piedroits being detached, they grew into a practicable gallery, as on the chapel of S. Aquilin near S. Lawrence of Milan,* and on the apsis of S. Sophia of Padua (A.D. 1223). Later on, by substituting detached colonnettes for piedroits they gave the perfecting touch to these charming little galleries of most graceful effect, which, during the twelfth and two following centuries, embellished the apsides, façades, sides, cupolas, baptisteries, and even the campaniles of so many German, Lombard, Tuscan, and Neapolitan churches.

I believe I shall confer an obligation on my readers if before leaving S. Ambroise I put in evidence another gross error into which several writers have fallen through having falsely interpreted the epitaph of Ansperto. I wish to speak of the ciborium or baldaquin which covers the high-altar of the basilica.

It is formed of a cross-vault, of which the four arches are supported by as many columns of porphyry, and surmounted with tympans. Archivolts and tympans are elegantly orna-

---

* If we may believe Hübsch and Dartein, the small exterior practicable galleries of the Lombard churches had a precedent in an edifice of the sixth or of the fifth century like the chapel of S. Aquilin. But I do not share their opinion, and I do not believe that the whole of this chapel belongs to its original construction. Also that S. Lawrence, which is close by, had submitted to innovations brought about by Lombard artists after the great fire of 1070; also, I believe, that under the same circumstances the chapel of S. Aquilin—formerly in my opinion resembling the temple of Minerva Medica of Rome, and several other similar buildings of the fourth or third century, that is to say, having a superior floor behind and pierced with large vaulted windows—was after the fire, and perhaps with the idea of solidifying the cupola, augmented with a practicable gallery. The style of the angular projections indeed seems to confirm this opinion.

mented with decorations and figures in stucco bas-relief. The angles are occupied by colonnette trunks supported by eagles, and the border of the tympans is gracefully adorned with small coping leaves. On the principal façade is figured the Saviour between the Apostles Peter and Paul; on that of one of the sides is S. Ambroise between two other saints, without doubt Gervais and Protais, who are presenting two monks to him, of whom one holds in his hand the model of the ciborium, which shows that it cannot be regarded as the work of an archbishop, but as that of the monks of S. Ambrose. It cannot, consequently, be anterior to the foundation of the convent (A.D. 789).

That was enough to make the Milanese historians one after another agree in attributing it to the Abbé Gaudens, placed by Angilbert, in 835, at the head of the monastery; but one does not see upon what reasons they base their conjecture. However, Dartein has not been afraid to say that, considered from the artistic point of view, it seems very probable, and he has permitted himself to stop there, making the remark in its favour that the erection of a precious altar might prompt the construction of a new ciborium worthy to cover so beautiful a work. Dartein has not been, up to this present, contradicted by any Italian, but on the contrary it is understood that Selvatico and his continuator, Chirtani, are of his opinion; but for my part, I think them grossly mistaken, for many considerations are opposed to their assertion.

The ensemble of the ciborium is not opposed to it, for we have already seen at Ravenna a pointed arch of the ninth century; but what contrast strikingly with this age are the details, both organic and decorative: the vault, for it is not a simple intersection like that of the Roman, the Byzantine, and those habitual in the eighth and ninth centuries, but an intersection with ribs like the Romanic in fashion after the tenth century; the divers ornamental decorations, for they exhibit by the variety, the originality, and the elegance of their motives, an art far more advanced than that of the ninth century; but more than all the rest the figures of the tympans, by the costumes of some of them, by the justness of the proportions, by the easiness and regularity of the attitudes, the science of the relief, the freedom of the folds, and the expression of the faces—all qualities which we look for in vain even in the least imperfect authentic Italian bas-relief of the ninth century.

The only parts of the ciborium which entirely preserve the *cachet* of the Italian-Byzantine style, and which can truly be referred to the former half of the ninth century, are, as I have said before, the capitals of the four columns.* The unskilful sculptor evidently proposed to imitate in them the modes of those elegant Byzantine capitals of the sixth century, which represent wicker baskets, from which issue flowers and leaves. However, with his clumsy and childish chisel he was not able to produce more than one thing above mediocrity; on this account the entwined osiers are shown in crossed lines instead of being

* The feet of these four columns (beautiful monoliths of porphyry) without doubt come from sumptuous Roman edifices, and their square bases, high as pedestals, are the only things which recall the basilica of the fourth century. It has been thought that the abnormal direction of the arch of the ciborium, which is not parallel with that of the basilica, was inspired by the same idea which dominated the building of so many Romanic and Gothic churches, especially in the North, in which the choirs present the same inclination, with the idea of symbolising the inclination of the Saviour as He died upon the cross. But the excavations of 1864 around the altar have made known that this curious inclination dates back to the period of S. Ambroise himself, showing that it existed even in the tombs, and that, in constructing the surrounding barriers, they had already endeavoured to disguise it by a process of gradual modification, till the exterior ones might be brought to fall perpendicularly to the axis of the church. This discovery dissipates the conjecture exposed above, for this strange custom did not see daylight till towards 1100. However, as it is not admissible to suppose that the constructors of the first S. Ambroise had not intended this inclination, I find no other way of explaining it than this: As they had not been able to set the basilica perfectly towards the east, as the liturgical laws then prescribed, S. Ambroise desired that the altar at least should be on the eastern side, and consequently the tombs which supported it and the ciborium which covered it. (I had the pleasure of noticing that, in his recent work on the Ambrosian basilica, Landriani, in so far as he treats of this originality of the ciborium, thinks exactly as I do.) But, however this may be, it is certain that this inclination has wounded the very sensitive eyes of our modern restorers, who, out of respect for the pedantic and more often than not anti-artistic law of eurythmy, ventured on the difficult, dangerous, and costly task of raising and turning round the heavy canopy in the foolish mania of setting it right. And to-day, when one visits the basilica of S. Ambroise in order to admire or study it, he finds it deprived of that peculiarity which rendered it still more important; but, by way of compensation, he can drink in at his ease the ineffable harmony which the whole edifice has gained by this easy but exceedingly important change!!!

wrought in relief. From the basket go forth large and heavy caulicules supported by palm leaves, and separated by rosettes. The abacus is formed of a band striated horizontally, and only broken in the centre by a square projection with vertical lines. I do not doubt that the superior part of the ancient ciborium was in perfect harmony with these capitals, composed of four arches garnished with as many slabs of marble and covered with ornamental bas-reliefs, precisely like so many other ciboria of the ninth or eighth century which we have already seen; and it is not improbable that the mosaic of the half-basin of the apsis (composed perhaps before the ciborium was retouched), repre-

Fig. 122.—Capital of the Ciborium of S. Ambroise, Milan—IXth Century.

senting nearly, in the scene of the sleep of S. Ambroise officiating, the existing ambo of the basilica, preserves also the physiognomy of the ancient ciborium, which would have had exactly four arches crowned with a horizontal cornice and a cupola. But I will not take leave of S. Ambroise without satisfying the just curiosity of the reader, who will surely ask me: if you deprive the ninth century of the glory of having constructed the naves and atrium of our basilica, to what age do you then attribute them? I hasten to answer him, even at the risk of departing from the lines which I proposed to myself in this work.

S. Ambroise is the edifice of Lombard architecture wherein, more than anywhere besides, the greater part of the sculpture is redolent of the Italian-Byzantine style of the ninth and tenth centuries; but this fact must not lead us to believe it anterior to the eleventh century. First, because, more or less, all the buildings of the Lombard style preserve, as I have said elsewhere, the old manner of ornamenting by means of basket-work; and next, because S. Ambroise, included in the number of these buildings, presents others altogether new and more highly finished. Its numerous round faces of men and animals, though rude, yet manifest very notable progress in comparison with the horrible attempts of the ninth and tenth centuries, and certain foliage decorations, like certain organic forms, such as the interior galleries, speak plainly of the influence which Neo-Byzantine art exercised for the last time over Italian art towards the end of the tenth century and during the following one. In my opinion, no other church in Italy outside of Venice can furnish better material proofs than S. Ambroise of this influence, represented here by several works which could only have come from the hands of the Greek artists of the eleventh century or the commencement of the twelfth. Such are the mosaics of the half-basin of the apsis with its bizarre architecture, with its figures wherein appears the manner proper to the Byzantine renaissance; the incrustations of marble and the paintings of the hemicycle and the choir, which are in perfect harmony with the ornaments and mosaics. The decorations and membrures in stucco, which adorn this same apsis * all bear a Greek seal: the famous medallion also in stucco representing the likeness of S. Ambroise; and lastly, the superior portion of the ciborium of the high altar.† In all these works, and everyone should recognise it, the Lombard school is completely absent, while, on the contrary, in their ornaments (of which the fineness, moreover, belongs less to the merit of the century wherein they were executed than to the material of which they were made) ‡ are shown all the Byzantine character and grace, especially in the creeping leaves of the tympans of the ciborium, and in those that frame the medallion of S. Ambroise. In looking at the

* At the time of the last restorations some traces of paintings which adorned the walls were found, and there remain some of the designs (see Dartein). On the other hand, the stuccoes, which were found in their place in pretty good preservation, were destroyed by our sapient restorers because, according to their view, they did not harmonise with an apsis of the sixth century ! ! !

† All these stuccoes submitted to chemical analysis gave results almost identical, proving their contemporaneity.

‡ As I have observed in the preceding chapter in speaking of S. Maria-in-Valle de Cividale, the works in stucco are always inferior as to care and skill to those of the same epoch sculptured in marble ; and I add here that as jewellery, the ceramic art, weaving, and arts of the same nature, had subjects of decoration in general quite different from those of architecture, so must it have been with the art of the stucco decorator, for one does not otherwise know how to explain the novelty and the variety of the subjects which we see in the rare stuccoes which remain to us—subjects which are scarcely ever found in the works in marble of the same period.

figures in bas-relief mentioned above, one almost believes that he has before him in larger proportions those covers of the Gospels which the Byzantines enriched with pictures and stories cast in precious metals. If we now set ourselves to discover under what circumstances all these embellishments could have been effected in the church of S. Ambroise, we must consider that the mural paintings of the choir indicated above appear executed after the construction of the crypt, for they finish regularly at the level of the upper floor; and as the crypt, to judge by the style of the arches which remain of it, must have been built at the same time as the naves, it follows that the embellishments above-named were added to the choir when it became necessary to harmonise it with the richness of the new construction. The desire to have mosaics occasioned recourse to Greek artists, and to them also were confided the other decorations in marble, stucco, and in painting.

All these considerations induce me to believe that the existing naves of S. Ambroise rose in the second half of the eleventh century, and the atrium towards the commencement of the following one, a little before the new campanile, which, as is well known, dates from 1129. Therefore, to resume, the most probable history of the restorations effected on the celebrated basilica is, in my opinion, this :—Archbishop Angilbert lengthened the upper portion from 824 to 829, built the three apsides entirely, and very probably repaired the ancient naves. Archbishop Ansperto, from 868 to 881, finished the restoration of the church by reconstructing the quadriportico. In the second half of the eleventh century the three naves and the vestibule were rebuilt, while holding intact the apsides of Angilbert. They built the crypt, the superior part of the ciborium, and the ambo, and decorated the choir with stucco, mosaics, and paintings. In 1129 the second belfry was erected, and in 1196 they repaired the damage caused to the edifice by the fall of an arch in the principal nave, restored the damaged ambo, and raised the cupola again.*

But if S. Ambroise of Milan can still exhibit a portion of its construction anterior to the eleventh century, the not less celebrated basilica, S. Michael of Pavia,

The apsis of S. Ambroise of Milan, with its little niches, its vertical projections, and its arched cornices, is the more precious, not only because it becomes an excellent guide to the assignment with certainty to the same century, or that following it, of several other important buildings whose age has been until now an inexplicable enigma, but especially because it teaches us what are the true origins of the Lombard or Romanic style; origins which archaeologists, led astray by prejudice, have not known how to discover, and which Dartein, notwithstanding his immense labours, has declared still wrapt in obscurity.

The apsis of S. Ambroise is not, then, a unique specimen of its kind. Milan itself offers four others which go back without any doubt to the ninth or tenth century. These are the apsides of S. Calimero, S. Vincent-in-Prato, S. Eustace, and S. Celso.

The architects of the Ambrosian apsis, the oldest of all, so far as one can judge by the vague historical souvenirs of this epoch, had contrived as much as they could with the simple and easy adjustment of long vertical projections to give lightness to the walls and, at the same time, to enrich them at but slight expense. It is for that reason that we see two more of them on the apsis of S. Calimero, that is to say six in all, so that the wall is divided into seven fields. The upper part of each of these encloses three inches framed by the usual little hanging arches.

But the most precious edifice preserved in Milan is neither presents, to my sight, nothing of that kind. Many conjectures have been made in order to determine the divers buildings and restorations to which this church has been submitted in consequence of the disasters from which it suffered in 924 and 1004 ; but here again it is well to remember the old prejudice relating to S. Ambroise, which has deceived so many archaeologists. It is not surprising that they have gone equally astray when speaking of S. Michael of Pavia. Let us leave on one side those who still pretend that the existing church goes back to the seventh century. To those who, like Reynaud or Dartein, will have it that it was built almost entirely in the tenth century, I would say that the artistic progress presented by the sculptures of this church in comparison with those of S. Ambroise, and the visible affinity of the decorations with those of *San Pietro in Ciel d'Oro* of Pavia, a church that was consecrated in 1136, bring me to believe that S. Michael of Pavia was built at the beginning of the twelfth century, and perhaps after the famous earthquake that overthrew so many churches in Upper Italy, and thus brought about so many rebuildings.

this nor the apsides just mentioned, nor the little church of S. Satyrus, but an entire and passably large basilica which has been closed to students for nearly a century, and for this reason and because it is hidden away in a sufficiently remote corner of the town, it has remained unknown to nearly all savants; it is the church of S. Vincent-*in-Prato*. The first who drew public attention to it as a discovery was not this time a foreigner, thank God! but the Count Charles Belgiojoso in 1868.* It was then reproduced with drawings by the lamented Count Edouard Mella in one of those small but valuable monographs which he was in habit of publishing in order to shed light on some obscure and interesting monument of Lombardy or Piedmont—an honourable and useful example which should have many imitators.

S. Vincent-in-Prato is, then, a church of basilical form, with three naves, separated by sixteen columns, supporting semi-circular arches, covered with open roofing *à cuchevêtrures*, and terminated by three apsides. One is the entrance door, rigorously rectangular, with the architrave lightened by a semi-circular arch. The façade is bare, as are also the other walls, except the back-wall, which on the exterior tympan is ornamented with little projecting creeping arcades, and with a little cross-window closed by a large tabernacle formed of two slim demi-colonnettes of terra cotta and feeble cornices with bricks disposed in zig-zag. Below bends the central apsis, in which may be seen the same vertical projections, small niches, arches, and cornices which we have seen in S. Ambroise, and, what is more, in the same quantity and in the same order. The interior has smooth walls, in which are numerous broad and high arched windows,† that abundantly light the church. There is no artistic work there except the capitals of the columns, which are very varied both in dimensions and in style. They are in great part Roman and Christian of the first centuries, coming very likely from the ruins of an ancient church. There is, however, one which, as I said in a preceding chapter, betrays the Byzantine chisel of the eighth century, and several others that doubtless belong to the same period as the church, though

* In the Report of the Lombard Institute.   † M. 2.40 × 1.20.

250

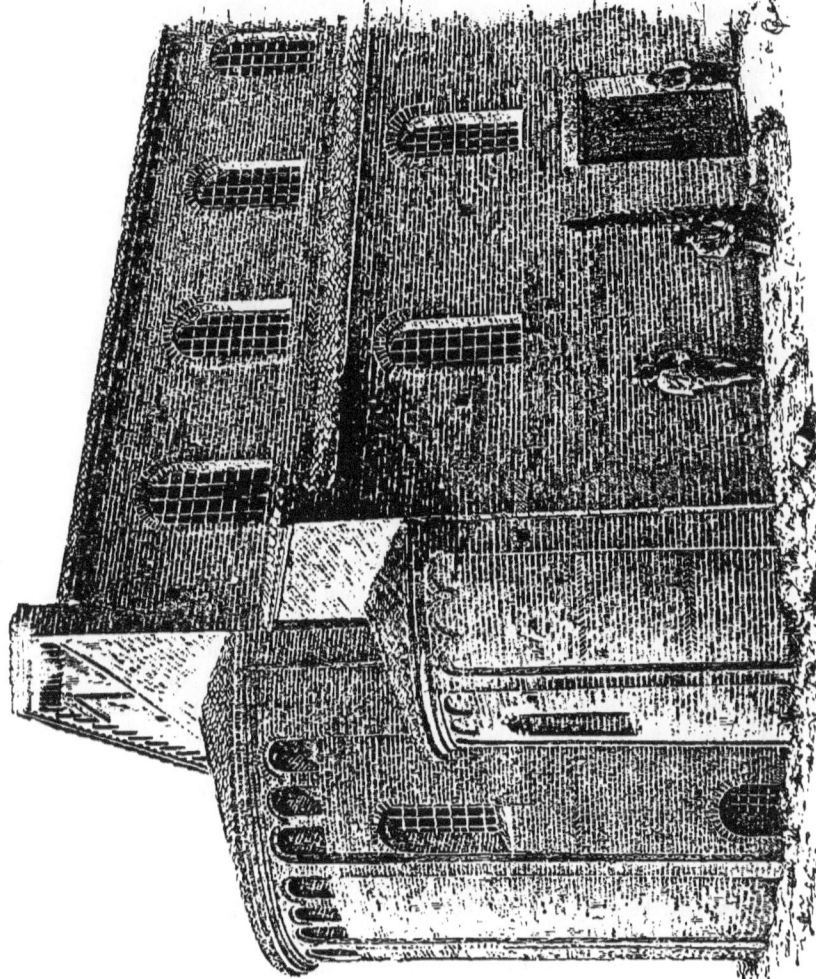

FIG. 123. — Apsides of the Church of S. Vincent-in-Prato, Milan—IXth Century.

without ornaments, and of an original form. But with very little reflection one sees there the rudimentary ensemble of the capitals of the ciborium of S. Ambroise, whose physiognomy, full of expression, suggests the style of the ninth century. It is in that place a proof of contemporaneity which finds

Fig. 121.—Capital of the Naves of S. Vincent-in-Prato, Milan— IXth Century.

confirmation in the evident resemblance of the apsides of the two basilicas. The bottom of the great nave, in the part corresponding to the three last between-columns and to the apsis, is occupied by a crypt which has its level a little below that of the naves, and on that account goes out considerably, raising the choir by more than two yards. It is formed of numerous cross-vaults, supported by colonnettes of antique production and of very varied forms, including that of the fifth century.

Such is the church of S. Vincent, whose basilical form, simple structure, and capitals, for the most part very ancient, have made Mella, Paravicini,* and almost all the writers who concern themselves with the art, believe that it was anterior to the Lombard period, with the exception of the posterior part and the crypts. Dartein, on the contrary, but without speaking freely, seems inclined to believe that it was erected during the Lombard domination of the seventh to the eighth century. But these opinions, notwithstanding the merit and the science of their authors, are in the present case of very slight import, for they rest upon a false idea, according to which the eighth and ninth centuries witnessed the flourishing of Lombard architecture, whose churches with banded pilasters and cross-vaults must necessarily be relegated to the seventh, sixth, or fifth century, those of basilical form suggesting a more ancient art. They made an exception of the apsides; but, in truth, there is too much unity of construction throughout the edifice for seeing

* Guida artistica di Milano.

therein posterior rebuilding, whereas, by the researches that we have just made, we prove that the whole church announces clearly the ninth century. And now it only remains for us to give a glance over the historic recollections that belong thereto.

Benvenuto d'Imola, Torre, and Castiglione have written that the church was founded by Desiderius, last king of the Lombards. But this date, which would have attributed a venerable antiquity to the edifice, has not found favour with modern historians, who have judged this church to be worthy of the first Christian centuries; therefore they have either confined themselves to assigning it to the apsis alone, or have rejected it as a mere fable. I have no reason, on another account, to believe it without foundation, for I have recognised in one of the capitals of the naves the Greek style of the time of Desiderius, who may have dedicated to S. Vincent, not the actual basilica, but a chapel of small dimensions. It is precisely because it was small, that it was not sufficient for the Benedictine monastery that was joined to it in 814: and here is why we see it replaced by the existing church, which, according to all appearance, was the work of the monks of the ninth century. The lists of donations made to the monastery by the Archbishop Giselbert, in 833, and of the great riches bequeathed to its fraternity in the wills of Archbishops Scaptoald and Angilbert, and of Garibaldes, Bishop of Bergamo, seem to correspond to the time when the monks had the means of commencing this work. Thus then the historic data and artistic observation confirm one another with marvellous agreement, and assure us that this precious basilica, which owes its conservation almost miraculously to the decadence of the monastery, to its abandonment which followed thereupon, and to its situation in a quarter of the city only a few years ago still isolated and lonely, goes back in effect to about the middle of the ninth century.

Perhaps an objection will be made relative to the age of the high presbyterial crypt,[*] which has certainly much more the form

---

[*] The number of August 15, 1888, of the Florentine review, *Arte e Storia*, contains a note by Professor Paul Tedeschi, which runs thus: "In an article printed in December, 1882, on 'l'Archivio storico Lombardo,' I have tried to show the necessity

and character of the Lombard churches than of an old basilica; but to that I can reply, first, that its capitals do not offer the least trace of the Lombard style, whilst their grotesque variety harmonises perfectly with the fragmentary mass of those of the superior naves; and, secondly, that several other basilicas of this century, of which we will speak later on, are also provided with a synchronical crypt very much raised; a raising to which quite an important significance was attached, as we shall have occasion to explain in speaking of the primitive basilica of S. Mark at Venice. However it may be, it is certain that the crypts were constructed for depositing the bodies of saints, and we know, in fact, that towards 859, the church of S. Vincent-in-Prato received the bodies of S. Nicomedes and Quirin. Does this event correspond to the date of its consecration? Certainly nothing is endangered by admitting it.

Milan itself here offers for our study the little church of S. Satyrus, which, as we have seen, was constructed by the Archbishop Ansperto. Its plan is a square cut by a cross, whose centre is determined by four isolated columns, and its extremities, except that of the entrance-door, by small apsides. The spaces between the columns and the angular walls are covered by semicircular arches and by little cross-vaults, the little arms of the cross by caisson-vaults, and the apsides by semi-basins whose axis is at the height of the mullions of these vaults. The centre is to-day covered with a little modern cupola, which does not permit of our divining what was there originally—probably a simple cross-vault. To-day the exterior wall of this little church

of demolishing the elevated choir (of S. Vincent), added later. My weak voice has not been heard, so in this unique specimen of a Romanic basilica, restored at Milan in these latter days, we have the hideous spectacle of a huge barrack and a crypt dating several centuries later." I ask Professor Tedeschi's pardon, but I can only felicitate the Commission of the Monuments of Milan for not having listened to him. It ordained that the old crypt should be entirely preserved. Before destroying anything it is wise to reflect. Conservation, however excessively indulged in, does not run the often irreparable risk which the mania for destruction brings with it. I should warn the reader, who may be visiting the basilica as it is " restored " to-day, that the ambos on either side of the choir are modern, imitated from the antique. The style of the ninth century has been well reflected in the ornaments of the parapets, but not in the cornices and capitals.

is circular, pierced with several niches, but it can no longer be called the original wall; it is a strengthening revêtement added in the fifteenth century, when the edifice was decorated within and without with bricks. In the interior, besides the four isolated columns, there are four smaller ones, of which a row

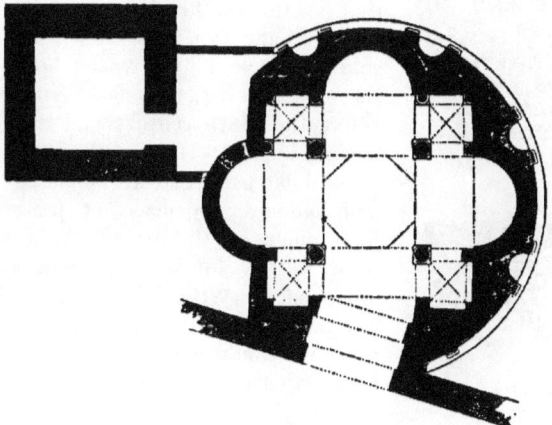

FIG. 125.— Plan of the Church and of the Belfry of S. Satyrus, Milan—A.D. 879.

are enchased in the lateral walls of the altar in order to enrich the little chapel at the end. The capitals are in part Romanic, in part modern (substituted for the old ones during some restorations), and in part are contemporaneous with the construction of the edifice. One distinguishes three of them which, by their barbarous richness, their style, and the ensemble of their forms, betray a close relationship with one of those which we shall see in the crypt of the church of Alliate, a construction of the same period. It is a clumsy imitation of the Corinthian; they have leaves that look as though they were piled up in a species of shell, rough caulicules, crosses with double volutes, and the customary shabby abaci.

No one would know how to oppose me in suggesting that the little church belongs to a less remote period, and that the capitals of more ancient buildings have been adapted to it: first, because it offers the characteristics of no architecture used in Lombardy dating from the eleventh century; secondly, because these three capitals have the air of having been sculptured for

the shafts which support them, and because the latter are of different diameters; that is to say, for the one with large columns and for the two with small columns. One cannot reasonably suppose that the church had been constructed before the ninth century and merely restored by Ansperto, for the reasons expressed on page 228 are opposed to it, and, moreover, it does not present the least index of the art of the centuries prior to the ninth. Its plan and its organism, on the contrary, decisively acknowledge the Neo-Byzantine style, so that one would not be astonished to see it at Athens, at Thessalonica, or at Constantinople.

Fig. 126.—Capitals of the Church of S. Satyrus, Milan.—A.D. 879.

One is in the habit of regarding generally as the work of Ansperto the old belfry which rises near the church of S. Satyrus. I do not hesitate to declare that this opinion does not appear to me destitute of foundation, and I accept it willingly.

The use of bells can be traced back further than is commonly believed. Fleury has demonstrated, with examples, that in the sixth century many churches were already provided with towers and very large bells, and this is confirmed by several bells, for the most part cylindrical, at Ravenna, which in their structure, in the nature of the materials which compose them, and in the characters of their sculptures, undoubtedly acknowledge the sixth century. History does not, then, in the least oppose the antiquity claimed by the belfry of S. Satyrus, still less does an artistic examination of the bell, of which the great twin doors, and the friezes with little pensile arches, of the greatest simplicity, have their equivalent in analogous parts of edifices of the ninth century. Add to this, that the axis of the plan of the belfry is perfectly parallel to the axis of the contiguous church, erected by Ansperto, and the fact that the two edifices are of the same epoch appears to be confirmed.

The belfry of S. Satyrus is, then, very probably the most ancient belfry of artistic character which remains to us after those of Ravenna, and is the prototype of the characteristic Lombard belfries, which are invariably square and subdivided into several zones, ornamented with vertical projections of little pensile arches.

ALLIATE.—The ancient basilical style is also shown outside S. Vincent of Milan, by the church, not less cherished and not less precious, of the village of Alliate, in Brianza. This church, as I have before said, owes its origin to Archbishop Ansperto, who, according to the tradition, erected it in 881. It were truly desirable that all traditions of this kind might find, in the monuments to which they relate, a confirmation as complete as that offered to us by this church of Alliate, which acknowledges the ninth century in every part. It has three naves, separated by columns—here, as in S. Vincent, of a fragmentary character. But this poor country was not, like Milan, rich in Romanic capitals, which might, on occasion, be pressed into the service of the church. Moreover, with the exception of a solitary one, dolphin- and shell-shaped, very small and which consequently required a very large abacus, the others are only reverses, bases, or fragments of funereal cippi, invariably raised by means of high abaci. One of the columns actually

FIG. 127.—Belfry of S. Satyrus, Milan—A.D. 879.

presents a Romanic inscription upside down, a proof that it was a miliary column. The last two arcades of the naves, half as large again as the others, were very probably opened later, to the detriment of four arches of less importance, with the object of enlarging the staircase of the choir, which is situated at the side.

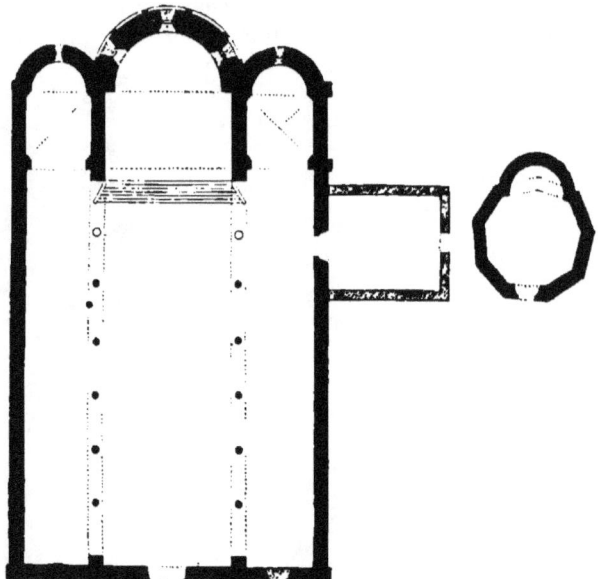

Fig. 128.—Plan of the Church and Baptistery of Alliate—A.D. 881.

Arched windows of moderate dimensions open under the roof of the great nave, which presents the usual open overlappings.

But where this church exactly reproduces S. Ambroise of Milan is in the three apsides of the fond, preceded by compartments, separated by walls, and forming, in the centre, a choir covered with arched vaults, and, laterally, two little chapels with cross-vaults. Here also the choir is found to be raised on account of the crypt, and must originally have been much more so, before the level of the naves had submitted to the present raising. The crypt, to which access is obtained by two little doors, which open in the small side chapel, is divided into three little naves by colonnettes, supporting little cross-vaults. It is here only that we find capitals sculptured expressly for the edifice. One of them, of barbaric richness, much resembles those which we have seen in the small synchronical church of S. Satyrus at Milan. All the others, while they acknowledge the ninth century, show a certain leaning towards later Romanic forms, though their rudimentary execution makes us think of the clumsy workers of the country who, without doubt, sculptured them.

Outside, let us remark the principal entrance. It is the only door ornamented in ninth century style with which I am acquainted in Lombardy, presenting, like certain doors of the same period to be found in Rome and the Venetian Isles, the jambs and architrave ornamented in front, and (on the side) the usual curvilinear interlacings peculiar to the Italian-Byzantine style. This central door, precisely level with the interior naves, required to be slightly raised, but that has not been done to one of the lateral doors, which has consequently remained closed and hidden away, while preserving intact its rude architrave flanked with two large square bricks and surmounted by the characteristic semi-circular abutment, as at S. Vincent of Milan. Lastly one notes, on the exterior, the central apsis, whose windows are larger than those of the naves, and which is ornamented by four long vertical projections and the inevitable little false niches, which are very rough and distributed without taste.

Fig. 129. — Capitals of the Crypt of Alliate — A.D. 881.

Another edifice which we owe to Ansperto is the baptistery attached to this same church of Alliate, which — strange circumstance! — is enneagonal in place of being octagonal, is covered with a cupola, and has an apsis which, issuing from the body of the building, bizarrely covers two sides of it. Each side is pierced at the top by a very narrow window; above the windows extends a range of little and very slightly projecting arcades

Fig. 130.—External Wall of the chief Apsis of Alliate—A.D. 881.

of feeble impost, and above that, instead of below, and concentric, as we have seen them hitherto, penetrate the little false niches, which, as in the adjoining church, are rough and considerably removed from one another.

We should pause here to consider two facts of decided importance. One is that the windows, which had before been made large, begin in this church of Alliate to become more narrow, and finish in its baptistery by resembling true loop-holes. The other is that they present a double splaying, a natural consequence of the narrowing of the window in order to gain a compensation in light for the interior. Now, the very narrow windows with the double obliquity were, dating from this epoch, one of the most marked characteristics of Lombard architecture. Archæologists have put themselves to much trouble to discover the motive which could have induced the constructors of churches from the tenth to the twelfth century to abandon large and luminous windows for these miserable holes, avaricious of the daylight and worthy of a prison. Some have sought in it the intention to render the place a little sombre for the sojourner, and thus to give it a certain air of meditation and mystery. Others have

Fig. 131.—External Wall of the Baptistery of Alliate—A.D. 881.

sought a reason in the foresight which built the church so that, in case of war, it could be converted into a fortress capable of resisting the attacks of the enemy. In such a contingency there would be no need of large and dangerous windows, but merely of true and useful loopholes. Finally, others have found a reason in the fear to prejudice the real solidity of the edifice by too large openings.

This last conjecture is fashionable to-day, but, to my mind, it lacks reasonableness as much as the second; for it does not appear logical to believe that such fears had begun to manifest themselves at the moment when the constructors abandoned the ancient manner, reputed weak, to adopt a very robust system, such as that of the Lombard churches with vaults. Consequently, of the three suppositions, the first appears to me to be the most reasonable and the most probable. During preceding centuries they also sometimes used very narrow windows, but these examples are either isolated exceptions, like S. Agatha and S. Victor at Ravenna, and the parish church of Bagnacavallo, or mausoleums like the mausoleum of Galla Placidia or that of Theodoric at Ravenna; and in these last they threw them out, not from a fear of weakening the edifice, but simply because this mysterious daylight added to the character of them. This nearly sepulchral darkness of churches, dating from the beginning of the eleventh century, harmonises, in my opinion, wonderfully with the mysterious and diabolical sculptures of beasts, with the terrible representations of the last Judgment, and with the sombre and fantastic shadows of the subterranean crypts.

BIELLA.—To this group of edifices of the ninth century is linked, by resemblance of style, the baptistery of the cathedral of Biella. Its plan is a perfect quadrilobe, on which rise four large half-circular niches. The central square is bounded by four arches supporting a story or gallery of very curious form, for exteriorly it presents an octagon of equal sides, and angles alternatively nearly right and very obtuse, giving in front an angle instead of a side; and interiorly it presents a square, rounded at the angles by curved sides, which, as they ascend, grow larger and larger until the square is changed insensibly into a circle, and becomes the base of a hemispheric cupola. The cupola and apsides are covered with a roof inclining to the rectilinear, resting directly on its arches. On the summit of the edifice a small square tower, having a double window, rises, which would seem to be a subsequent addition. Below, the octagon is enlivened by the habitual little niches very close together, and framed by small projecting arches, reproducing by that, even better than those of Alliate, the others of Milan. On each of the sides of the octagon there opens a small balistraria with double sloping.

The lower quadrilobate floor is equally ornamented below the cornice with similar niches, but here the little arches in relief are by four and four, supported by long vertical projections which

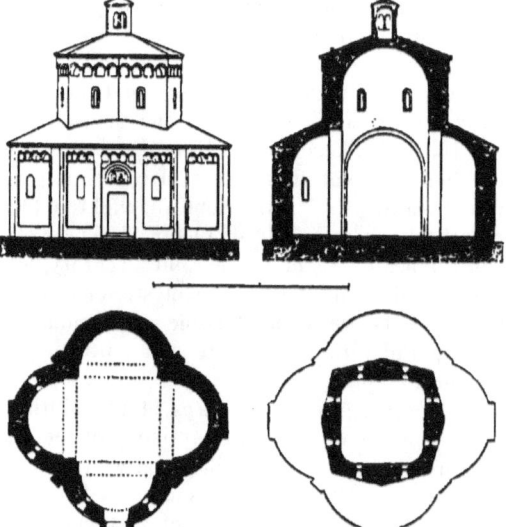

FIG. 132.—Plans and Elevations of the Baptistery of Biella— IXth and Xth Centuries.

descend to the base. The windows of the apsides are a reproduction of those above. The door, like that of S. Vincent-in-Prato, is not graceful). It is composed of a stiff rectangle, of which the architrave is lightened by a flying buttress, semi-circular, after the Byzantine manner. Here, therefore, remains the organic essence of the doors of Romanic architecture, starting from the first years of the eleventh century, however rich they may be in colonnettes and sculptures.

In the presence of this baptistery of Biella, quite devoid of ornaments and in part of bizarre if not barbaric structure, we cannot help praising the fine proportions of the exterior, nor withhold the observation that these builders seemed seriously pre-occupied with the difficult study of arches and their effects. On the outside of the apsidal chapel of S. Ambroise, and of the church of Alliate, stands out pilasters in strong relief, which, projecting in perfect agreement with the interior arches, give birth to the suspicion that whoever set them there already understood the organic value of counter-forts. Now, this is a fact confirmed by the baptistery of Biella, whose exterior angles, reappearing in the middle of the apsides, are occupied by four projecting pilasters, not at angles, but straight: these then are the veritable counter-forts of the interior arches supporting the cupola.

These edifices, and some others of the same kind which we shall see in Venice, are the architectural examples which the ninth century affords us in Upper Italy. But with the exception of some small structures, such as the sacellum of S. Satyrus, and the baptisteries already cited, structures which, being of small dimensions, could be at all times easily covered with arches, and cannot represent the progress of architecture, there only remain to us the churches of S. Vincent of Milan, and of Alliate, representing truly the state of religious architecture in Italy during the eleventh century. They show us, clearly enough, that she still followed the ancient basilical manner, and though she began to depart from it to a certain extent, in the basement chapels for instance, she was still a long way off those discoveries which gave birth to the Romaic church.

This conclusion will, perhaps, discourage the writers on Italian art who, after having proclaimed up to this time, not without a certain pride, that Italy was the cradle of the Romanic style, and that she had the honour of teaching other nations in the tenth century, now see themselves under the bitter necessity of confessing that this style, far from being born in the seventh century, and having given during the eighth the proofs of an abundant life, had not, one may say, yet appeared at the close of the ninth. And, in effect, what are these vertical projections and cornices with little arches in relief, if not purely decorative and not even original elements of the Romanic church, in face of its true and principal characteristics such as cross-vaults furnished with nervures, banded pilasters, and vigorous counter-forts, elements which we have certainly not met with up to this time. Must Italy, then, renounce this honour, and recognise that instead of having formed she has followed other people? Was the Romanic style born in France or Germany, as a large number of writers beyond the Alps have pretended, and still pretend? And will my writings have the result, deplorable for us, of confirming their conjectures? I dare flatter myself that it will not be so, and my hope will not be deceived.

In the interval comprised between the building of the basilica of Alliate and the end of the tenth century, when, according to Raoul Glaber, historian of the eleventh century, S. William, after having visited Italy, passed into France with a troup of Italian artists, and began to build sumptuous churches there, not less than a century had slipped by. If architecture in Italy at the end of the ninth century had not made great progress, it had, at all events, taken a good direction, as we have already seen, and as we shall see further on, and we may thereby conclude that, during the long space of another hundred years, it may have approached perfection more and more, and have arrived towards the beginning of the eleventh century, at least in part, at the precious characteristics above indicated; insomuch that S. William could carry among the Gauls, I will not say the fruits, but at least the flowers, of the new Romanic style. The limits imposed on me by my strength, and the labour claimed by my work upon S. Mark, have not permitted me to pursue my researches in Northern Italy upon a scale enabling me to enumerate here a long list of monuments belonging to this epoch, capable of representing the continuous and progressive development of Romanic basilical architecture. But the reader may, nevertheless, be assured that I am not taken unawares, and that the few but precious edifices which I propose to point out to him will answer for the moment the purpose of more abundant enumeration.

The use of arches, the generating principle of Lombard religious architecture, has only been revealed to us, thus far, very feebly and imperfectly by oratories and apsides, by the chapels and crypts of large basilical churches, before the extent of which it seems that the constructors of arches still recoiled. Perhaps the need and the courage to roof large naves with arches was born when the sumptuous marble columns, furnished till then by Roman ruins and the most ancient basilicas, began to fail, and it became necessary to substitute thick pillars of brick or stone, alone capable of bearing a considerable weight because they were susceptible of any dimensions. To substitute pilasters for columns certainly was no novelty, for, from the sixth century, the abbey of S. Peter at Bagnacavallo, and S. Victor and the Holy Ghost at Ravenna, had been obliged partly to content themselves with modest supports in bricks, and that, doubtless, because among the few Roman *débris* of this town the columns had long been exhausted, insomuch that, in order to build the principal basilicas, importations from the quarries of the East had been found necessary, as is proved by the uniformity of the materials and the ribs of the summit and the listel of the foot of the columns.

MILAN.—A church in Milan, rebuilt towards the end of the ninth century and the beginning of the tenth, and which will serve to represent the first transition from monolithic columns to clustered pilasters, is the celebrated basilica of S. Eustace. Of the old building, founded by S. Eustace himself in the sixth century, nothing remains ; for the apsis, which has the air of being the most ancient part of the present edifice, is so similar to those which we have just studied, that we cannot be permitted to doubt their contemporaneity. Here also are the same vertical projections, cornices, and little arcades in relief, and the same zone of arches. The rest of the church appears to have been remade during the centuries which followed the eleventh, with the exception of the two unornamented arcades, the last ones of the naves, supported by pilasters which seem to date back to the epoch of the apsis to which they are attached. It has been thought that they were formerly isolated, and that they corresponded very nearly to a field similar to that of S. Ambroise and of Alliate; but in 1869, after the restoration of their present supports, they brought to light the old brick balustrades, at the summit of which they found the original of the jamb of the two other arcades, cut, when the church was redone in the Romanic style. So one can conclude from that, that the naves of the basilica of the tenth century were entirely separated by pilasters in lieu of columns.

But this is not the only peculiarity of the old church of S. Eustace. When they were constrained to use ranges of massive pillars the architects thought to profit by them in adding to the solidity of the edifice, whose materials were in no way precious. They also resolved to throw across the little naves numerous arcades, which, strengthened by a wall, would become a solid buttress for the high walls of the major naves. To this end they projected piedroits from the lateral walls, and others corresponding with the ranges of pilasters, which assumed thereby the form of a T, and above those they caused the said arcades to rest, of which two still exist.

A considerable step towards the Romanic system of cross-vaults was taken on the day when they thought to complete the organic idea of the transversal arches of S. Eustace by projecting them equally on the great nave, by which proceeding they obtained a reasonable and solid chain round the whole edifice. Hence it came about that, in loading the pilasters of the naves with four distinct cross-arcades, four piedroits requiring to be prepared below, the pilaster, in the ensemble from its base, assumed a cruciform shape. This important advance in Italian-Byzantine architecture has never been regarded as an insignificant attempt, but as an invention so perfect in itself that it was applied with conspicuous success to a great number of remarkable churches in the eleventh and twelfth centuries. We find it already employed in 1013 in S. Miniato of Florence, and if it had so early crossed the Apennines, it is more than logical to suppose that well before this epoch it was in use in High Italy.

VICENZA.—In support of this we have at Vicenza a very precious and totally neglected church: that of SS. Felix and Fortunatus, which rises outside the town at a short distance from the railway station, and announces itself by a picturesque fortified belfry.* A historical document teaches us that in the year 1895 Bishop Raoul, having found it "omni cultu monastico et divino officio destitutam ob negligentiam pastorum et barbaras gentes quae in Italiam nuper irruerunt," recalled to it the Black Benedictines and restored it "ad honorem SS. Martyrum Felicis et Fortunati, Viti atque Modesti." This church suffered in the course of centuries, restorations, retouchings or mutilations until 1614, when it was barbarously transformed, but not corrupted to the point of retaining no trace of the ancient edifice. The principal door, a mixture of Romanic and Neo-Byzantine elements, bears the date of M·C·LXXXIII; the apsis that of M·C·LXXIX; the windows of the crypt that of M·C·LXXXIII; the steeple that of M·C·LX. All these dates, at first sight, permit of the suspicion that the church restored by Raoul was completely rebuilt in the

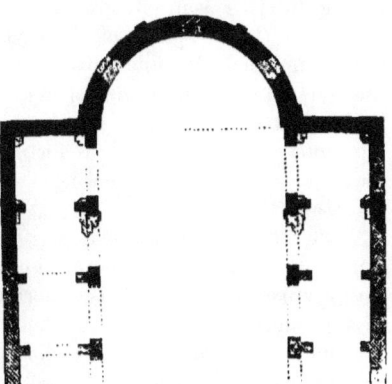

FIG. 133. Plan of the ancient Church of S. Eustace at Milan—IXth or Xth Century.

* See "Grande Illustrazione del Lombardo Veneto: Vicenza e il suo territorio," by J. Cabianca di F. Lampertico, p. 796.

twelfth century; but an attentive examination of the edifice soon dissipates this idea, and makes it certain that the works which belong to this century are the only ones provided with a date, with the exception of the crypt and some portions of the walls, and that Raoul's work was not a simple reparation of the old church, but an almost total reconstruction. It was in the sixteenth century that it suffered the greatest damage, when the monks, having wished to fortify the belfry by surrounding the upper story with corbels and battlements, judged it necessary to isolate it.

They then took away a part of the little northern nave, which, thus contracted, was terminated by a little chapel covered with a cross-vault; they also sacrificed the corresponding part of the meridional nave in order to utilise the space for an apartment devoted to some useful purpose; they walled in the arcades corresponding to the portion destroyed, and without doubt transformed into big columns the pilasters of the ancient church in the part which remained intact.

Now this reform has been a fortunate one for us, for it has saved for us—although they are stopped up—six arcades of the ancient naves, with their original supports, which show us ranges of pillars alternating with columns. Here, then, is a fresh advance towards the Lombard church, in which the nature of the vaults exacts that the supports of the naves should be alternatively strong and light. Towards the meridional nave an intact column is preserved, and a pilaster on the side of the northern nave. The first door bears an Ionic capital, grossly imitating the richest of the ancient ones by means of ornaments in the Italian-Byzantine style, and crowned by a large abacus, ornamented with interlacings. The second presents forms which are at once new, and simply Lombard. By that which remains of it we may judge that the ground plan was originally cruciform, that is to say, formed of two pilasters and two columns, the first the length of the longitudinal axis of the nave, the second the length of the transversal axis. Everyone will easily see in this pilaster the most ancient attempt known at grouping pillars. It teaches us that in the second half of the tenth century this characteristic feature of Lombard church architecture was already in course of formation. The structure tells with sufficient clearness what kind of arches it supported, and if to-day we have no longer those which rested on the demi-columns traversing the naves, as at S. Miniato, there nevertheless remain traces of them. But there is more. Pilasters and demi-columns (those at least which give on the small naves) are crowned with a common capital which is developed all round in a uniform pattern; and while by its rude sculptures it recalls the style of the tenth century, by its conception and proportions it anticipates all the similar capitals of the Lombard churches of the eleventh and twelfth centuries, as for example some of those in the church of Aurona of Milan, now destroyed.

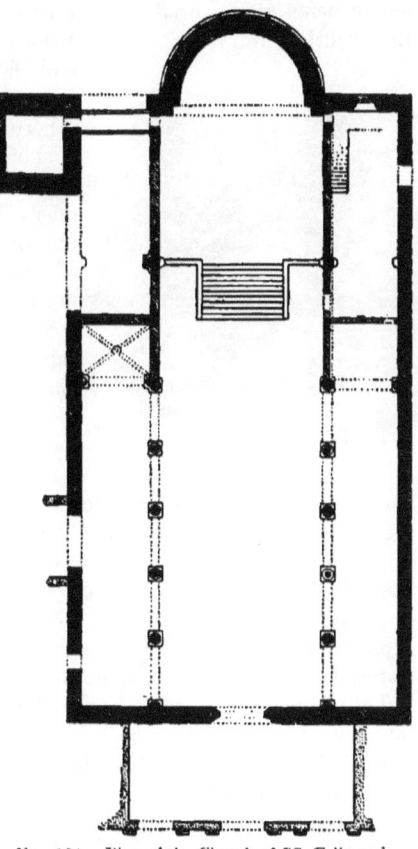

FIG. 134.—Plan of the Church of SS. Felix and Fortunat, near Vicenza.¹

The foot of the pilaster also merits our attention, for it presents a Lombard profile as pure as

¹ I owe the design of this plan to the obliging kindness of Chevalier Flaminio Anti, of Vicenza.

that of S. Ambroise, and shows at the angles of the plinth below the demi-columns a sort of buttress in the form of a small loaf, which is an essential characteristic of the Lombard style. In the twelfth century they were transformed into a thousand varied and fantastic ornaments and figures, which the Gothic style inherited later on, and during a short time even that of the Renaissance. S. Felix of Vicenza offers, then, the most ancient known example of pilasters alternating with columns, the most ancient specimen of clustered pillars, the most ancient capitals of a freely Lombard character, and the most ancient model of bases furnished with buttresses. It is consequently a monument of the highest importance, and the most precious example of transition from the barbaric Italian-Byzantine to the Romanic style.

Fig. 135.—Capital of S. Felix, near Vicenza—A.D. 985.

If one was tempted to believe that that which I attribute to the year 985, belongs, on the contrary, to the twelfth century, the crypt and exterior of the apsis, work incontestably of that century, afford us several fragments which have been used as old materials, and suggest, evidently, the Italian-Byzantine style, and the same chisel which has sculptured the capitals of the columns and of the pilasters above them. Such are some pieces of small pilasters covered with interlacing, with roses and honey-suckle ornaments which must have belonged to the old choir, and five capitals, of medium dimensions, which are the probable remains of ancient ciboria. The three in the best preservation are of a uniform design, decorated with stiff volutes and coarse palm-leaves.

The Milanese basilica of S. Celso, erected a little before 988 by Archbishop Landolpho, shows us, perhaps, a more pronounced tending towards the Romanic church if its naves had not been reconstructed in the twelfth century, as is seen clearly by that which remains of it.

The only relic that we have of Landolpho's church is the apsis, which presents on the exterior the same ornaments of small arches in relief, and the same niches that embellish the apsides of the ninth century.

But although the tenth century drew from the organic study of churches the qualities that gave us S. Felix of Vicenza and S. Miniato of Florence, I do not believe that it ever succeeded in roofing them entirely with cross-vaults. No monument anterior to the eleventh century permits us to believe it, not even those of the first half of the eleventh century, whether in Italy or in France and Germany, although the Lombard style made more rapid progress there after the year 1000 than in Lombardy. Then, if the exceeding breadth of the grand naves of the basilicas daunted the most skilful builders of arches during the first half of the eleventh century, with much more reason might it frighten the timid workmen of the tenth century. For it was truly the one great obstacle. We have the proof of this in several churches erected in France during the first ten years of the eleventh century, such as the abbey churches of Cerisy-la-Forêt and of Mount S. Michael, wherein the principal nave was still roofed in timber work, while the lateral naves were covered with sturdy cross-vaults. And this was natural. In the arts risky attempts are always on a small scale; first because, as several trials are often necessary, it is well that time and expense should be respectively economised, and next in order that, where success is uncertain, the damage may be less considerable, and the catastrophe less felt. It is thus that the sculptor proceeds before working in the marble, and it is thus that the architects went to work in the end of the tenth century and in the beginning of that following it. Before extending their system of roofing on a vast scale, they made a trial of it on edifices of small dimensions, or on little naves of large basilicas. That is the highest degree of progress that we can accord to the architectural art of the tenth century, and it seems to me that we are authorised thereto by an important monument in Verona.

VERONA.—The church of S. Stephen, built to all appearance towards the middle of the fifth century, demolished by order of Theodoric and afterwards rebuilt, was probably subjected to complete restoration during the second half of the eighth century, if the thirty capitals of this period which are found there were sculptured expressly for it. We are obliged to recognise in the existing building the fruits of two separate periods. To the first, that is to say, in my opinion, to the tenth century, should be attributed the apsis; to the other, that is to say to the twelfth century, the façade, the naves, the choir with turriculate cupola, and the crypt situated below it. But it is precisely the apsis that is the most original and the most precious part of our church, for it is formed of a semi-annular nave, a veritable perpetuation of the ancient little naves no longer in existence, and, moreover, surmounted with a gallery of equal dimensions, which excites the suspicion, otherwise well founded, that it formerly extended over the little naves and formed real galleries.

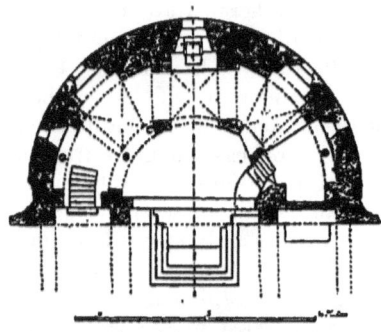

Fig. 136.—Plan of the Apsides of S. Stephen (inferior stage)—Xth Century (?).

This very singular nave presents, then, the most ancient example of galleries after those seventh century ones of S. Agnes-without-the-Walls of Rome, and is the oldest specimen that I know of this kind of hemicycles, as rare in Italian churches as they are common in the French churches, where they are called *pourtour*, and develop themselves in a circular series of chapels constituting one of the special characteristics of the Gothic cathedrals of the North.

But the structure of this apsis of S. Stephen, though agreeably conceived and rich in columns, has, from its proportions, and a disagreeable succession of vaults (as many cross- as caisson-shaped), columns and pilasters, the aspect of a barbarous monument. The little ornamentation which it presents is formed of Roman fragments and capitals of the eighth century, accumulated without taste, and frequently mutilated in order to fit the stems. This fact excludes the possibility of the building's dating back to the eighth century; but, at the same time, its barbarism and absolute lack of any architectonic ornament of the same epoch, sufficiently demonstrate that it cannot be a fruit of the twelfth or the eleventh century. We are, therefore, led to assign it to one of the intermediate centuries, and preferably the tenth, on account of its vaults. Moreover, this apsis, though rudimentary and without grace, deserves very close attention as being the most ancient essay known to us of naves covered in this manner, and consequently it represents one of the boldest strides towards the Romanic church before the year 1000.

The examples which I have hitherto adduced, though few in number, will not, I hope, be declared insufficient, or without due weight, and will not fail, I think, to establish the fact that, in the eleventh century, the system of vaults, of clustered pillars and buttresses, which the Lombard church reproduced after the year 1000, was already approaching its maturity. This conclusion, certainly, hardly accords with the opinion of those who have assigned the birth of Lombard architecture to the seventh or eighth century, but, besides that, it disagrees with another not less erroneous opinion (though absolutely opposed to the former error) which has been rather prevalent for some time past: the dogmatic assertion that, from the second to the eleventh century, Art did nothing but decline more and more, and that consequently Romanic architecture is entirely posterior to the year 1000.

Unfortunately, fashion is a hypocritical and pitiless tyrant, who slowly and noiselessly imposes himself on everything, on all men and (who would believe it!) even on the appreciations of the historian. To-day, custom has so far prevailed, as to raise an impassable barrier between the tenth century and that which came after the year 1000, an epoch when people were awaiting the end of the world, and which has been painted in the most sombre colours as the fatal bugbear before which everything, and consequently the arts themselves, must have recoiled. But I greatly fear that those who speak thus, measure the terror which they attribute to the generation which lived in the year 1000, merely with that which they imagine they would themselves experience under similar conditions. Although one is willing to believe that the prospect of the approaching end of the world made many people reflect, it was not, after all, an article of faith, and we should be wrong to exaggerate the consequences of it.

This terrible shaking up of the Christian populations of the tenth century, which, as several people pretend, should have struck minds with sterility, or have withdrawn them from every terrestrial and artistic pre-occupation, is in no way confirmed by the study of monuments. Greek art had none the less arrived at a true renaissance, as we shall see later, and, towards the year 1000, far from falling into decay, it was hastening towards Italy, bearing a new fertilising germ, which resulted in the furtherance of the renaissance. At Venice also, in the tenth century, Art, aided by the Greeks, progressed from day to day so well that, towards the fatal year 1000, there was no town in Italy where it was more advanced, and the century during which they constructed most churches at Venice was this very tenth century. If one must believe Galliciolli, they built twenty-nine in the tenth century—two of them even in 995—so great was the fever of construction notwithstanding the dreaded date. I acknowledge that the Greeks and Venetians, absorbed then by an active commerce, and favoured by fortune, were much more protected from funereal thoughts of the life beyond the grave than the other Italians, whose political situation was more precarious; but, however that may be, we can only say that in comparing the Italian artistic productions of the seventh century with those of the tenth, we recognise, in the intermediate period, a continuous progress towards an amelioration full of promise.

Also I willingly acquit of levity those who, unduly preoccupied by these fears, declare that, since the epoch of the Antonines up to the year 1000, Italian art did nothing but decline more and more, and who make of this blessed epoch the last stepping stone of a profound decadence. But those who sustain this theory are sluggards, whom patient and minute researches weary overmuch, and who seek to hide their ignorance conveniently behind the darkness of this pretended decadence of so many centuries.

But, at the first appearance of the eleventh century, it is beautiful to see their eagerness to expand oppressed hearts, to awaken minds from a deep sleep, to cause new blood to circulate, to infuse limbs with unaccustomed vigour, to set spirits on fire with noble thoughts: in a word, to show forth an instantaneous and marvellous resurrection which embraces the whole Christian world, and raises up immediately a cloud of witnesses in the form of monuments in a style new as the life which circulates on all sides. But the history of Art can be written neither by rhetoric nor poetry, but with facts acquired by the conscientious study of authentic monuments and with the deductions which reason draws from them.

I do not follow, at all hazards, those who are possessed with a mania for increasing the age of monuments and assigning Lombard architecture to a remote origin; but, at the same time, I am not disposed to range myself on the side of those who wrongly pretend that it originated after the year 1000. That edifices where the Lombard style exclusively reigns, even in the least details, may be posterior to the year 1000, I admit, but not that this style was born as though by the enchantment of the joy of having escaped from the end of the world: such prodigies may only be effected in certain imaginations. In fact, if we see this new style appear immediately after the year 1000 in all its brilliancy, it is very reasonable to suppose that it had passed during preceding centuries through the long series of experiences and applications; for an architecture such as Lombard architecture cannot be formed from one day to another like a decorative caprice.

So, when the last hour of the year 1000 had struck, Lombard architects must have held in reserve, if not all, at least the principal elements of their art, the fruit of slow but continual studies which were developed in their country during the space of two centuries, and to which the last edifices which we have seen render indisputable testimony.

CHAPTER IV.

ARCHITECTURE IN THE LAGOONS OF VENETIA.

FROM THE BEGINNING OF THE NINTH CENTURY
TO THE YEAR 976.

IT would be a waste of time to look for monuments anterior to the ninth century in Venice. Before the seat of the Venetian government was established there it was but a group of detached islands, some near together, the others remote, and some perhaps uninhabited. The largest or principal group of these isles was called Rialto, and was sufficiently populous to merit the Tribunal seat; but, notwithstanding all, its importance was always mediocre, and certainly below, not only that of Malamocco and Grado, but also of Heraclea, of Jesolo, of Torcello, and even of Murano. Rialto owed to the safety of its position, defended and surrounded by vast lagoons, and to its compact crown of little islands, susceptible of easy enlargement, the insignia and perilous honour of becoming, towards the year 810, the seat of the government of the Republic. It is certain that it was only from the date of this epoch that the Rialtine islands began to rival their sisters in the importance and splendour of their edifices, for the transfer of the government naturally drew industries and artisans from the abandoned capital. To tell the truth, if we may believe certain writers, these islands had no reason to pride themselves on their new monuments, for the most part sorry buildings of wood thatched with straw, whether private houses or public buildings or even churches were in question; but I am not disposed to share that opinion. That wood was much employed in constructing the more modest habitations I can readily believe; it was a widely-spread custom of the middle ages, and the large fires which then desolated towns compel belief in it. That some churches began by being poor wooden oratories may also be admitted, but not in order to draw the illogical inference that all the dwellings and all the churches of that period were mere wretched hovels of wood and rushes. To that the numerous stone ruins of these ages, which have been found all over Italy, are opposed: to that good sense is also opposed, for it cannot be admitted that the strongest, most feared, and richest people in Italy would content themselves with contemptible and rude buildings, while the neighbouring islands abounded in edifices which were magnificent for that period. But that which is above all opposed to it is the fact that Venice still preserves the traces of divers monuments of the ninth century.

It is impossible for us to know whether, before 810, Italian-Byzantine art had penetrated the islands of our lagoons, for the town which, better than any other, could have responded to such researches, the unfortunate Malamocco, having been swallowed up by the sea in 1110, and consequently despoiled of all kinds of monuments, does not permit us any investigation of that sort. But one may suppose, if one reflects, that towards the end of the eighth century Italian-Byzantine art had already shown itself in the neighbourhood at Ravenna, and if one studies the numerous works of this kind contained in Venice, some of them by their extreme rudeness seem to belong precisely to the end of the eighth century or to the beginning of the ninth; but this cannot be affirmed with certainty, for not one of them is marked by a date that dissipates all manner of doubt.

Saint Hilary.—Italian-Byzantine art must have been already planted on our shores when the Doges Agnello and Justinian Partecipazi founded, towards 820, on the margin of the lagoons at the west of Venice, the celebrated abbatial church of S. Hilary and S. Benedict on the spot where there had existed a small oratory, dedicated in the seventh century to the same saints. This church had to suffer great damage caused by Ezzelin: it recovered shortly after, but finally succumbed, on account of the alluvion of the waters, the filling up of the surrounding lagoons, and ensuing malaria, so completely that in the last century the exact spot where it had stood was not known. Happily, some years ago, excavations undertaken to recover the materials of an old wall brought to light the remains of the ancient basilica, that is to say, a good part of the walls of the enceinte, a portion of the original floor in mosaic, and some fragments of sculpture indubitably of the time of the Partecipazi.

The ichnography of the church was clearly drawn, presenting the ordinary basilical form with three naves, separated by columns, with the walls of the enceinte united. But the far end of the three naves furnished a subject of study. They terminated in three distinct apsides, much deeper than those common to churches of the preceding ages, that is to say, prolonged by slabs of wall forming little compartments between them and the naves. This commencement of the choir is analogous, though less marked, to that built shortly afterwards in S. Ambroise of Milan, and my supposition that it was thus designed for the convenience of the monks finds support in the fact, that the church of S. Hilary has been from its origin confided to monks. This church, then, may be regarded as the oldest known example of the basilica with three apsides that was built in Venice, and one of the first in Italy wherein the apsides began to be transformed into chapels. But the importance of these ruins was not understood either by those who discovered them or by those who were sent to examine them. Let the reader not be astonished, then, if, betaking himself to S. Hilary in the hope of visiting these precious relics, redeemed from the hands of a private individual and preserved to history and the study of the learned, he finds there, on the contrary, the poor joke of a ploughed field!

The ichnography of this church bears no trace of Greek genius, but, on the contrary, the seal of Italian or Lombard artists of its period. It is also an Italian hand that is suggested by the more considerable and precious remains of the ancient basilica, namely four fine pieces of its mosaic floor drawn from the ruins and deposited in the Municipal Museum of Venice, and several other fragments possessed by private persons. They were of *opus vermiculatum*, like the ancient pavements of Christian basilicas and of a great many pagan edifices, formed of small cubes of white, black, and red marble. The designs of these mosaics reproduce faithfully the subjects of decorations adopted by the Italian stone-cutters of the ninth century: fields with intertwined bandelets, curvilinear and mixtilinear, knotted loops, flying creatures with branches in their beaks, Pegasi, palms, small interlacings and other capricious or insignificant representations. The technique is rude, the design careless, and the figures only stand out thanks to a severe black outline, frequently simple, and sometimes traversed by hard lines or covered conventionally with chequer-work to express wings or feathers. These fragments of mosaic of every fashion are most precious, for, being the only specimens that survive of so many floors of the same kind which, in far-away centuries, embellished the churches of the Estuary, they serve to give us a just idea of them, and to make us understand how the Venetians of that day, notwithstanding the rudeness of the age and the infancy of art, were anxious to adorn richly and lovingly even those parts of their buildings which, in better times, have very often been neglected.

Among the remains of sculptures discovered at S. Hilary, and indubitably of the time of the Partecipazi, were found, beside the clumsy feet of the church columns, two broken marble plaques on which are coarsely sculptured small arches supported by little pilasters and enclosing wretched crosses and lilies. We have hardly commenced the examination of the Italian-Byzantine works of the lagoons, which it is already well to suspend for the insertion of a large parenthesis, and to note the influence of a foreign art. The absolute domination of Italian-Byzantine art in the lagoons was of very short duration, for it soon found itself face to face with Greek art, which disputed its place, and deprived it of many opportunities for self-exercise before vanquishing and annihilating it altogether. However, the continual relations and intimate ties that united Venice to

Among the debris disinterred there may still be seen on the ground fragments with lines in the form of circles and crosses which seem to belong to the seventh century, and two sarcophagus covers which served perhaps to close the tombs of the Doges, founders of the basilica. Why are not these relics transported to the town Museum?

Greece justify, and even give birth to, the conjecture that Byzantine art often landed on her islands and embellished the churches upon them; but here in place of a simple conjecture we are in the presence of a fact which is affirmed by history and monuments.

Sansovino relates to us, in fact, in his "Venetia," that the doge Justinian Partecipazio, returning from Constantinople, crowned with honours, rebuilt the church of S. Zachariah and founded the adjoining convent, following the desire of the Emperor Leo V. (813–820)," "who not only sent him money, but men and excellent masters in architecture, in order that they might build a beautiful church and finish it soon. In homage to Leo he caused the imperial eagles to be sculptured on the capitals of the columns, which are still to be seen in the ancient church."

Unfortunately not a solitary stone of this church has been handed down to us, a church which had otherwise been our most precious example of the Greek art of the ninth century. I have rummaged in the most hidden nooks and corners of our existing churches, ancient and modern, which, however, have not changed since the time when Sansovino wrote, but I have not found the capitals of which he speaks.† Most people have taken the crypt still existing under the choir of the old church for a relic of the first reconstruction, relying on the fact that it existed in 1105, if, as Sabellico relates, the terrible conflagration which happened this year caused the death, by asphyxia, of a hundred religieuses who had taken refuge in the crypt

As Della Rovere has justly remarked in his pamphlet on S. Mark, Sansovino was deceived in calling the Fourth the Emperor Leo V. the Armenian, as also in giving the year 827 as the date of the foundation of S. Zachariah, whereas it must naturally have preceded the death of the emperor, which took place in 820. He might have said, however, that the church was finished and consecrated in 827. Justinian, consequently, must have founded the monastery during the lifetime of his father Agnello, and whilst he was associated with him in the government.

† In spite of all that, it seems to me legitimate to suppose that their form did not differ from that of certain capitals of S. Demetrius of Thessalonica and the façade of S. Mark of Venice, in which the eagles sustain the angles of the abacus whilst one or two rows of leaves turn below. It was impossible that they should approach the form of those of the new church, in which it has been desired to reproduce eagles in order to recall the old ones.

in the hope of finding safety there. It is possible that the present crypt may be that which served as the tomb of the unfortunate religieuses, but that is not a reason why it should date back to the time of Justinian, for we shall see by documents that it was constructed a little later. *Per contra*, a small portion of the mosaic pavement existing in the little chapel of the ancient church, as well as the picturesque belfry (with the exception of the cornice of the crown, which may perhaps be a work of the fourteenth century), belong to the twelfth century.

The only thing which, in the present old church of S. Zachariah, could recall the original building, is, I think, the plan of the perimetral circuit of its walls. That it had been respected in subsequent reconstructions can, in my opinion, be deduced from the ensemble of the perfectly basilical proportions, but more particularly from the fact that we see a single apsis and lateral naves terminated by rectilinear walls; though this form, common to all the most ancient basilicas, was scarcely fashionable in the fourteenth century, when the present old church was rebuilt, and they preferred, on the contrary, to build numerous light Gothic apsides. For the rest, the apsis itself, such as it appeared in its oldest part, corresponding to the crypt, semi-circular in the interior, polygonal on the exterior, as in the Byzantine churches of the fifth and sixth centuries, bears the stamp of the Greek genius.

It would result from this that S. Zachariah of the Partecipazi was not a large church, but of small enough proportions, and that it was divided into three naves by two ranges of columns, and preceded, according to the usage of the time, by a portico. To one or another of them may have belonged the beautiful Greek marble stems of the twenty-two columns (some of which are fragmentary) which support, by groups, the very graceful apsis of the new church.

If such was the form of S. Zachariah as constructed by Byzantine workmen, should one then see in it the type of the Greek churches? Certainly not. It is not admissible to suppose that these Greeks who, from the sixth century, had abandoned the old basilical style in order to follow the system of vaults and cupolas of which S. Sophia is the most finished model (and which they constantly adopted in the tenth and eleventh centuries), should, in the ninth century, have returned to the old style. Also, if we see them erect in our country churches which do not conform with their plans, it is because they were obliged to adapt themselves to our customs, and to the wishes of their commissioners, who did not leave them full liberty in what concerned decorative details.

GRADO.—The architects sent by Leo were, without doubt, the first Greek artists who saw Venice in the ninth century, but not the first who penetrated into the lagoons; in fact, before S. Zachariah was built, several of them had already landed on the shores of Grado, then the Jerusalem of the lagoons, and had wrought several works there.

When we think of Grado in the commencement of the eleventh century, we immediately remember that fiery nature, that famous Patriarch Fortunato (803–826), of whom the old histories speak so often and with so much enthusiasm. He was the principal supporter of the Frank party in the lagoons, who just at the time had seen (according to the Chronicles) the sword of Pépin, and he fought vigorously against the Greek party. He subsequently ended his days, covered with opprobrium, in a village of Normandy, leaving us a testament the more precious because it contains detailed mention of all the works and sacred ornaments of great value with which he had desired, as second dignitary in Italy, no way inferior to the Pontiffs of his time, to enrich the metropolis. Tradition speaks of the lamps of inestimable price which he caused to be made, of which one in gold and one in pure silver bore a hundred small lights; of balustrades of silver which he had placed before the high altar of the cathedral; of altars in gold and silver with ciboria and images of the same material which he had dedicated to the holy martyrs; of great censers of gold; of ornamental draperies, &c.; of the church of S. Agatha of Grado, which he rebuilt, and in which he placed two rich sarcophagi made to his order at Constantinople that cost him twenty-five pounds weight of gold. And among other precious objects and buildings of his devising, it is said, that at the cost of the holy Empire of the West ("de dono sanctis imperii"), he roofed the church of S. Mary: that he imported artists from France ("feci venire magistros de Francia") to restore the baptistery of S. John: and that in France he had despatched fifty pounds of objects and diamonds to enrich and ornament a chalice.

I pause here, to inquire whether it was really worth while to bring artists from France to the eastern extremity of the lagoons to restore a small building like the octagonal baptistery of Grado (which we know already), as if there had been no workmen in the Estuary and the rest of Italy capable of repairing it. If there is not here room for a suspicion that under the name of France, Fortunato wished to indicate all countries, including Italy, under submission to the Frankish emperor, I incline to believe with Seguso that the Patriarch only resorted to Frankish workmen from the political motive, that the partisans of the Eastern Empire might flatter the Greek artists, in order that both might become instruments suitable to keep rival party spirit awake in the Venetian isles. A proof that the lagoons were not deficient in artistic talent at this period is, that Fortunato confided to one Murino of Grado splendid pieces of goldsmiths' work, and sent Venetian masters to Ludovic, Duke of Lower Pannonia, to aid in fortifying his places. (See Muratori, Art. Ital.)

If Fortunato favoured Frankish artists, the patriarch John Junior, deacon (814–818), who administered the church of Grado during the interregnum of the former, protected the Greeks, on the other hand. He has clearly indicated the works that he caused to be carried out, and they remain to us still in great part. Sagornino asserts in the chronicle that the Patriarch John "*Ante sanctorum martyrum Hermacorae et Fortunati, seu Yllarii et Datiani corpora, nec non et sancti Marci capellam, marmoreis columpnis et tabulis honorifice choros componere studuit.*" Guided by this indication, let us enter the cathedral. We see standing at the end of the apsis a beautiful seat, enriched with sculptured marbles and protected by a roof supported by two colonnettes. Many people see in it the ancient

" Della Sponde marmoree o Vere da Pozzo."

pulpit of the patriarchs, but it is, in truth, only a picturesque falsehood ingeniously contrived of ninth century fragments. One sees there two parapets, covered with very complicated mixtilinear interlacing, which some call executed with the spirit of contemporary Italian art, but which betrays the refined cunning of the Greek chisel; several friezes decorated with plaits and caulicules which serve as architraves above the colonnettes of the balustrades, and two of these last with short shafts, furnished with their capitals, and placed on

FIG. 137.—Frieze and Capital of the Balustrades of the Cathedral at Grado.

little pilasters, on the front of which are seen squares and braidings, and on the sides grooves which were originally intended to receive the parapets. These capitals are of the Corinthian free and simple style, with palm leaves and four small volutes on each front. Eight others, quite similar in dimensions and ornamentation, are found in the church, six are in the existing ambo, and two are upside down, condemned to serve as stands. They should have crowned as many colonnettes of the choir built by the Patriarch John. Those who would wish to have a material proof of the age and paternity that I assign to these same sculptures, can see in the court behind the cathedral a fragment of an architrave, ornamented like those above described, with braids and caulicules, and bearing the graven name of this same patriarch. "IOHANNES IVNIOR SOLII DI . . . ." We may mention for its elegance another architrave in the same court, with a frieze composed of nine small arches, decorated with notching, supported by twisted colonnettes, and filled in by large and beautiful wild acanthus leaves.

Sagornino, whom I have just cited, after speaking of the works with which the patriarch John enriched the cathedral, adds: "*In sanctae vero Dei genitricis Mariae ecclesia supra altare ciborium peregit.*" Of this ciborium there also remains something, namely, three fragments of its monolithic arcades and a portion of architrave, which one sees to-day barbarously enchased in the pavement of the church. The arcades are diversely and gracefully ornamented with doves and some with decorative motives, tolerably pleasing and novel considering the epoch, in which a certain spontaneity of forms contrasts with the rudimentary caprice of the chisel. They are also decorated with the inevitable tresses, which present here, however, a peculiarity highly characteristic of the Byzantine style of the ninth century; they are formed of bandelets, not, as in the past, marked by equidistant rays so as to pourtray rushes, but by two lines engraved along the borders, leaving a large band in the middle. The architrave is ornamented by ordinary caulicules, and two rows of squares like those of a chess-board, alternated and in very slight relief.

FIG. 138. — Fragment of Archivolt of the Ciborium of S. Maria at Grado — A.D. 814-818.

In my opinion that fact, supported by the above inscriptions, and their entire conformity to the description of them given by Sagornino, proves that the sculptures which we have just examined belong to the ninth century. And, as one remarks here an art too superior to the Italian art of the early years of this century, and, at the same time, a conception and character too different for him to believe them the fruit of native chisels, it appears to me that he can quite naturally draw the conclusion that these sculptures can only be attributed to Greek artists. Their frankly Byzantine style certainly permits of no doubt. On the other hand, they cannot with their poverty adequately represent the Byzantine style of the ninth century, which, while departing lightly in its decorative conceptions from that of the eighth century, does not the less constantly preserve its varied and fantastic spirit. For examples we have the works of this style which are preserved at Venice, and especially at S. Mark.

VENICE.—I should never have done if I were to set forth here all the arguments which have led me to fix the form, dimensions, and details of the primitive basilica of S. Mark. The reader will find them fully developed in the second part of the great work published by Ongania on the basilica, wherein I give the architectural history of the edifice; therefore I shall limit myself here to the conclusions reached by this study.

The erection of the basilica, instigated by the arrival of the body of S. Mark and decreed by the Doge Justinian Partecipazio, was only carried out by his brother and successor John, in 829. It has been known for a good many years past, thanks to the articles published by Selvatico and Foucard,* that the present basilica should be considered as a structure of the second half of the eleventh century, and that that of the ninth century, restored in the tenth, was of far more modest dimensions and simple basilical form, like all the Italian churches of the same period. Their conjecture, according to which the width of the longitudinal arm of the present basilica corresponds to the width of the ancient one and the lateral walls of the transept belong thereto, is confirmed by discoveries made during the recent restorations; but not their assertion that the interior of the church of the Partecipazi was as long as the existing one, and that the lower part of the apsis remains. An examination of the crypt, less superficial than theirs, gives quite contrary results, showing that the interior of the ninth century church was about ten yards shorter than that of to-day, and that its small naves ended just where the balustrades of the chapels of S. Peter and S. Clement rise. Perhaps the walls which sustain them, and those corresponding with them in the crypt, are remains of those which bounded the ancient small naves in a

* "Monumenti artistici e storici delle Provincie Venete," 1859. That which relates to S. Mark has been reprinted by Selvatico in his last work, "Le Arti del Disegno in Italia," Vallardi, 1883.

straight line, whereas the old apsis was entirely destroyed in the eleventh century.

These writers are not less mistaken when they allege that the floor of the present crypt corresponds with the plan of the choir of the old church, for this supposition requires that the level of the square should have been two yards and a half lower in the ninth century than it is at present, which is in complete contradiction with the law of ground-rising known by experience, and especially with the nature of the soil of our islands. The pavement of the choir in the church of Partecipazi was not lower than that of the naves of the present church, whereas the pavement of the ancient naves was a yard lower than that of to-day. These data are furnished by the little subterrane now impracticable, for it is much deeper than the actual crypt, which extends for a certain distance under the central cupola of the basilica, and of which Selvatico has thought to be able to explain the existence by the aid of absurd conjectures. I am convinced that it is, on the contrary, a portion of the crypt of the primitive church, a crypt which would be raised like the present one, about a yard, and correspond to the ancient choir. We have material proof of this elevation in certain little windows which may yet be seen in the wall at the end of this subterrane, and which would formerly give on the great nave and light the interior exactly like the analogous small windows of the present crypt.

The presence of a high presbyterial crypt in a church of the ninth century should not be able to astonish us, who have already seen at Milan and Alliate two belonging to this very century. Apropos of the latter, I have said that a meaning attached to their raising which we were able to deduce from the study of S. Mark of the Partecipazi. I will now explain myself. The Altinate Chronicle, and a manuscript in the Library of the Vatican, teach us that the primitive basilica of S. Mark was built by its founder "*secundum exemplum quod ad Domini tumulum Ierosolimi riderat.*" This assertion surprises us greatly at first, and, not knowing in what the basilica of the Partecipazi could imitate that of Cavalry, we are almost tempted to relegate this information to the limbo of dreams. But, after reflecting that it is equally applied by ancient chronicles to the Venetian churches of S. Saviour and S. Zachariah, and that these are provided with a crypt similar to S. Mark's, one arrives at the understanding that it is not of the whole edifice, but merely of this part, that the chronicles speak. The crypt, in fact, rising almost in isolation at the bottom of the church, and enclosing a revered tomb, the object of pious pilgrimages, recalls to a certain extent the most characteristic part of the famous sanctuary of Golgotha, that is to say S. Sepulchre, whose isolated monolith was placed by order of Constantine in the midst of the ancient apsis which, later on, was converted into a Rotunda.

This precious cryptic relic, the only ruin dating from the ninth century remaining to us at Venice, and consequently the oldest of all, is covered with several cross-vaults, sustained partly by walls and partly by two columns. Their united capitals may be defined as cubes with the lower corners cut and rounded—prototypes of that species of capital which was in considerable use after the year 1000 in constructions of the Venetian-Byzantine style.

The naves of the original basilica were, without doubt, separated by columns, which may, in whole or in part, still exist to-day in the present basilica ; but it is useless to search for one of their capitals belonging to the age during which the church was built, for the few which are not of the tenth or eleventh century are either ancient Roman or Byzantine of the fifth or sixth century. But we must not conclude that the basilica contains no sculptures of the ninth century. It is, on the contrary, abundantly provided ; we may count not less than eighty examples. In the midst of so great a quantity of marbles belonging to this period, there are very few that represent the Italian-Byzantine style ; almost all, on the contrary, suggest the Greek style. And as among these last we distinguish a group composed of very varied elements, and at the same time uniform in style, which we may easily guess to come from the same edifice, we are quite naturally brought to see in them the decorative remains of the primitive S. Mark, and to declare that this church was built by Byzantine artists, the same, very probably, who were sent by the Emperor Leo, and who built S. Zachariah.

This group of sculptures, wherein I see the decorative remains of the original church of S. Mark, is composed principally of choir parapets, small pilasters, capitals, small consoles, balustrades, cornices, archivolts, cymatia, doors, and other fragments. The basilica must have had at least four doors, and there are, in fact, four cymatia, ninth century style, which are still preserved, and serve to crown four other doors. The largest, which is the most decorated, and which must have crowned the principal door of the church of the Partecipazi, is found in the Zeno Chapel above the entrance leading to the baptistery. Two others, smaller, less ornamented, and with a uniform decoration which one sees at the entrance to the crypt, should originally have served for the small doors on each side of the principal one, and the fourth, which on

FIG. 139.—Cymatium, formerly above the door of S. Mark of the Partecipazi, A.D. 829.

account of its size and richness is placed between the first and the two others, and which will have crowned one of the doors of the basilica, opening doubtless on one of its sides, is situated above the little door that gives on the terrace of the southern façade of the existing church. Their form, like that of a large number of church door cymatia of the fifth and sixth centuries in Syria, consists in a single inclined plane terminated by listels, and their decoration in minute arches supported by colonnettes, the one single the other joined, furnished with thick socles in steps, and little flat capitals which recall those of the crypt. These little arches almost always enclose palms of strange shapes, varied by hemispheric convexities, sculptured with crosses or openwork curvilinear interlacing. The largest cymatium is also distinguished by a very bizarre cross, and by certain capricious ornaments formed of foliage bound by bandelets cut out below and bent, which recall certain friezes in terra cotta of ancient Pompeii. It is to be remarked, that this capricious decoration, as well as some other fantastic ornaments of the cymatium, have been reproduced by a clumsy local workman on a sarcophagus of the ninth century existing in the Museum at Murano. It is an evident proof of the age and the original destination of these sculptures of S. Mark, and of others of which I am about to speak.

It is, in fact, by study of the ornaments of these cymatia and the works of Grado, Athens, and Constantinople, that one comes to distinguish, among so many parapets contained in S. Mark, those that belong to its first construction, and there are not less than twenty.

I am not going to describe them all. The limits imposed on me do not allow me to do so. Those who desire to go into these small details have only to open my book upon the basilica. I

FIG. 140.—Parapet of S. Mark of the Partecipazi, existing in the Gallery above the Altar of S. James—A.D. 829.

have there described every one of them, and they have been all reproduced by phototype. I content myself here with grouping them into three different classes which I describe *en masse*. One category is composed of those which are covered with interlaced rushes or basket-work, whose structure recalls the species of the eighth century. Such is the parapet in two fragments which may be seen in the vestibule of the basilica, and which is orna-

FIG. 141.—Parapet of S. Mark of the Partecipazi, existing along the little Ambo Staircase—A.D. 829.

mented with concentric foliage, often knotted together and enclosing a rose, reminding us very much of that of the sixth century in Ravenna, which we have seen on page 86. Such are

FIG. 142.—Sculpture existing formerly in the Vault of S. Mark—A.D. 829.

also four other parapets of interior galleries for the most part the length of the transversal nave. These last show the ornamentation of the ninth century on the reverse, and are covered with

fine and complicated interlacing, executed with such ingenuity
that they recall the parapets of the cathedral of Grado to the

FIG. 143.—Lacunar of the Tomb of S. Mark in the Crypt—A.D. 829.

FIG. 144.—Parapet of S. Mark of the Partecipazi, existing in the South Transept
—A.D. 829.

point of making one believe them to be the work of the same
artist, so identical are their respective designs.

I have grouped in a second category, and it is both the most numerous and the most characteristic of the ninth century Byzantine style, parapets, which though decorated with interlacings, exhibit them formed of bandelets similar to those in the ciborium of S. Mary of Grado, and distributed in accordance with an ornamental idea often quite different from that which guided the artists of the preceding century. In these interlacings, that which most often serves as basis is the square set at angles, or the rhomb; round these figures turn circles and semi-circles, always knotted and often empanelling roses and half roses in rayed or girandole fashion similar to those of the eighth century; or else crosses, palms, doves, or other caprices. The most characteristic of these parapets is a plaque seen encrusted in the exterior wall of the Treasury, and one other which covers the tomb in the crypt that encloses the body of S. Mark.

I have found a third category of a few parapets which, belonging in their ensemble to the same style as those I have just described, deviate from it in the centre, where they present a large openworked hemispheric convexity, made of interlaced curvilinear bandelets, similar to that on a much smaller scale which we have seen on the cymatium of the fourth door.

All these parapets united together by small pilasters, or by colonnettes, and perhaps at the same time by both, that is to say, by little pilasters converted later into colonnettes, would surround a large part of the top of the choir of the original basilica; others the high altar; others the tomb of the Evangelist in the crypt. One of these little pilasters may be seen among the capitals of certain columns of the atrium; it is covered with osier interlacing, which at the top is changed into a cross with lilies and small palms.

I recognise the style of the Greek artists who built S. Mark on four small capitals that decorate the tomb of the Dogaressa Felicia Michiela in the vestibule of the basilica. They present in the ensemble the basket forms of those of the crypt, but cut into leaves and fir-apples, distributed after a very elegant design which is borrowed from certain capitals of the sixth century with which the East, and especially S. Mark, are abundantly furnished. I note further, eight small consoles in marble, existing in the atrium, on which is sculptured a plain cross with double cross-beams planted on a plinth with steps. The intact and very precious ninth century balustrade of the church of S. Luke of Athens, presents an appearance that warrants the supposition that these consoles stood out round the cornice of the balustrades in S. Mark of the Partecipazi.

Among the marbles having most in common with the parapets are two monolithic pieces of balustrade which now serve to close an arcade of the galleries of the basilica to the south. There are in all sixteen small semi-circular arches with rather raised feet supported by colonnettes with very simple base and no capitals. They seem almost imitated from the

Fig. 115.—Cornice in the Church of S. Mark of the Partecipazi.

arches that are cut into palm-leaves. The character of these balustrades, the timidity of the few ribs which are found above, and a certain rudimentary aspect, make these important remains the most ancient model that I know of balustrades with colonnettes.

The existing basilica, in the chapels of S. Peter and S. Clement, along the walls of the transversal nave and in a large niche of the vestibule, preserves about seventy yards of cornices which indubitably belong to the church of the ninth century. They are formed by a raised shell terminated by a listel and ornamented with leaves of the wild acanthus, and certain heavy lapels, divided in three, that recall the rudest of the eighth century. The leaves alternate with the calyxes of the baluster.

The most remarkable piece of sculpture that remains of the ancient S. Mark is certainly a large marble plaque, rectangular in form (m. 2·68 × 0·83), which is to be seen in the baptistery. It is decorated on both sides as if it had been a party wall. On one of the sides is sculptured a long plain cross resting on a globe and graded base; on the other, on the contrary, are rich and elegant bands with small graceful palms in the Greek style with quadrilobes knotted together, enclosing rose-work of elegant forms.

There is in this same baptistery another sculptured stone of small dimensions which bears a very graceful composition. It is an elegant arch of horse-shoe pattern ornamented with charming little leaves, supported by two long colonnettes with bold network capitals, and enclosing a beautiful cross-pommé flanked with branches, doves, and stars. It is one of the most exquisite and sympathetic compositions that the Byzantine artists of the ninth century have left us.

I will cite finally two beautiful round and sculptured stones which to-day adorn the north façade of the basilica, and in which, as in the plaque that I have just described, there shines forth all the grace and skill of the Greek artists. In one, an ingenious net-work of woven fillets, figures a cross in a circle; in the other, a very elegant interlaced osier is wedded to palm-leaves. These two patterns are framed by a ring artistically cut out.

FIG. 146.—Bas-relief existing in the Baptistery of S. Mark of the Partecipazi—A.D. 829.

It would have been imprudent to judge the Byzantine art of the ninth century by the few fragments of Grado, but not by the large number offered to us in the basilica of S. Mark. That which encourages us to do so without fear is, most of all, the great variety of forms and elements that are there presented to us; hence the probability that their authors came directly from the principal artistic home of the East, that is to say from Constantinople, and finally the fact that their style is found in perfect harmony with the numerous sculptures that are still preserved in Constantinople and Athens. The reader may convince himself of this by looking at the photographs of the ancient cathedral and of the museum at Athens, or the works of Salzemberg, Pulgher, and Castellazzi. The most impartial judgment, then, that one can pronounce is that the Byzantine art of the ninth century is, in perfection, nowise superior to that of the preceding century, insomuch that it would certainly not be an exaggeration to apply to it the epithet of barbaric. This barbarism applies especially to the representations of animals (for human figures are absolutely wanting in it), wherein form,

FIG. 147.—Parapet existing at Constantinople—IXth Century (after Salzemberg).

design, and model leave much to be desired. The elegance of certain decorative compositions cannot soften this judgment, for one recognises in them the preceding century.

All the same, the Byzantine art of the tenth century imported into Italy could triumph over Italian art, and could do so the more easily at the beginning of this century since our artists had scarcely emerged from the abyss into which they had fallen during the preceding age. If the sole fact of having come from afar frequently invests strangers with an aureole of reputation and respect, sometimes false and ill bestowed, we can imagine with what veneration and with what favour the Venetians would welcome and consider artists such as these, who came strong in position because they had been sent by the Greek Emperor from Byzantium, the richest and most admired capital of that period, and were able, moreover, to show by their works how greatly superior they were to our own. That the Venetians hastened to utilise them to the best advantage of their new city, in the construction of religious and civil edifices, has been testified by the splendid remains of S. Mark, and many other sculptures of which I am about to speak.

Among the sculptures which must belong to the churches let us cite a parapet, to-day set in the façade of a house in the Calle lunga at S. Simeon-the-Little, and some others on the façade of the church of S. John and S. Paul. They are ornamented with roses and

Figs. 148-150.—Parapets in the Church of the Mother of God at Constantinople — IXth Century (after Pulgher).

knots on a square or rhomboidal base, and in these parapets both the idea and execution show an evident and close relationship with the analogous sculptures of S. Mark of the Partecipazi.

The same may be said of a small balustrade pilaster of the choir which has been employed as material in the construction of the southern wall of the cloister of S. Gregory's Chapel, and on which the fine mixtilinear interlacing framed by small plaits betray a Greek chisel. It is perhaps a remainder of the original S. Gregory, which Galliciolli declares to have been built in the ninth century.

In the State Archives of the Fraria a mutilated capital belonging to S. Hilary is preserved, which recalls, by the conception and style, the portion of the tomb of the Dogaressa in the vestibule of S. Mark. However, in this, the style of the ninth century is more directly suggested, on account of the use made of the conventional leaves then in vogue.

Fig. 151.—Parapet in the Church of the Mother of God at Constantinople —IXth Century (after Pulgher).

We find several other sculptures due to the same chisels in the Municipal Museum. There is a stone plaque, also belonging to S. Hilary, to be seen, on which is carved in bas-relief a rough and unornamented cross, set on a demi-disc, and flanked above with two Ω, below with two Δ, both hanging from this cross. The bent extremities of the cross, resembling handles, betray a Greek hand.

Let us mention yet one more stone, brought from the Island of Poveglia. Its religious purpose is shown by the great monogram of the Saviour, in the form of an openwork wheel, which occupies the upper part of it, while a cruciform rosette in bas-relief, set in a flowered square surrounded by four palms, ornaments the lower half of each band of the parapet.

To the Greek artists who built S. Mark is attributed a

certain vase, without bottom, in the same museum, finely ornamented with bas-reliefs, representing vases from which spring fir-apples flanked by peacocks, griffins, and harpies, alternating with large palm leaves. The chiselling of it is timid and the design rude, but not without a certain grace and correctness.

Another mutilated fragment, of unknown origin, in the Municipal Museum, suggests the Byzantine style of the ninth century. Nevertheless it presents in its interlacing and rosettes too rigorous an executive perfection to allow us to attribute it to the artists that ornamented S. Mark. It belongs, without doubt, to the close of the ninth century, and was probably sculptured in Greece by an artist who had, up to a certain point, submitted to Mahommedan influence. It has certainly a Mahommedan touch on the exterior moulding, ornamented with insipid and capricious reliefs which one would take at first sight for Arab characters.

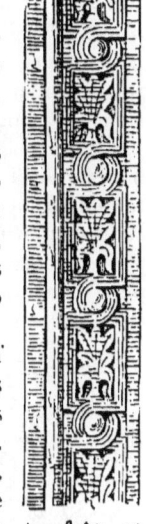

Venice can offer us what no other town of Italy affords, namely, some remains of houses of the ninth century. If the seventy metres of cornices with large leaves, which we saw in S. Mark, did not testify, by their style and quantity, that they belonged formerly to the primitive basilica, we should know it by the sole fact that several houses and palaces of the town possess similar cornices. There are some of them on the façade of a house on the quay of the Shambles, near the *Via Sansoni*; on another house at S. Cassiano, on the Grand Canal, where the lamented painter Favretto died; on the Da Mosto palace in the passage of the Holy Apostles; on the Bembo palace, also on the Grand Canal; on a house contiguous to the Prefecture; on the side door of the Carmelite Church; and on a house situate on the bank of the Carbon, near the little Dandolo palace, where the cornice, which exists

Fig. 152.— Jamb of a Door found at Athens —IXth Century (after Castellazzi).

in little fragments, is (though a sister of the others) a little
less rough. These cornices never form the crown of the
edifice, but that of the ground floor, like the cornices of
similar character, though of better style, which one sees on the
houses of the tenth and eleventh century. In the last house
of which I spoke, the cornice seems never to have been
touched, for above it, on the two extremities of the façade, rose
two long little arches in bas-relief, of which one is still in its
place, formed of heavy membrures and terminated on the summit
by a cornice with reversed gorge of Byzantine character, of which
traces remain on the other extremity. Here we have the least
ruined remains of houses dating from that remote period which
time and man have respected; this is next to the palace of
Theodoric at Ravenna, the most ancient portion of a house of
the middle ages left in Italy. It is then very precious, as much
because it witnessed the splendour and riches of Venice at a
period so poor and barbarous, as because it informs us that the
purely Venetian type of house was already completely formed in
the ninth century; for these decorative arches and cornices show
in their composition an
agreement with the analogous
details of more recent palaces,
such as the Da Mosto palace,
so perfect, that one may
reasonably believe that, even
for the rest, the rich habitations of the ninth and tenth
centuries resembled those of
the following ages. And
nevertheless, this house, precious as it is, will soon fall,
with many others, under the strokes of the pickaxe, guided by
that insensate mania for blind destruction which seems to distinguish the Municipality of Venice, who only substitute for
the ancient edifices monstrous buildings, ten times more un-
shapely than those produced by the barbarous ages.

More rich and not less precious Byzantine fragments are

Fig. 153.—Parapet found at Athens—
IXth Century (after Castellazzi).

furnished by another house, also doomed to demolition, close by the preceding; but all do not suggest the character of the ninth century. To this period belong, in my opinion, the two angular stones, ornamented with bas-reliefs, of which one rests on the ground and bears, under an arch ornamented with notches, superposed on a listel, a large cross in low relief, with extremities terminated by demi-circles. The other, slightly elevated above the ground, is formed of two little twin arches ornamented with braids, supported in the centre by an octagonal colonnette having a capital on which thorny acanthus leaves are feebly cut. Under the small arches, and along the little pilasters at the side, appear also the original notches of the other stone.

I know two other angular stones of our most ancient palace. One is to be found at the Municipal Museum, the other at that of the Estuary* at Torcello.

The former was recently discovered in digging the foundations of the new wing of the Museum itself, and offers three little arcades, supported laterally by two little octagonal pillars, and in the middle by two colonnettes which, at midshaft, embrace one another like serpents. It is the oldest example of ophitic columns with which I am acquainted in Italy—a bizarrerie due doubtless to the Byzantines, as is evident to anyone who studies the Greek antiquities of the ninth century. If the Lombard artists of the twelfth century knew it, and made great use of it, it was suggested to them in that case by Byzantine art, and they taught it, without any doubt, to Venice. Between the interlacings of these two colonnettes is niched a cross, of pure Byzantine character, of the century which we are studying. As much may be said of the large basket-shaped capitals, the bases, and the divers other mountings.

The angular stone of the Museum of Torcello, which comes

* This is a new museum containing an important collection of ancient objects, put together by M. le Com. Cæsar Augustus Levi, whom one cannot thank too heartily for having generously offered them to the public. One may see there, safely deposited, several precious objects which the carelessness of the Municipality of Venice and the Curators of the Municipal Museum had condemned to dispersion. Thanks, then, be given to M. Levi! May the gratitude, owed him by all those who are devoted to the study of the memories of their fatherland, encourage him to persevere in his noble enterprise, for there is still much to save in Venice.

from Venice, is ornamented on each side by a single arcade sustained by two colonnettes. The rudeness of the chisel, the negligence of the workmanship, and the character of the mouldings, date back to the ninth century, and recall the style of the preceding one.

All these sculptures are of the same epoch and of the same style as the well-mouths still existing at Venice—one in the Repository of Antiquities, which Signor Marcato possesses in the environs of S. Martial, the other in the Cour Battaggia ai Birri. The first is a Roman cubic cippus, converted into a well-mouth, on two sides of which little arcades, single or coupled, have been executed, sustained by angular octagonal colonnettes, and by a little central pilaster, ornamented with little groups of palm-leaves. The capitals of it are simple or rude, the archivolts cut into little leaves, the upper edge ornamented with a braid, and the intermediary fields with faces of harpies or of twin leaves. It is necessary to observe the cylindrical form given to the central cone below the little arches, perhaps with a view to give more relief to the angular colonnettes, or to isolate them.

We see this idea developed and all but brought to perfection in the other well-kirb at Birri. It offers the picturesque aspect of a cylinder enclosed in a cube pierced with eight joined arches, supported by small pilasters, which in the angles remain altogether isolated. The bands of the base and of the coping, the little pilasters and the archivolts, are abundantly and variously ornamented with interlacing, foliage, cordons, branches, and palms which, even through their roughness, betray the elegant and facile chisel of the Greek artist, or to say the least his intervention. Flowering shrubs, peopled with rudely wrought little birds, enrich the surface of the cylinder, while the curious indenting that we have seen on the quay of Cabon appears again under the archivolts of this precious well-mouth.

As remains of a habitation, and of Byzantine work, I have but one fragment of a cornice to produce, existing in the State Archives of the Frari, and belonging to a house close to the

* See "Raccolta delle Vere da pozzo esistenti in Venezia," F. Ongania publisher, 1889.

passage of the Madonnetta. It is a gorge gracefully carved with small palms in the Greek style, enclosed by listels and cubic notching.

The last sculpture of Venice, in which I can recognise the Greek seal of the ninth century, is the front of a sarcophagus, found in 1807, in the now demolished church of S. Dominic of Castello, and that can be seen at present in the court of the Patriarchal Seminary. The short fascia of the centre, bearing the following inscription: "+ IHC REQVIISCIT : VITALES ET PAVLINA IVGALES EIVS:+" is surrounded with complicated osier interlacing which, like that of certain parapets of S. Mark, show all the elegant *désinvolture* of the Greek chisel.

TORCELLO.—Outside Venice and Grado, we find in the lagoons no Greek work of the ninth century, except in the museum of Torcello. It is a capital of a column of medium size, which, like those of S. Mark and S. Hilary, presents in the ensemble the basket form, and is ornamented with bandelets fluted and bent, with little palms, laurel leaves and roses, the whole distributed with a certain grace. It recalls certain balustrade capitals of S. Luke, near Athens, work of the ninth century.

Beyond the Venetian Lagoons I have found traces of the Byzantine style of the ninth century only in three towns, Padua, Bologna, and Ancona. However, what is seen in these places is limited to fragments of little importance, which may have been transported from the lagoons long afterwards. But this supposition does not destroy the possibility that a Greek artist, after having worked at Venice, was called from thence to some other city, and exercised his talents there.

As for the remains at Padua, they consist of several yards of cornice with large leaves, altogether resembling that of the ancient S. Mark and the Venetian houses, which is found under the balcony of the façade of S. Anthony. It has served as a model for many other less ornamented cornices, which run the length of the fronton of this same façade, and of certain others which are seen on the exterior of the old Town Hall—works of the ninth century.

At Bologna we have two parapets, of which one is mutilated, on view in the Museum of this town. In the one, which bears a rhomb attached to a rectangle and at the same time to circles enclosing rosettes in low relief, one sees evidently the same style as that on several parapets of S. Mark. The other, on the contrary, wanders widely with its knotted circles, which, in turning on their own account, produce new circles and enclose crosses and leaves.

What I found at Ancona consists in some rare fragments of small pilasters and parapets, ornamented with the habitual interlacing of bandelets and rosework, set in the middle of certain arches of the bizarre façade of S. Maria-in-Piazza.

As in the eighth century poor Italian artists derived great advantage from the example of the Byzantines, so did in their turn those who resided in the lagoons from the ninth century. Their profit would probably have been greater if the art of their masters had been more perfect. But if Byzantine art maintained itself at a very inferior level, our artists could, nevertheless, learn something good from it, as the monuments bear witness.

VENICE.—The Italian-Byzantine art of the ninth century, and of the first half of the tenth, is no longer represented in Venice by any building, for the only one which remains for me to point out, showing in its details the Byzantine style rather than the Italian, cannot witness to the intervention of indigenous art. Such is the crypt of the church of S. Zachariah. One reads in the "Annals of the World" of Stefano Magno[*] to Pietro Tribuno (year 888–912) : "The annals say that this Doge had built for S. Zachariah a monument in imitation of that of our Lord, to which access was given by a double staircase, and that later on, when Helena Donado, Abbess in 1460, would pull down the church, the tombean was taken from its place under the portico until the new church was finished, and then placed under the high altar." " Sono annalj dicono questo Doxe in san Zacharia haver fato far uno monumento al muodo de quello de

---

[*] Municipal Museum, manuscript Cicogna, 266, page 66 *au verso*. I owe the knowledge of this valuable document to the courtesy of the learned Doctor and Engineer Jean Saccardo.

nostro Signor, al qual se andava per una scala in do rami, el qual poi in tempo de Helena Donado, abadessa in el 1460, volendo desfar la giesia fo trato de li et posto soto el portego fin fo fato la giesia nova et poi fo messo sotto lo altar mazor."

By this monument or sepulchre, made in the manner of that of the Saviour, only the crypt can be understood, to which the descent was actually by two staircases. One of them still exists in the minor chapel of the old church, while there is only an indication of the other. The simple annalist has also confused the crypt with the sarcophagus that was to have enclosed the body of S. Zachariah, as he shows by the statement that it was placed under the high altar of the new church. This crypt is a small subterraneous place corresponding to the end of the central nave, that is, to the presbytery of the old basilica, divided into three small naves by two rows of octagonal columns supporting cross-vaults. Like the ensemble, the details, that is to say the capitals, imitate those of the antique crypt of S. Mark, having basket forms and headings adorned by dentels. The majority of works of Italian-Byzantine style existing in Venice are composed of well-mouths, seventeen in number; but of these, seven are in the possession of dealers in antiquities and therefore in continual peril of exile from the lagoons, six are preserved in the Civic Museum, three in private habitations, and one only in a public courtyard. Whilst the well-mouths of this epoch, to be seen in Rome, all present a cylindrical form, those of Venice are often externally cubical, and sometimes scooped out of antique cippi or bits of Roman columns, to which were added crosses, palms, roses, spirals, or symbolic animals. There are two of this kind in the Civic Museum, derived from Torcello, and therefore to be regarded as Roman remnants of unhappy Altino. Certain well-mouths of Venice were certainly adapted to this use at this time, since they are merely large Corinthian capitals of ancient date.

But, whether round or square, these well-mouths are, in general, very roughly ornamented. On their sides we easily recognise all those motives of decoration that we saw on the parapets of the various churches of the ninth century in Italy and Dalmatia. We find invariably the same mixtilinear braidings: the same little arcades enclosing crosses, palms, rough vases or barbarous volatiles; the same knotted circles, cross-bearing lambs, roses, laurel-leaves, lilies, spindles, cordons, and all those details and caprices that belong to this style, so that it would be tiresome and useless to describe them one by one. Some of them, however, deserve special mention, because they are inspired rather by Greek modes of the eighth century than by Italian-Byzantine modes. These wells, which I persist,

Fig. 154.—Well-kirb belonging to M. le Chevalier Guggenheim, Venice - End of the VIIIth Century (?).

nevertheless, in assigning to the ninth century, may be seen, the one in the Corte del Pestrin at S. Maria Formosa, the others in a house at S. Antonino, in Calle dell' Arco. A distant reflection of certain Byzantine forms is seen in the crosses of a curious well-mouth, of cubic form, in the possession of Cav. Guggenheim, though the egregious crudity of the chiselling shows a very inexperienced hand. I judge it to be the oldest well-mouth that remains in Venice; certainly it is not unworthy of the eighth century.

On the other hand, a little cylindrical well-mouth, adorned by little arcades, palms, and spirals, that once embellished the courtyard of a house at S. Margaret, and now is in the possession of Signor Marcato, marks a certain progress in Italian-Byzantine art.

But what could show better than anything else the profit derived by the Italian artificers from the study of Byzantine

Fig. 155.—Well-kirb formerly at Venice—Second half of the IXth Century.

works was removed from Venice some years ago. But I keep the photograph from which Fig. 155 has been taken, and it gives a good idea of the admirable proportions of its fine fasces and the good taste of certain details: indeed there is so much grace and harmony in its ensemble that, if we did not find similar merits in other works, undoubtedly Italian, which we shall see hereafter, we should feel inclined to attribute it to a Greek chisel.'

<small>Some have thought that the cylindrical well, in the courtyard of the Lorédan Palace, now belonging to the Municipality, was a work of this epoch, and at first</small>

The few other sculptures of the ninth century that Venice possesses correspond to this improvement, under Greek guidance, of Italian-Byzantine art. One is a stone with the customary symbolic representation of a cross between trees placed under an arch, to be seen in the baptistery of S. Mark. Two others, similar and of more careful workmanship, though of rugged design, may be seen in the Civic Museum, together with a third, covered with floral, interlaced circles, whose ribbons are furrowed in the contemporaneous Greek style. They come from the Farsetti palace.

The front of a sarcophagus of this style, rich in braidings and inscriptions, is preserved in a room of the Ducal Palace. A few fragments of another sarcophagus, adorned by the usual crosses between palms and roses, may be seen in the Patriarchal Seminary, and some other sculptures of varied importance are possessed by antiquaries. Venice would have been extremely rich in such sculptures had she not been sacked by the buyers-up of antiquities for foreign museums. However, people think her much richer in antiquities than she really is, and continue to export from her a quantity of works, apparently of the ninth but really of the nineteenth century. If the authentic works were separated from the bogus ones, certain museums of the North, and especially America, would be left decimated and perhaps even bare!

TORCELLO.—The only works of Italian-Byzantine architecture spared to us by past ages are at Torcello. The deacon John in his chronicle, referring to Torcello, wrote that from 864 " Ecclesia Sanctae Dei Genetricis et Virginis Mariae (that is to say, the cathedral) quae vetustae pene consumpta manebat, a Marini patritii filiis consolidata est." In examining the cathedral, we soon learn that the work of 864 was not a mere consolidation of the edifice, but an almost general rebuilding of its perimetral walls, including an augmentation of its area.

We are induced to suspect that the Greek artists who built

sight its decorations may appear to be of the ninth century. But, observing it more accurately, one discovers from certain details in the style of the Renaissance that it was a face cope of a Byzantine well, made in the sixteenth century.

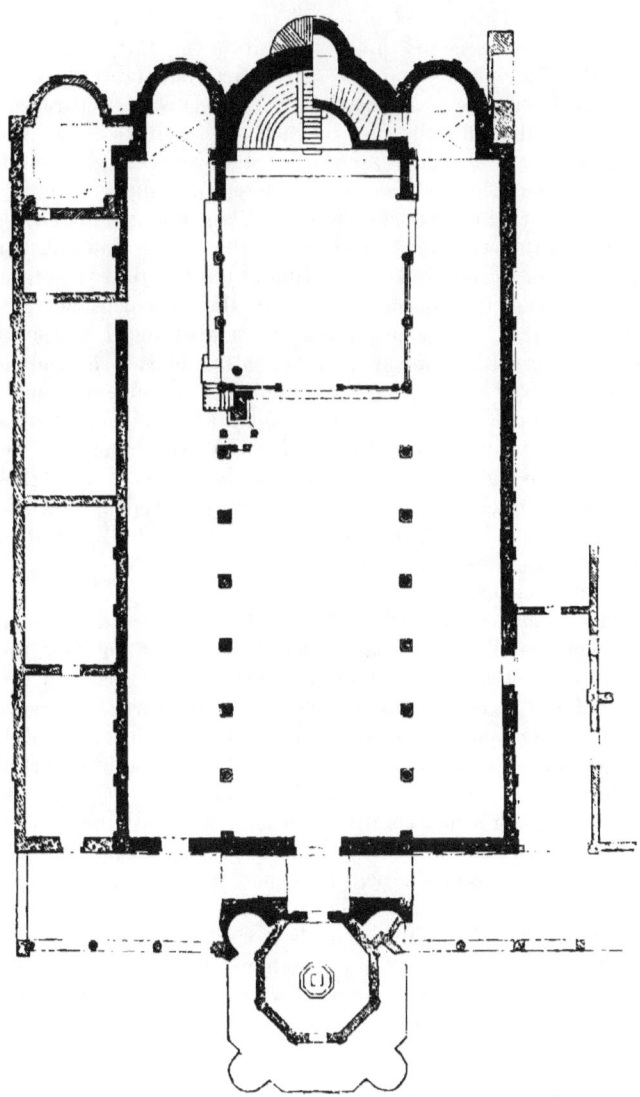

Fig. 156. Plan of the Cathedral of Torcello at the present time.

S. Mark were either dead or had departed from the lagoons by this time, because in this refabrication of the cathedral of Torcello there is no trace of Greek art, but everywhere the stamp of Italian-Byzantine style. The apsis is all that remains standing of the old walls, and on each side of it, to prolong the minor naves, two chapels were erected, covered by cross-vaults and terminated by little apsides. These appendices give us an idea of the synchronical churches at Milan and Alliate, and we shall be further reminded of them by the architectonic decorations of the external walls, consisting of long vertical projections which, around the apsides, finish in the indispensable little pensile arches. These projections were also added to the old wall of the central apsis, and, as the nature of the soil did not allow of a crypt like that of the Lombards, recourse was had to the expedient of a shallow semi-annular subterranean chamber along the internal wall of the apsis, for which reason the considerable raising of its vaults had to be masked with those splendid internal staircases, a true presbyterial hexahedron, known to us all. Then it was that, outside the apsis itself, another (little) apsis corresponding to the crypt and receiving the altar was attached.

The façade of the cathedral was also adorned by the same projections as the sides; but, being much nearer together, they were capable of combination above by means of an arch over each field. The passage existing between the lower part of the centre of the façade and the ancient baptistery was then covered by barrel-vaults, which exist to this day, and form a robust portico. No one could doubt the age that I attribute to these constructions, since their own decorative architectonic details most clearly proclaim them to be of the ninth century. Thus the little brackets that sustain the pensile arches of the apsides, support sculptured crosses which evidently belong to that epoch : the internal arcades of the little chapels repose on little cornices cut into braids and leafage of pure Italian-Byzantine style. The same may be said of the imposts of the vaults in the atrium, where antique Ionic-Roman capitals, reversed, are obviously enriched by sculptures of 864.

But all these details do not so well represent to us the value of these artificers as other works of sculpture that exist outside the cathedral or in the sacristy. The doorposts of the great door (which Selvatico attributes to the fourth century) are splendidly rich with very various designs in spirals, circles,

Fig. 157.—Parapet of the Cathedral of Torcello—A.D. 874.

braidings, pearls and crosses, vigorously carved, and with a sureness of effect, and a certain grace, inherited from Grecian art. Of the same character is a mutilated parapet, which one sees set in the exterior, near the side door of the cathedral, together with other fragments, of divers epochs, and certain fragments of doorposts that adorn the *lavabo* of the sacristy. Two capitals of the front portico, north of the baptistery, one adorned by rugged acanthus leaves, the other by caulicules capriciously distributed, are connected, both by style and age, with the preceding sculptures.

At the same time as the cathedral, or shortly after, but by the same workmen, must have been built or rebuilt the adjoining church of S. Fosca, which then presented, without doubt, the aspect of a little basilica with three naves terminated by three apsides. The two little lateral apsides, whose style differs from that of the centre and that of the rest of the present edifice in showing the Italian-Byzantine manner (one of them, too, having a bas-relief with a cross and roses), are, I imagine, remnants of the ninth century church. The same epoch is acknowledged by two sculptured stones encased in the sides of the great door, and bearing representations of crosses under arcades among roses, palms and vine-branches, in the elegant and almost Grecian style that we admired in the neighbouring cathedral.

Numerous are the sculptures of this style, more or less perfect or precious, in the two museums of Torcello. In the first rank figure certain parapets with sculptures of wheels with superposed squares enriched by roses, lilies, palms, and braidings; many capitals of small dimensions, and many cymatia or bracket-formed abaci, richly adorned—remains, perhaps, of some presbyterial chancel; and many crowning friezes carved in braids or caulicules, often accompanied with inscriptions.

MURANO.—The island that is richest in Italian-Byzantine sculptures is Murano. Its celebrated cathedral certainly must have undergone rebuilding or radical restoration in the ninth century. The numerous sculptures of Italian-Byzantine style still preserved on its external walls bear witness to this, and so do the many fragments which reappeared in the last restorations of the present edifice, built about the year 1100. The style of these sculptures is similar to that of the works of the cathedral and of S. Fosca of Torcello, and, like the latter, represents that degree of perfection, unattained, at that time, in any other region of Italy—an improvement which, without doubt, was due to the profitable example of the Byzantine works. This close analogy between the sculptures of Torcello and those of the cathedral of

Murano alone witnesses to an evident synchronism: but we have another proof in that famous mutilated inscription which appears on one of the usual friezes or architraves of choral chancels, adorned both by braids and caulicules, which is set in the outside of the church at the side of the apsis. It runs thus : ". . . T SCE MARIE DI GENETRICIS ET BEATI ESTEFANI MARTIRI EGO INDIGNVS ET PECCATVR DOMENICVS T . . ."; and if, as is probable, this last T is the beginning of the title *torcellanus episcopus*, the Domenicus there mentioned can only be that Caloprino whose see was between 871 and 880.

The two most remarkable and best preserved pieces of sculpture are two great parapets, one of which is to be seen in a chapel inside the church, and the other closes the last intercolumn on the right of the exterior balcony of the apsis. They are bordered and traversed by large fasces, which divide the fields into two squares; and they are distinguished by the distribution in good taste of the braidings of withes, the circles and spirals furnished with palm-leaves, the semicircular superposed arches which one sees on Greek works of the eighth century, laurel leaves, rosettes, and beads. Other stones also merit consideration, on which are sculptured crosses and palms under the customary arcades adorned by rampant caulicules, and, above all, several archivolts of ciboria more or less mutilated, having been used, about the year 1100, to form the arches of the balustrades on the balconies of the apsis. For elegance and freedom of decoration they are not inferior to the parapets named above, even as those Corinthian capitals which we see employed externally on the side of the apsis, and which, without doubt, served originally to sustain the aforesaid archivolts, are superior to any other capitals of Italian-Byzantine style. Their svelte proportions, elegant novelty of detail, and the accuracy of their execution, show a real progress in art.

The museum also of the island, embellished by many spoils from the old cathedral, the baptistery, now destroyed, and an antique cemetery adjoining, can show very many fragments of Italian-Byzantine sculpture, such as archivolts of little ciboria, parapets, pilasters, and friezes always covered with rich ornamentation, and sometimes with often illegible inscriptions. Very important are certain sarcophagi ruggedly ornamented with braidings, crosses, palms, roses, and cross-bearing lambs. The most precious of all is the one whose front, carved with a double zone of ornament, shows linked circles and some curled arches and strange plants, that clearly show an almost servile imitation of certain motives used by the Greek artificers on parapets, and especially on the heading of the great door of the basilica of S. Mark.

JESOLO.—Sarcophagi of the same style recently came to light among the ruins of the cathedral of Jesolo, rich in ornaments that express the manner of the eighth century, or in braidings so distributed as to remind one of S. Abbondio of Como.

CONCORDIA.—In the atrium of the baptistery of Concordia several parapets are preserved, adorned by braided circles, palms, lilies, and the usual motives, which in conceit and execution recall the best works of the style that we have seen at Murano, Torcello, or Venice.

Thus Italian-Byzantine art, in penetrating the lagoons, found at the outset a rival in Greek art; but, having once passed the middle of the ninth century, it became sole master of the country, and, profiting by the excellent example of its rival, was able to reach a degree of perfection unattained by the art of the other Italian cities. But the same cause that served to accelerate its perfection in the lagoons contributed, towards the end of the tenth century, to its utter extinction, as we shall see in the following chapter.

CHAPTER V.

ARCHITECTURE IN THE LAGOONS AND IN VENETIA.

FROM THE YEAR 976 TO THE MIDDLE OF THE ELEVENTH CENTURY.

VENICE.—The basilica of S. Mark, as built by the Partecipazi, lasted till the year 976, in which year the people rose against the doge Pietro Candiano IV., and, having set fire to the Ducal Palace, the flames gained the church and made great havoc therein. The detested prince having been killed, the ducal crown was placed on the head of Pietro Orseolo I., whose first care was to restore, at his own expense, not only the palace, but the basilica of S. Mark. Do not believe, however, as it was believed for too many centuries, that he reconstructed it from the foundations, and still less that he enlarged it. His work was confined to the reparation of the injuries suffered by the edifice, which, as far as we gather from the chronicles, only extended to the half, the part towards the east, which was nearest the palace. The restoration, therefore, could not have occupied a long time; in fact, two years after (A.D. 978), we find the church already opened to the public, and services carried on. It must, therefore, at least in its organic parts, have been already restored. Having assured ourselves, then, that the church of Orseolo was neither longer, larger, higher, nor different organically from that of the Partecipazi, let us see if we can recognise among the innumerable sculptures of the present church those that have reference to the restoration or embellishments of 979.

It is certain that, after this date, the edifices of Venice and of the islands, of which we know the exact year of foundation or of restoration, and of which some things still remain, such as S. Maria-delle-Vergini (983), the cathedral of Torcello (1008), and the cathedral of Caorle (1038), show, in certain of their details, a uniform originality of forms, which cannot easily escape the eye. There are, in the first place, fine composite columns, of delicate intaglio and excellent effect, which have no counterpart in others of any preceding century; there are cornices carved into leafage with equal perfection, parapets magnificently and elegantly arabesqued with every manner of ornament, which depart from the models of the ninth or eighth century, and also from the style of the sixth and fifth; they are, in fact, a harmonious ensemble of forms, which announce an art both new and complete. And since these details do not consist of fragments picked up here and there, but, and especially at Torcello, of sculptures executed expressly for the edifice which holds them, one must conclude that that art, even if not born in our lagoons, was certainly imported there and cultivated. Now we find it also in S. Mark, represented by a considerable number of works, which while they are perfectly analogous to those named above, sometimes even approaching nearer than they do to perfection, yet offer us such conditions as to assure us, that though they were made on purpose for S. Mark, they could neither have been made for the modern church nor for that of the Partecipazi.

We must, therefore, recognise in them the works ordered by Pietro Orseolo, and the Neo-Byzantine style. Without doubt the Doge, who wished to restore the basilica at his own expense, also wished that his work, far from leaving occasion for people to regret what was lost, should be so beautiful and perfect as to make them bless the destroying fire. In order to attain that result he knew that he must resort to Byzantine artists, who, since, even in the preceding centuries, they had justly earned the glory of being the masters of our artists, might claim it as a right in the tenth century, because their art was then in a state of true renaissance.

The causes of decadence in art, that is to say, civilisation and a people's prosperity, produce also its renaissance. From the day in which the artificers who erected S. Mark set sail from Constantinople to the day in which the new restorers left it, more than a hundred and fifty years had passed, and, in the meantime, the fate of the Greek empire had had to improve, and Greek art to revive. The Byzantine empire, so Bayet writes,[*] was never so flourishing and potent as under the domination of the house of Macedonia (867-1057). The great princes of the period had a surer intelligence, an energy superior to that of Justinian himself : they better understood the interests of Hellenic civilisation. Intrepid warriors, able administrators, they knew how to give development to whatever might be favourable to the moral and material grandeur of the empire. The founder of the dynasty, Basil the Macedonian, opened the way, in which he was followed by Nicephorus Phocas, John Tzimisce, and Basil II. The empire valiantly defended itself against the invasions which overflowed its provinces from north and south ; the Slaves were repulsed, the Bulgarians arrested, Cyprus, Crete, and Cilicia reconquered from the Arabs. On all sides Hellenism recovered a portion of the ground that it had lost. At the same time, industry and commerce brought a marvellous augmentation of wealth to the great cities. Constantinople became the centre of the commerce of the world, and served as an emporium for the East and the West. There met together the merchants of Arabia and France, Italians and Asiatics. Constantinople was the medium of their exchanges, whilst she sold to them at the same time her jewels, her embroidered stuffs, her carpets, her arms, her ivories, and many other precious objects, amply paid for, which were destined to propagate the Byzantine influence in the most distant countries. To this increment of industrial and commercial life, a new manifestation of intellectual life corresponded. Constantinople had a university, in which philosophy, rhetoric, and mathematics were taught ; from thence the emperor selected those whom he judged to be worthy of the highest charges. The schools of Athens arose anew ; France, and England itself, sent students to them. This general renaissance also extended to art. The emperors showed favour to it, and Constantine

---

[*] Bayet, " L'Art byzantin " (Paris, A. Quantin).

Porphyrogenitus himself described with complacency the edifices which he built and adorned.

The basilica of S. Mark, having the good fortune to become the prey of the flames at a moment in which Byzantine art arrived at the apogee of this first renaissance, was restored magnificently and enriched with beautiful productions. Let us then examine it, certain of finding in the above-named monuments, which I intend to describe, the most ample justification of my choice. The dimensions of the basilica of the Partecipazi and of Orseolo permit one to conjecture that its naves were divided by ten or eleven columns on each side. The most precise information that we derive from the Chronicle about the damage suffered by the church through the fire of 976, is to the effect that half of it was burnt. Now among the capitals of the large internal columns of the present basilica, and of those which from their size might have separated the naves of the primitive one, I find ten of the time of Orseolo, which, divided by two, exactly corresponds in number to one-half of the church. They now crown the eight twin columns of the transept that arise behind and in front of the two little altars of S. Paul and S. James, and the two columns of the altar of the Blessed Virgin.

They are all composite, but of that composite without ovoli, rich in leafage of wild acanthus, which was the predilection of the Byzantines ever since the fifth century. Nevertheless, it may be divided into two classes, one of uniform and regular leafage, the other confused and often capricious. The five of the first class are adorned by two rows of large and well-carved leaves of wild acanthus, of excellent taste and sure and agreeable effect. In their ensemble they appear to indicate certain proto-Byzantine capitals of the fifth or sixth century.

Nearer still to these come the five of the second class, in the minuteness of the intaglio of the leaves, often excessively trite, and in the volutes, that have the pared corners gracefully ornamented. Two of them attract our curiosity, by certain capricious and most original leafage opening chalice-wise and rolled into curled cornet-like volutes very minutely notched.

The common characteristics of both classes are these: the short zone, which in the composite Roman capitals is reserved to the egg pattern, is here, on the contrary, cut up in little leaves, and the abacus above has its corners cut at right angles, instead of being pared away. Abaci of this fashion are seen among the ruins of about the sixth century in Central Syria, but they are isolated examples, and so few in number that they cannot, as in the present case, constitute a special characteristic of the style. After the tenth century we see them used very frequently, both in Byzantine and Romanic monuments.

From this group stand out four other capitals of various measures that appear to have been sculptured in the time of Orseolo. The two largest are those of the columns now in the presbytery where the apsidal curve begins; the other two, much smaller, are seen under the Gothic tabernacle at the south-east angle of the meridional façade of the basilica. They are embellished by one or two rows of wild acanthus leaves, rolled up and folded one over the other as if beaten by the wind: a most elegant conceit, which is visible in Byzantine architecture as early as the fifth century, as certain capitals of Syria, and others of Thessalonica or of Ravenna, bear witness, besides many that are visible in S. Mark's Church itself at the sides of the principal door.

I said above that there were sculptures in S. Mark's that proclaimed themselves works of the Orseolo basilica. Such is the architectonic decoration

FIG. 158.—Little Arcades forming the Base of the Choir of S. Mark's—A.D. 976.

that forms the base of the chancels of the present presbytery, and corresponds with the elevation of

the crypt on the pavement of the naves. It is not a collection
of fragments nor an ensemble of stones of various forms, such as
might make one suppose one's self in the presence of a composition of remnants of marble collected and imported here ; but a
long series of arches of uniform measure, supported by regular
columns provided with base and capital ; in fact, a work that
must have been executed on purpose for our church. But at the
same time their style, too perfect to be assigned to the ninth
century, and the presence of many other of those little arches,
placed as old, mutilated, and incongruous, under the staircase of
the present ambo, are arguments that, while they exclude the
possibility that they were made for the Partecipazi church, or for
the restoration of the eleventh century, are sufficient to persuade
us thoroughly that they were ordered by Orseolo in 976. These
little arcades must have decorated splendidly three sides of the
base of the choir corresponding to the antique crypt, and we have
in their height the exact elevation of the presbytery of the
ninth and tenth centuries.

Considered artistically, those arcades constitute the loveliest,
most elegant, and finest work that Orseolo caused to be executed
for S. Mark. They are semicircular, posted on short octagonal
columns, slightly diminished at the two extremities, and half
enchased in a smooth pilaster in the background. They are
poised upon bases which are also octagonal, of pure Byzantine
profile, and they are crowned by graceful Corinthian capitals,
finely carved in little acanthus leaves and volutes, in which the
style and the chisel of the larger capitals mentioned above is
reflected. Here two architectonic novelties worthy of notice
present themselves. The first consists of certain little abaci,
or rather cymatia, that are placed between the foot of the arch
and the capital, forming, as it were, the crown of it. This is
no longer that high entablement, almost like a second capital,
that was so much used by the Greeks of the fifth and sixth
centuries, and that in the eighth century we find to be almost
fallen into disuse, but it is among the most ancient examples
that I have met with of those graceful headings that we shall
henceforth find constantly used by the Byzantine architects, as

much in the constructions raised in their native land as in those erected among us, and not abandoned by the Venetian architects till the sixteenth century. The other novelty appears in the little archivolts, and consists in their being limited in the *arête* of the intrados by a baguet. And this is one of the oldest examples of the very reasonable use of this robust member set to guard the fragile right-angled corners in the place most exposed to damage.

Over the archivolts to finish the stylobate runs a dentellated listel, and the mixtilinear intermediaries are splendidly arabesqued with charming and very varied ornaments, sometimes so delicate and beautiful as to appear works of the Renaissance. There are little bushes of leaves, enlaced spirals, stems with blue-bells and other flowers, loose vinesuckers, all manner of leaves, roses, palms, pomegranates, all distributed with that fine beauty-sense that was ever distinctive of the Greeks. It is natural that over a basement so magnificent the eyes of the restorers could not tolerate the old parapets, both because, in comparison with it, they must have seemed antiquated and almost barbarous, and because they must have been spoilt for the most part by the conflagration.

However that may have been, it is indubitable that Orseolo caused eighteen or twenty parapets to be sculptured, and we can still admire them in the present basilica. The ornaments of the little arcades of which we spoke, and the parapets which we shall see in the cathedral of Torcello, are a sure guide for their recognition.

Two of them are seen used to close the lower part of the intercolumns of the sepulchre of the Dogaressa in the vestibule of the basilica; the rest are all preserved in the interior, and for the most part serve to make the internal galleries more beautiful, distinguishing them from all others by splendour of ornament and elegance of composition. Many of them are finely corniced with a braid of withes, not flat as in the preceding ages, but in relief and slightly convex. Sometimes the braid is limited by rows of spindles in **Hellenic** style; sometimes it is replaced by large leaves grafted one on the other. The compositions that embellish the interior fields for the most part consist of rich acanthus plants which develop themselves in vigorous foliage, or else in vases in which are set fine spiral branches with diverse leaves of various intaglio, out of which issue bunches of grapes, pineapples, roses, palms, lilies, and cups. There is scarcely a parapet that does not show figures of animals in the midst of the

Fig. 159.—Parapet of S. Mark, made by order of Pietro Orseolo I.—A.D. 976.

leafage. There are little birds, peacocks, lions, hares, and sometimes fantastic monsters, such as a single body to which are attached the heads of bulls and horses, or else fishes that turn into plants, or trees that bear quadrupeds' heads for fruit.

Many others of these parapets of 976 have their fronts subdivided into several squares corniced with listel mouldings, shell-work, and batons sometimes cut into cords, and enclosing less pompous compositions, which are, for the most part, vases with short vine-branches and lions' heads, fountains with rampant griffins beside them, or simple scenes of animal life, that is to say, creatures in strife, e.g., a griffin striking down a hare, a griffin mounted on an elephant engaged in tearing off its proboscis, a lion throwing down and killing a calf, or a large duck. More than in the novelty and elegance of these parapets, the merit of their sculptors appears in the animal figures, which, though certainly falling short of perfection, are yet often finely formed, have very natural poses, show a certain study of anatomy, a sufficient relief; in fact, are a thousand miles apart from the deformities of the preceding century.

Besides the chancels of the choir restored by Orseolo, we have remnants of the ambo that he caused to be made; not of their curvilinear parapets, but only of those of the staircase which led to them, and they may be seen on the reverse side along the stairs of the present ambo of the epistle and over the west gallery of the basilica. They were trapezoidal, like those we shall see in the cathedral of Torcello, and they offered in a very large frame formed of varied mouldings, and quite Byzantine, symbolic decoration of rather archaic character, though of accurate and free chiselling; that is to say, an arabesqued cross, between roses, spirals, and palms on graduated bases, or else a crown of laurels with roses and leafage.

In the year 976 appeared two door-cornices richly adorned, which came to light during the last restorations of the principal façade of the basilica, and are now preserved in the courtyard behind the same. The larger of them is formed of those characteristic mouldings of various profiles that we took note of around certain parapets and by the sides of the ambo; here, however, they are enriched with elegant leaves and doubly dentellated. Let us stay a moment before this last decoration, because it is the most ancient example that appears in the lagoons, perhaps even in Italy, of this dentellation, which was afterwards preferred and so profusely used by our artists in their architecture till the fifteenth century, as to become a conspicuous characteristic of the Venetian style. The only difference that separates these Greek dentels of the tenth century from those of the following is, that while the latter are rectangular, the former are perfectly square—a feature which helps to make them more elegant. The aforesaid mouldings run round the doorposts, and are only interrupted in the centre of the architrave by a medallion enclosing a bust of the Saviour in the act of benediction; one of the few figurative bas-reliefs, though unfortunately mutilated, that have remained to us from those times.

The doorposts of the other (smaller) door are moulded in the usual manner and carved into elegant leaves, which turn gracefully about, being interrupted in the centre of the architrave by a little cross.

The various figurative representations of the parapets serve as a guide to us in recognising the work of 976, in a considerable number of decorative bas-reliefs that now adorn the basilica towards the *Piazzetta dei leoncini*. We saw in the preceding chapter, two circular stones, adorned with braidings, which belonged to the church of the Participazi. Well, the conceit of those decorative discs was not neglected by the restorers of the tenth century, but rather re-adopted by them, giving rise to a decoration which afterwards became essentially characteristic of the Venetian palaces of the three following centuries. These are the well-known pateræ, on which are sculptured symbolic animals, mostly bizarre representations of fighting beasts. Of this kind are those nine stones that one sees enchased in the walls of the façade above named, wherein the same chisel is seen and, in great part, the same conceits of the bestial scenes seen upon the interior parapets of 976. There we see lions, griffins, or eagles hunting hares, a monster formed of four bodies of lions with only one head, an open-winged eagle which seizes a serpent, a peacock on a ball with its tail displayed which forms a niche—a graceful idea, which seems suggested by the antique flabelli, and which we find twice represented over an internal parapet; a nude Orpheus, playing the flute, while a lion carries him meekly on his back through a wood; a man struggling with a lion; and lastly a naked man with a drawn sword, riding and menacing a fantastic monster, half ox and half wolf.

Always relying on the sculptures of the Cathedral of Torcello, and those just seen, we may, in all security, regard as a work of the year 976, a certain little female figure in bas-relief, which is also seen set in the northern façade of S. Mark. The figure stands out in relief from a rectangular background, framed by a pretty branch of olive leaves; it has an antique vestment drawn up by a rich girdle on the hips, a pearl necklace on the throat, naked arms braceleted at the biceps and the wrists, a jewelled crown on her head, under which loose locks flow down.

With her left hand she holds a long palm branch ending in a
bunch of grapes, and with the right she raises a crown of leaves
merely sketched out, while on her right hand arises one of the
usual conventional palm trees, very like those sculptured on the
remnants of the ambo. What does this woman represent?
Excluding the idea of a saintly image, because there is no nimbus
and the costume is too profane, I opine that she must be a
Victory without wings ; the kind of dress, the crown, and the
palm, speak clearly. Very probably this figure formed part of
an ensemble of bas-reliefs, now lost, from which the allegorical
signification that I attribute to it might more easily have
been gathered. A bas-relief of the same epoch of the cathedral
of Torcello will explain better the hidden symbolism.

As to the artistic value of the latter, and of the few other
figurative bas-reliefs of this time, offered to us by S. Mark and
the cathedral of Torcello, one should be grateful when one
thinks of the barbarism of two centuries ago, but eyes that seek
perfection in art have little here to enjoy. The proportions are
often mistaken, the limbs heavy, the heads too large, the
expression nil, the drapery hard and sharp.

However, the splendour of the new ornaments lavished by
Pietro Orseolo on the restoration of the basilica of S. Mark,
must have procured infinite honours and advantages for the good
Greek artificers who had conceived and executed it. The rare
good fortune of being able to dispose of the best artists that
Italy then held, must have spurred the Venetians to exercise
their compass and chisels in employing them in the construction
of churches and palaces.

Pietro Orseolo I. perhaps employed them also in the restoration of the Ducal Palace, a restoration that, together with
the construction or rebuilding of a sumptuous private chapel,
was completed by Pietro Orseolo II. But nothing remains to
us of this edifice.

Till a few years ago there existed in Venice the church of
S. Maria of Jerusalem, or of the Virgins, a church which
Galliciolli affirms was erected in 985, and, according to San-
sovino, was rebuilt by the Doge Pietro Ziani in the twelfth

century. It was a basilica with three naves divided by columns; which, when destroyed by our modern Vandals, to make the Arsenal a trifle larger, were sold together with their capitals to the sculptor Signor Dorigo, and some of them may still be seen among his marbles. Those capitals are divided into three distinct classes. Some of them belong to the sixth century, and are fragments from more ancient churches; several others show the Venetian-Byzantine style of the time of Ziani, and, lastly, two have the Neo-Byzantine style of the tenth century, fully confirming the date affirmed by Galliciolli. In these last, of *srelte* forms, with large, well-cut leaves of thorny acanthus, and with a third row of the same capriciously replacing ovoli and volutes, it is easy to recognise the same chisel that worked on those of S. Mark under Orseolo.

The four composite capitals that in 1460 were employed in the construction of the Door of the Arsenal, are, without doubt, relics of some rich edifice due to the same artificers. Like the preceding one and the greater part of those of S. Mark, they are encircled by two rows of fine leaves of the usual acanthus; they have volutes at the angles, and offer the peculiarity of two branches full of leaves extended under the abacus.

About the end of the tenth century the church of S. Euphemia at Giudecca had to be rebuilt, and the columns and capitals of the present church are of that epoch, intermingled with others of more ancient date. The first, however, although they show the Neo-Byzantine style, are not to be regarded as works of Greek artists, but rather those of some Venetian chisel in rugged imitation of their manner. And in the frequently minute intaglio of the leaves we trace the artificer's efforts to copy a model of the sixth century existing in the church itself.

The too-neglected church of S. John the Baptist, which, according to Galliciolli, was built at Venice in the year 1007, is more important, and, in fact, its three naves validly confirm this assertion. They are separated by five arcades on each side, turning in a double half-circle with a semi-oval curve inclining to the acute form, almost like that of the palaces of the Sassanides. They are supported by eight columns with capitals of the Venetian school, very superior to those of S. Euphemia, although they remind one of them. At any rate the continuation, or rather the last reflections of the Italian-Byzantine art of the preceding centuries is evident in them, modified and improved by the recent examples of the work of the Greek artificers. This precious remnant of a church, the most ancient in Venice, owes its preservation to having been spared by the many conflagrations that desolated the city in the twelfth century.

Venice preserves a sufficiently considerable number of Neo-Byzantine sculptures, of the end of the tenth century or the beginning of the eleventh, which once adorned houses and palaces of that period, and were afterwards employed in new constructions. The works seen by us at S. Mark, and those which we shall see in the cathedral of Torcello, will serve to us as sure guides for their recognition.

Keeping in our mind the fine leaves of thorny acanthus that adorn the capitals of the two churches just named and those of S. Maria-of-the-Virgins and of the Door of the Arsenal, whose originality is chiefly conspicuous in the characteristic reverses, we find them multiplied and translating themselves into long cornices on some of the habitations of the city. They are to be seen, for instance, on the two façades of an old palace which gives on to the Corte del Milione and the Corte Morosina at S. John Chrysostom. Similar ones appear on a house near the Ponte Storto at S. Apollinaris, and on a third near the Palazzo Widmann at S. Canciano. All three are furnished with numerous decorative paterae of equal age, which, like those of S. Mark, show struggling animals, peacocks, or eagles, with spread wings and tail, or griffins in pairs. The same cornices appear also on the Bembo Palace, and on a house near the Prefecture, both on the Grand Canal, and both provided with other cornices of the ninth century, whose rough leaves are a striking contrast with the elegant ones of the tenth century.

In addition to sculptured cornices and figured stones, the palaces erected towards the end of the tenth century were embellished with archivolts and friezes, gracefully arabesqued, of which fragments may still exist here and there. The door of the Malipiero Palace on the Campo S. Samuele is crowned with a delicately sculptured pointed arch whose curves, imperfectly concentric, may be easily recognised as fragments of an ancient semi-circular arcade of Neo-Byzantine style. It is adorned with spirals of leaves and bunches of grapes, with doves, rabbits, and a peacock with outspread tail, which originally must have occupied the summit of the arch. The little door is limited externally by a cornice formed by a listel, by dentels, and a moulding cut into little leaves which bear great analogy to those that frame two parapets of the chancel at Torcello (see Fig. 165); while those of the archivolt, in little groups of three, recall certain other parapets at S. Mark and a great sculptured stone (*formella*) of Murano, which we shall see farther on.

Many are the churches and palaces of Venice on which it is easy to recognise decorative stones of the style which we are studying; but it requires very expert eyes to distinguish them from the quantity which were sculptured in the succeeding centuries. Horizontal friezes in our style are found in a smaller number, while there are hundreds of metres of those of the following ages. One rare fragment of a frieze sculptured in the style of the parapets of Torcello, in spirals, with grapes, various leaves, and a dove, is in the possession of the writer.

Amid the abundance of well-mouths of Byzantine style which Venice still possesses, there is not one that appears to be the work of the restorers of S. Mark and of the cathedral of Torcello. There exists one, however, which, though neither sculptured by them nor a work of their time, yet shows their style, imitated with such faithfulness of motive and such character of design, as to enable us to regard it as a most diligent reproduction of one of their works now lost. This is a most beautiful well-mouth, which doubtless belongs to Venice, where it is now to be seen,* but at the beginning of the century it was stationed in

---

* It was on the point of passing the Alps; but the honourable directors of our Institution of the Fine Arts very sensibly stopped the proceeding, taking care to in-the village of Cessalto, near Oderzo. An inscription says it was sculptured in MCCCCLXVII. by Master Cristofolo di Martin, stonecutter, and a shield exactly of the style of the fifteenth century, and evidently contemporaneous with the whole, confirms the date, assuring us by a very rare but not unique example

FIG. 160. — Reproduction in 1467 of a Well-ring sculptured about A.D. 1000.

that in the time of the Renaissance the works of Byzantine style were sometimes lovingly reproduced, together with the Roman sculptures. In this well-mouth no one can better recognise than ourselves, knowing as we already do the production of the Greek artificers employed by Orseolo I., the impress of their style in the smallest details. Who, in fact, does not see in the octagonal columns which rise isolately at

form the Minister of Public Instruction of the great and exceptional artistic value of this piece. But the Ministry took no heed, and left the beautiful well-mouth to the chances of fate. It is highly desirable that the Municipality of Venice should purchase it for the Civic Museum. It may still be seen in a ground-floor room of the Institution of the Fine Arts.

its angles, in its bases and its capitals, the character and the conception of the columns of the basement of the presbytery of S. Mark? Who would not recognise in those timid dentels, in those graceful and varied archivolts, in those vases, peacocks, lions, and other struggling animals, the same mind that conceived the analogous things that we saw in S. Mark? The correspondence is so perfect that, without the shield and the inscription, one might swear that the well was of the time of Orseolo; and therefore, and because the obscure stone-worker of 1467 certainly could not have known how to create a composition so wonderfully coinciding not only with a style, but with a short and, till latterly, ignored period of a style already passed away and forgotten, I offer the reader the image of this well-ring as a most precious example of Neo-Byzantine and Greek genius.

TORCELLO.—Giovanni, deacon, left written in his chronicles, that on the occasion when Orso Orseolo was raised to the dignity of Bishop of Torcello (1008) his father, the Doge Pietro Orseolo II. "*sanctæ Mariae domum et ecclesiam, jam pene vetustate consumptam, recreare studiosissime fecit.*" There was, then, no ground for Selvatico's doubts as to whether the chronicles alluded to the cathedral of Torcello or to S. Maria of Murano, because the word *domum* could only refer to the bishopric of Torcello, consequently the church mentioned could only be the neighbouring cathedral. And even if that declaration did not exist the precious basilica would still remain, capable of dissipating every doubt, and assuring us that it must have been restored at that time. But Selvatico and everybody who has spoken of this church could not deduce anything from its numerous sculptures of 1008, for they erroneously regarded them as remains of the old basilicas of Altinate of the sixth or seventh century.

Perhaps in 864, when nearly all the perimetral walls of the church were re-made, and the little chapels and minor apsides still existed, the ancient nave was not touched; so that, at the beginning of the eleventh century, it was in such a ruinous condition as to require a radical rebuilding. At any rate, this is the only part of the church which was rebuilt in 1008, and which to-day remains almost intact. I say almost, because I have been able to convince myself that its eastern portion, corresponding to the presbytery, must in the second half of the twelfth century have undergone serious damage, as in that part, the lateral chancels of the choir and even some capitals of the larger columns, five in number, have been rebuilt.

The capitals of the other thirteen columns are all, except

Fig. 161.—Capital from the Naves of the Cathedral of Torcello—A.D. 1008.

one which is of the sixth century, work of the year 1008, and have so perfect an analogy with those of the S. Mark of Orseolo's time which we have already seen, as to make it quite useless to describe them. One alone differs, because it is an imitation of the sixth century, a very original capital of composite style, which has a row of very elegant little trees instead

of a lower row of leaves. Here, all the capitals of the nave are
crowned by low cymatia of red marble formed by a baton, a shell,
and a listel. On the cymatia rest the naked arches, the foot a
little raised, and this is the most ancient example in the lagoons
of those stilted arches which in the succeeding centuries formed
the delight of the Venetian architects.

FIG. 162.—Capital from the Naves of the Cathedral of Torcello - A.D. 1008.

Very well preserved and very precious is the front of the
chancels of the choir, formed by five intercolumns, the central
one of which is open and more spacious than the others, which
are closed instead by very rich and elegant square parapets.
The six columns of the chancel have rather heavy bases, formed
by a shell and a torus, which rest on a square plinth, the sides

of which present an enchasing going all round them in a concave semi-circle, a special characteristic of the Neo-Byzantine style. Among the upper capitals two are remarkable for fine intaglio and elegant composition. It is especially in a fifth parapet, which we find along the side chancels, that one can recognise the style of the richest of S. Mark, in the braids that frame it,

FIG. 163.—Parapet of the Cathedral of Torcello—A.D. 1008.

in the bush of acanthus at the base, in the central pine apple, and in the spirals forming curled up leaves and grapes, pecked at by birds. But in the four other parapets of the façade, though one recognises the same style and the same epoch, one is constrained to see the work of an artificer who left no sign of his chisel in S. Mark. They are, in all probability, the work of a Greek sculptor who came to the lagoons too late to be able to work in the Basilica Marciana, but in time to execute these

FIG. 164.—Parapet of the Cathedral of Torcello—A.D. 1008.

splendid parapets in the cathedral of Torcello. Their beautiful compositions, and the well-distributed spirals, rich in leaves and calixes and flowers of elegant *morbidezza*, are new to us. New.

too, is the conceit of those two peacocks, which climb up to peck at grain gathered in a vase, supported by a tall column; new is the technique used in the sculpture of the ugly lions, of the rabbits, of the birds, and above all of the big peacocks, which although treated with the utmost care and delicacy, yet do not equal the graceful and natural proportions of those of S. Mark, and much less the extraordinary elegance of that of S. Saviour of Brescia. New to us are also the ornamental motives of the framings, that is to say those original eggs of the baton, if we may so call them; those fasces with leaves agitated like flames, and, above all, that series of rings enclosing pretty rosettes. This last motive, being easy of execution and of sure effect, was much used by the Venetians of the following century, who availed themselves of it to adorn churches and palaces with friezes. But the same motive was also the favourite of those Byzantine artificers, who carved out in ivory certain elegant coffers, rich in representations of animals, or of struggling human beings, in pagan taste, but in which figures of saints seldom appeared.* These coffers were erroneously described as works of the Roman decadence, while they ought to be looked upon as fruit of the Neo-Byzantine art of the tenth and eleventh centuries. These parapets of Torcello and the sculptured stones of S. Mark bear witness to this.

Another parapet of this epoch is to be found in the basilica of Torcello, and comes most opportunely to prove a new error of those who take it, together with the above-mentioned coffers, for a Roman or pagan work. It is that symbolic-figurative bas-relief, mutilated and in fragments, that one sees enchased under the staircase of the present ambo. It is framed by hollowed mouldings, listels, and batons, enriched by cordons and braids, which acknowledge the Neo-Byzantine style; neverthless, the internal composition appeared to Filiasi and Selvatico to allude to the worship of Mercury, and to be a work of the sixth

* One sees them in several museums beyond the Alps, and in Italy, in those of Arezzo, Florence, Bologna, and Cividale. One of the most beautiful, preserved in the last-named city, was learnedly studied by Count Alvise Piero Zorzi, the illustrious director of that museum.

century. To Battaglini it seemed the figure of Fortune, a relic of paganism and of the edifices of Altino. But these figures breathe out the genius of the Greek artists who restored S. Mark and this cathedral. What, then, does it represent? One of the five figures is wanting, but I had the good fortune to find it two years ago among the fragments belonging to a marble-

FIG. 165.—Parapet of the Cathedral of Torcello—A.D. 1008.

worker in Venice, after its disappearance of so many centuries. The scene being thus completed, it was easy to understand that the semi-nude figure of a man on winged wheels which occupies the centre is neither Mercury nor Fortune, but the personification of Time—that time allotted by God to man that he may do good and combat his own bad passions. Such is the meaning suggested to me by the scales and the truncheon that he holds in his hands. On the right one sees the figure of an aged man who has let time pass away without profit. He is stroking his beard, but tears and grief await him in the form of a woman full of profound melancholy. On the left hand, by way of contrast, is sculptured a youth who seizes Time by the hair, and behind him a figure of Victory (which I recovered), with palm and crown, represents the joys of paradise reserved for him. The same intention and the same signification must belong to the Victory of the S. Mark of Orseolo, which so much resembles this of Torcello. From all this it follows that this composition, far from being a record of pagan scenes, aimed essentially at the synthesis of the Christian law, responding to the admonition of St. Paul: "*Dum tempus habemus, operemur bonum.*"

The cathedral of Torcello has preserved since 1008 important remains of the original ambo, which must have been placed within the precincts of the choir, flanked by two staircases after the antique fashion. It remained intact till the twelfth century, when, by reason of the repair of the presbytery, it was taken away and afterwards awkwardly replaced together with other marbles out of the enclosure, where it now remains. The curvilinear upper parapets, which originally must have been richer than those we now see, were used for the new ambo; but the four fine sides of the staircase were spoiled, being barbarously sawn asunder to serve as materials for the new construction. Then it was that the symbolic parapet, described above by me, lost the figure of Victory, which I afterwards found. In this mass of fragments with which the present ambo is grotesquely dressed up, the imagination of Ruskin conjured up nothing less than the haste and anxiety of the fugitives from Altino, who took refuge in Torcello in 641; and therefore regarded the fine sculptures as fruit of the fifth or the sixth century. On the contrary, they greatly resemble those stones of St. Mark's, in trapezoidal form, which are adorned, as we have seen, with symbolic archaic decorations. Here also we have the large frame of mouldings, enriched, moreover, with cordons, braids, leaves, and spindles. Here also there is an archaic symbolical figure in the field, which has the appearance of a lighted chandelier, with rows of spirals of vine-leaves at its base.

Among various other sculptures of 1008 contained in the church I will mention two little columns with graceful capitals which now stand in the episcopal cathedral; an elegant frieze that one sees beyond the meridional door together with other fragments, and the beautiful heading adorned with a vine-branch which crowns the principal door.

Torcello also preserves in its museums three important sculptures of Neo-Byzantine style of this epoch, and they are: a fragment of an arch of a ciborium adorned by a rude vase, out of which proceed spirals of vine-leaves, unique remains of a

Fig. 166.— Frieze of the Cathedral of Torcello—A.D. 1008.

ciborium of that time and of that style; a graceful framing of a little square window adorned with a shell in intaglio and with double dentels, with square fasces; and a sculptured stone (*formella*), arched rectangularly, framed by a baton of threaded leaves, and gracefully adorned by a tree with flowering branches, from which droop groups of curled leaves and bunches of grapes pecked by small birds. It is the most ancient sculptured stone of this species that I know, and the prototype of those of which, in the following centuries, together with the *pateræ*, they made so great a display on the façades of Venetian palaces.

MURANO.—A large stone in the same style (the largest that is preserved) may be seen at one extremity of the balcony which runs round the exterior of the apsis of the cathedral of Murano. Within a cornice formed of two rows of dentels, double and simple, separated by a baton, is a tree of luxuriant vegetation bearing roses and vine-leaves and grapes amid numerous birds. The nature of the foliage and the technique of the chisel, much assisted by drill-work, remind us of certain parapets of the basilica of S. Mark.

CAORLE.—The most remarkable construction that remains in the lagoon of the former half of the eleventh century is without doubt the cathedral of Caorle, built in 1038, and preserved almost intact. It is the most antique church of the Estuary, in which the old and severe basilical forms begin to yield to new and complicated forms. Nothing in this church causes one to suspect that Lombard art had helped in any way in its construction; yet its naves, instead of being divided by two simple rows of columns, are separated by columns alternated with pilasters, as had been the custom in Lombardy and other regions for more than half a century. For the rest, the cathedral of Caorle follows the traces of the usual basilicas with three naves, covered with wood and terminating in three apsides. The smaller ones do not project externally, and the largest is internally semi-circular, and externally polygonal. This detail is essentially characteristic of the Byzantine style; and the Byzantine hand also shows itself in the decorative accessories, such as the blind arcades of the wall of the apsis, and the cornice with fine thorny acanthus leaves, like those elsewhere described, that run round the imposts of the internal semi-basin. But perhaps several Venetian artificers worked in this cathedral together with a Greek one: so it would seem, judging from certain forms of capitals and the arches of the naves, in double rank, and with sharp semi-elliptic curves, which have their perfect counterparts in the Venetian church of S. John-the-Baptist, which we have seen was erected in 1007. With all that the capitals of the latter must yield to those of Caorle in variety and elegance of form and delicacy of execution; a circumstance owing, perhaps, to the progress made in Venetian art in the thirty-two years that divide them, or to the surveillance of a Greek master. They are always of Corinthian manner, with double caulicules and leaves of Greek character, and often of original form, crowned by cymatia much more expanded and higher than those of the cathedral of Torcello, and adorned with black incrustations of Byzantine design. It seems that we may attribute to the same period the curious belfry of Caorle, cylindrical like the very old ones of Ravenna, but covered by a cone, and adorned half way up by a false arched gallery supported by columns, and above by a saw-tooth frieze of Venetian-Byzantine character.

PADUA.—The Neo-Byzantine style of this first period has left its traces in Padua also. In one of the cloisters of the convent of S. Antonio is to be seen a sarcophagus of the fourteenth

FIG. 167.—Sarcophagus in a Cloister of the Convent of S. Antonio at Padua—Parapet sculptured about the year 1000.

century containing the ashes of a certain Guido da Lozzo. For the front a whole Byzantine parapet has been used, sculptured without doubt towards the year 1000, and for the sides two fragments of a second parapet like the preceding one. It is decorated by three arches with an intaglio of graceful leaflets, sustained by columns, and enclosing, in the centre, a simple monogram of the Saviour in a wreath tied with ribbons, borne up by the claws of an eagle with spread wings ; at each side is a vase, from out of which the symbolic vine arises, rich in leaves, grape-bunches, and vine-branches. The coarse technique, especially of the intaglio of the leaves, the wreath and the capitals, makes one suspect that the artificer was one of those who worked under Pietro Orseolo in S. Mark.

I also recognise the Neo-Byzantine style in the famous church of S. Sophia in Padua, a church that I believe to have been founded in the former half of the eleventh century, and not, as Ricci, Selvatico, and Dartein supposed, in the sixth or the ninth. Only the two lower stages of its vast and very original apsis * date from this epoch. Dartein without sufficient reason judged it to be a portion of a rotunda, but in my opinion it was, as it is at present, the end of a basilica, the minor naves of which turned around the apsis of the chief nave, exactly as in S. Stephen of Verona, which, as we observed before, belongs to the preceding century. S. Sophia was, from its origin, of basilical forms, as we may see by the niches of the lower part of its façade, which are absolutely like those of the great apsis. In it the central niche originally projected at the outside in a circular form, and only in the twelfth century was it changed to its present appearance. Perhaps even then the naves were divided by columns alternated with pilasters, like those of the cathedral of Caorle, and as they must have been in the following century. Certain coarse friezes and capitals on which crosses, caulicules, palms, and symbolic animals are sculptured, show the native chisels; but the profusion of niches and blind arches, certain fine cornices, and a Corinthian-like capital with accurate foliage of thorny acanthus, show the mind and the hand of a Greek artist.†

* Dartein has directed attention neither in his drawings nor his writings to the very marked character of the difference between the superior stage of the extremity of this apsis, formed of an arched gallery reposing on piedroits, and the two inferior stages. Whilst the latter are curvilinear, the former is polygonal. This difference is further increased by the regularity presented by the superior arcades in contrast to the embarrassed and even clumsy disposition of the inferior ones, by their imposing aspect, and by the variety of the archivolts. In a word, the superior gallery, while evincing the last influence of the Byzantine style which was implanted in Venetia during the second half of the eleventh century, proves that it must have been added at the time of the restoration of 1123.

† Several other capitals, in the style of the blunted cube, ornamented with beautiful leaves of wild acanthus, certain edicules in the centre of the church, and certain cornices of varied style, are so many Byzantine works of 1123.

AQUILEIA.—But where the beneficent rays of Neo-Byzantine art did not reach, the native art, even towards the middle of the eleventh century, remained still rude and almost barbarous, like that of the ninth century. This is clearly demonstrated by the cathedral of Aquileia, erected by the patriarch Popone between 1019 and 1025. It is a vast basilica, perhaps reconstructed on the foundations of one of the fourth century, as is proved by its plan, which is analogous to that of the Constantian basilicas of Rome, with transept and such large minor naves as to make one believe that they must originally have been subdivided. The patriarch Popone in rebuilding it reduced it to only three naves, prolonged the arms of the cross by constructing two apsidal chapels, and raised the sanctuary by many steps in order to hollow out a crypt under it, as was the custom of his time. The earthquake of 1348 very much damaged this basilica, so that its naves had to be rebuilt; and then it was that acute arches were planted on the old columns, and that the ranges of pillars of the transept, and the heads of the colonnades as well as the roof, were transformed into the same style. Notwithstanding all this, the basilica lost nothing of its importance, still keeping intact the columns of the ninth century with their bases and capitals, and, in the wings of the transept, even the original arches, which are semi-circular and planted on a high cushion, like those of the churches of Ravenna and Istria of the sixth century. Like the rugged bases and the dwarfed rough shafts of the columns, their Corinthian capitals also demonstrate the barbarous ways of those who built the church, adorned as they are with heavy leafage badly carved, and caulicules not a whit better than the sculptures of the ninth century. This enduring barbarism is seen still more plainly in the capitals of the crypt, with their intaglio of caulicules, palm-leaves, and tiny arcades so ruggedly treated that they seem to be from the same chisels that worked for Pope Adrian 1. at Rome. Indeed, one of the chapels

FIG. 168.—Capital of the Crypt of the Cathedral of Aquileia—A.D.1019-1025.

of the transept still preserves its original and almost intact chancels, whose rich bas-reliefs in knotwork and animals are so coarse, that certain writers, such as Mothes, Selvatico, and many others, took them for works of the eighth century. But in my opinion they err, not having observed, first, that the same roughness of detail prevails throughout the basilica; secondly, that those chancels were evidently executed expressly for the chapel that they enclose; and lastly, that the many braidings with which they are covered are formed with ribbons, not channelled with equi-distant furrows to imitate withes, like those of the eighth century, but by two incisions along their margins, precisely in the Greek manner of the ninth century, which we saw introduced into the lagoons in the time of the Partecipazi. As the influence of the Greek work in Grado executed by order of the patriarch John the Younger appears clearly in these parapets, we must exclude the possibility of an earlier origin for them.

The Romanic origin of the cathedral of Aquileia is also confirmed by the baptistery which rises before it, and which, like that of the fourth or fifth century, is square outside and inwardly octagonal, with four great niches. It is detached from the front of the basilica, sufficiently to yield space for a quadriportico even larger than that of Parenzo; and I do not doubt that once there was one. But, in the eleventh century, it was not reconstructed, for Popone limited himself to a three-sided atrium corresponding only to the larger nave, supported by pillars and columns, on the headings and capitals of which (here also charged with high entablements) the same rugged chisel appears, and the same barbarous motives of the capitals and the internal parapets. Perhaps in the second half of the eleventh century this atrium was attached to the baptistery by means of a large corridor in two floors, covered with cross-vaults and by a cupola, and having its walls pierced by large niches — forms that denote an

FIG. 169.—Capital of the Atrium of the Cathedral of Aquileia—A.D. 1019-1025.

artistic progress and the influence of the Veneto-Byzantine style.

If we now set out from Aquileia to Istria, without forgetting the cathedral of Popone, we shall see that it was the prototype of several churches erected along the shores of that peninsula, churches that belonged to the latter part of the eleventh century, and therefore had advantages in art over their model of Aquileia. But that would take me far from the programme that I proposed to myself, and which I trust has been sufficiently fulfilled, even though my researches must here be stayed. The result of these researches, as no one can deny, has overthrown the old history of the monuments of the centuries which we have observed; but will their latest consequences link themselves exactly, and accord with the commonly accepted history of Art in Italy after the end of the tenth century? I doubt it, and have reason to believe firmly that a study of the monuments later than that date, an ample, profound, minute study, free from preconception and party prejudices, would lead to results so unexpected and new as to change the aspect even of the history of our Romanic art. Such a theme has for me such seductive attractions that, if life and means should be granted me, it would be very difficult to escape the temptation of making it the subject of my future studies and of a new book.

APPENDIX.

Of Cordero I have spoken in the text. I give herewith my own appreciation of the works of the other authors there cited.

"*Storia dell' Architettura in Europa dal sec. IV. al XVIII.,*" per A. Ricci. The author belongs to the old Agincourt school. He has evidently seen no light in the midst of the barbarous ages, and is much more diffuse about their civil than about their artistic history, which he treats in an extremely superficial manner.

"*Monuments de l'Architecture Chrétienne depuis Constantin jusqu'à Charlemagne,*" par Henri Hübsch, 1860. In this remarkable work Hübsch shows himself an attentive observer, sufficiently exempt from the prejudices of the old school, and perhaps of all these writers he is the most independent; but this fact did not prevent him from forging fresh prejudices for himself which shackled him in his path. For him, for instance, Christian Architecture of the first five centuries has the same origin, the same nature and physiognomy, in the East as in the West; so that he finds it useless to call it by different names, and therefore denies the existence of the Byzantine style, and, consequently, its influence on Art in Italy during the fifth and sixth centuries—an error which often makes him see one thing for another, or at least leads him to points of interrogation. For the rest, he was incapable of throwing the least light on the artistic history of the barbarous ages, showing that he did not know the greater part of the monuments of this epoch even by sight.

"*Étude sur l'Architecture lombarde,*" par F. de Dartein. This voluminous work, very valuable for all that it contains regarding the monuments of Lombard architecture in Northern Italy, and the acumen with which the nature and character of this style is studied and analysed, is, on the other hand, utterly useless for what concerns its origin. Dartein is certainly not of the old school, but he could not escape far from it, and therefore maintained confusion and darkness in the artistic history of the barbarous ages and gave unknown sources to Lombard Art, and a development illogically precocious, succeeded by an equally impossible immobility.

"*Le Arti del Disegno in Italia — Storia e critica,*" per Pietro Selvatico. Parte II., Vallardi, 1880. This illustrious writer, who had opened his career as Art historian in 1847, by publishing his well-known work on architecture and sculpture in Venice, which, if not quite free from errors (very pardonable in a first work), at least gave great hope for the future, showed in his last work, which his death prevented him from finishing, that in the long period of thirty years he had scarcely made any progress in that species of study. In this work he had proposed to himself to handle the artistic history of the ages of decadence in an original manner; but in substance he only followed in the footsteps of Dartein and others, adding very little of his own. The result is a work whose poverty and confusion of erudition, incredible contradictions, multitudinous and blameworthy errors and inexactitudes, make it desirable for the sake of his good fame that it had never been written.

Selvatico's chief fault, one inveterate and widely spread, especially in Italy, was that of frequently describing the monuments not on the spot, but at his own desk; not with photographs before him, but ugly and inexact engravings; not after notes, even old ones, taken by himself before the original, but too often after such imperfect descriptions of our things as are given every now and then by certain foreigners on the other side of the Alps. In glancing over Selvatico's last work, the attentive and intelligent reader will be astonished to find him contented with so little, with nearly nothing, in fact, when he ought to descend into the pettiest details and the most minute research; and he will not be able to explain this defect without attributing to the author a great amount of carelessness or laziness.

To all those, and they are many, whose absolute emptiness of personal opinion makes them accept avidly and blindly, like the manna that rained on the Hebrews, all that a man known to fame says or prints, these expressions of mine will certainly seem exaggerated, malignant, and self-conceited: they will seem otherwise to those who do not stop here, but will have the patience to follow me through the long course of these pages and the future ones on S. Mark's Church at Venice, where (not for the pleasure of making of the ruin of others a footstool for myself, but for pure love of truth) I shall, much against my will, be constrained to point out many of the infinity of errors committed by Selvatico.

"*Storia dell' Arte Christiana dal I. secolo all' VIII.,*" per R. Garrucci. The author therein wrote some remarkable pages on the monuments of the early centuries, but became exceedingly superficial and quite lost his road when touching on the works of the Lombard era.

"*Die Baukunst des Mittelalters in Italien*," von Oscar Mothes. Iena, Herman Costenoble, 1882-84. If Mothes, in writing the history of the architecture of these ages of decadence, had not erred in following the tracks of the old writers, he would have given in this work the amplest and most orderly history of the mediæval monuments of Italy. It is useless to say that he scattered over the centuries anterior to the eleventh a great quantity of works that belong to the eleventh and following centuries, and that he gave himself much useless trouble. Nevertheless, he often showed himself a good connoisseur of the products of the art of the fifth and sixth centuries, that is to say, of that proto-Byzantine art that flourished in Italy during the Gothic domination; but he, like a good German, would have it that the Goths themselves brought to Italy many of these elements, and this is a gross error. Let us add that several drawings offered by him to the reader are full of frightful falsehood: he invents monuments that do not exist, creates ideal ruins, and widens, lengthens, and complicates at pleasure the plans of certain churches!!! On the other hand, he may be profitably consulted by the studious for the dates of constructions, restorations, and rebuildings of monuments which he has collected and published with the greatest care.

"*La Messe: Études archéologiques sur ses Monuments*," par Rohault de Fleury. Paris. Rohault de Fleury is, of all the above-named authors, the one who, in his valuable volumes, has enumerated the greatest number of works of art belonging to the barbarous ages, and is also the one who, in fixing their epoch, has stumbled less frequently than the others. Perhaps he might have avoided several gross errors, and found the right road, if, before setting himself to search for specialities (chiefly decorative) which were to assist his work, he had thoroughly studied the various architectonic monuments about whose history he pronounces no opinion.

INDEX OF THE MONUMENTS
DESCRIBED OR MENTIONED IN THIS VOLUME, AND OF THE CITIES OR PLACES WHERE THEY MAY BE FOUND.

A.

		PAGE
ADRIA .	. Bocchi Museum . . .	128
"	Church of the Sepulchre . . .	128
AIN-SULTAN (¹) . . .	. Fragments of Christian Sculpture	91
AIX (²) (in Provence) .	Cloister of S. Saviour	164
AIX-LA-CHAPELLE (³)	Rotunda of Charlemagne 218
ALBENGA . .	Baptistery of the Cathedral	155–56
ALLIATE . . .	. . Parish Church . . . 102 (in note), 232, 256 (et seq.)
"	Baptistery . . . . 232, 258 (et seq.)
ANCONA .	. . Church of the Misericordia . . . 96
" . .	Cathedral	197
" . . .	. Church of S. Maria-in-Piazza .	303
AQUILEIA .	. Church of S. Felix .	62
"	. Baptistery .	76
"	Cathedral	342
ARBE . .	. . . Cathedral	215
ARLES (⁴)	. Museum	164
ARSAGO .	. Baptistery	. 242
ATHENS	Tower of the Winds .	64
"	. Old Cathedral . . .	85
"	Church of S. Luke	293
"	. Museum . .	295

B.

BAGNACAVALLO . .	S. Peter's Church, called the Pieve—	
	128 (et seq.), 241, 260, 264
BAQUOZA (⁵) .	. . Church . . .	94
BEHIOH (⁶)	Church	89
BENEVENTO	. . Cloister of S. Sophia .	163
BERGAMO . .	. . Sozzi Museum . . .	142
BIELLA . .	. . Baptistery	260

(¹) Mauritania. (²) France. (³) Prussia. (⁴) France. (⁵) Syria. (⁶) Syria.

		PAGE
BOLOGNA .	Tomb of the Foscherari	133
„	. Church of SS. Peter & Paul, near S. Stephen	134 (et seq.)
„	. . Museum	303
BRESCIA	. . . Old Summer Cathedral	62
„	. Old Winter Cathedral or Rotunda . . 142 (et seq.),	217
„	. S. Saviour's Church . . . . 212 (et seq.)	
„	Christian Museum . .	150
BUDRIO	. Marble Cross . .	205

C.

CAPUA . .	Fieramosca Palace	162
„ . . .	. Campano Museum	162, 194
„	. S. Michael's Church . .	195
CAORLE .	. Cathedral	338
„ . .	. Belfry	339
CARTHAGE . .	. Christian Ruins	91
CATTARO	Cathedral . . .	216
CÉRISY-LA-FORÊT([1])	Abbatial Church	. . 270
CIMITILE	Church of S. Felix	93
CIVIDALE . .	. Baptistery	104
„	Church of S. Martin	108 (et seq.)
„	. . . Church of S. Maria-in-Valle	114 (et seq.)
„	Museum	. . . 118
„	. Cathedral	209
COMO	Church of S. Abbondio . .	220
CONCORDIA . . .	. Baptistery	123
CORNETO .	Church of S. Maria di Castello	49 (in note)

F.

FERENTILLO . .	. Abbatial Church	. . 102
FERRARA .	University	131
FLORENCE .	. . . Baptistery	59 60 (in note)
„	. Church of the Holy Apostles	. 199
„	. Church of S. Miniato . .	266

G.

GRADO .	Cathedral . . . . 60 (et seq.), 123–4, 281 (et seq.),	291
„	. Baptistery	. 65, 282
„	Church of S. Maria . .	66
GROTTAFERRATA . .	. Church	99

([1]) Africa.

J.

		PAGE
JERUSALEM ([1])	. . . Church of Calvary . .	. 50, 286
„	. . . Sepulchres of Judah .	89
„	. . . Mosque of Omar	167
JESOLO	Cathedral . . .	313
JOUARRE ([2])	. . . . Church of S. Paul . . .	164

K.

KOKANAYA ([3])	Sarcophagus	89
KHARBET-EL BEIDA ([4]) Ancient Castle		89
KALAT-SEM'AN ([5]) . .	Church of S. Simon the Stylite .	. 171, 241

L.

LIBARNA	. Fragments of Stucco	. 155
LUCCA .	Church of S. Frediano	55-6
„	„ S. Michael-in-the-Forum	. 55-6

M.

MILAN	Archæological Museum . . .	. . . 137-141
„	. . . . . Church of S. Vincent-in-Prato	141-2, 249-53
„	„ S. Ambroise . . .	. . . 223-48
„	„ S. Satyrus	. . 252-3, 253-6
„	„ S. Nazairo	. 242
„	„ S. Lawrence . .	. . 242
„	. . . . . Chapel of S. Aquiline	. . 242
„	. . . . . Church of S. Calimero . .	. . 248
„	„ S. Eustace	. 264-5
„	„ S. Celso	. . 269-70
MODENA .	Cathedral	. . . 132
MONSELICE	. Public Museum . .	. . . 127
MONZA	Cathedral .	. 57 (et seq.)
MOUDJELEIA ([7])	. . A House	89
MOUNT S. MICHAEL ([6]) Abbatial Church		270
MUGGIA VECCHIA .	. Church of S. Maria	210
MURANO . . .	Public Museum	. 312
„	. . . . Cathedral . .	. . 311

N.

NARNI (Environs of) .	Church of S. Oreste . . .	160
NOLA	Basilica of S. Paul	66

([1]) Palestine. ([2]) France. ([3]) Dalmatia. ([4]) Syria.
([5]) Syria. ([6]) France. ([7]) Algeria.

		PAGE
NONA .	Church of S. Croce (Holy Cross)	215
NOVARA . .	. Baptistery	242
NOVEGRADI .	Parapet	216

O.

ORLÉANSVILLE ([1]) .	. Ruins of a Church .	91
ORVIETO	Museum	197
OSIMO .	. Epitaph of Bishop Vitalianus .	. . 157
OSSERO .	Church . . .	215

P.

PADUA	. Museum	. . . 208
,,	Church of S. Sophia . . .	. 212, 340
,,	. ,, S. Anthony	. 339
,, .	. . Cloister of S. Anthony .	 339
PARENZO	. . . Cathedral	38, 62, 68, 210
,,	. . . Baptistery	. . . 76
PAVIA . .	. Church of S. Michael .	. 217 (in note)
,,	Palazzo Malaspina	154
,, . .	. . Church of S. Maria delle Caccie .	 155
PERUGIA	Church of S. Angelo . .	. 38 (in note)
,,	. Museum . . .	. 157–8
PISA	Cathedral	. 198–9
POLA ([2]) .	. Church of S. Maria Formosa of Canneto	. . . 68, 214
,,	. Museum . .	. . 118–214
,,	. Cathedral	. 214
,, ...	. Baptistery . . .	. . . 214
PORTO (Tiberino)	. . Lateran Museum	178

R.

RAGUSA .	. Church of S. Stephen . .	. . . 216
RAVENNA .	Baptistery of Ursiano.	38, 128, 211
,,	. Belfries	. 255
,,	Cathedral	. . 33, 46
,,	. Mausoleum of Galla Placidia .	. 33–4, 260
,,	,, Theodoric .	260
,,	. Museum of the Archbishop	200
,,	,, of Classe	. 201
,,	. Palazzo Rasponi . .	. 29, 204
,,	Church of S. Agatha	260
,,	,, S. Apollinaris-in-Classe—	
	31–5, 64, 68, 73, 199 (et seq.)	
	SS. John and Paul	28–9

([1]) Algeria.　　　　　　　　　　([2]) Austria.

			PAGE
RAVENNA	. . . . .	Church of S. John the Evangelist .	38, 61
,,	. .	,, S. Peter Major (S. Francis)	. 241
,,	. .	,, the Holy Spirit	201, 261
,,	. . . .	,, S. Vitale	32, 38, 68
,,	. . . .	,, S. Victor	241, 260, 264
,,	. . . .	Little Tomb of Bracciaforte	205
ROME	. . . . . .	Mediaeval Belfries	172 (in note)
,,	. . . . .	Cloister of the Lateran	177
,,	. . . . .	,, S. Laurence-beyond-the-Walls	. 193
,,	. . . . .	Roman Forum	190–1
,,	. . . . .	Office of the Ministry of Agriculture, Industry, and Commerce	192
	. . . .	Artistic-Industrial Museum	161, 191, 192
	. . . . .	Lateran Museum	178, 188
	. . . . .	Palace of the Cæsars	191
	. . . . .	Ponte Salario	45
	. . . . .	Church of S. Agnes-beyond-the-Walls . . .	53, 189
	. . . . . .	,, the Holy Apostles	189
	. . . . . .	,, S. Cecilia in Trastevere . . . 54 (in note), 189
	. . . . . .	,, S. Clement on the Cælins . . . 39–41, 188
	. . . . . .	,, S. George-in-Velabro . . . 41, 48, 55, 187
	. . . . . .	,, S. John at the Latin Gate	192
	. . . . . .	,, SS. John and Paul	48
	. . . . . .	,, S. John Lateran	67
	. . . . . .	,, S. Laurence-beyond-the-Walls— 41, 46 (et seq.), 193
,,	. . . . .	,, S. Laurence-in-Lucina	176–7
,,	. . . . .	,, S. Maria-in-Ara Cœli	192
,,	. . . . .	,, S. Maria-in-Cosmedin	170, 176
,,	. . . . .	,, S. Maria-in-Domnica . .	. 188
,,	. . . . .	,, S. Maria-in-Trastevere	185, 189
,,	. . . . .	,, S. Praxedis	41, 67, 181, 183
,,	. . . . .	,, SS. Quattro Coronati	189
,,	. . . . .	,, S. Saba	43–4, 174–5
,,	. . . . .	,, S. Sabina	45, 184
,,	. . . . .	,, S. Stephen Rotunda	36–8, 52
,,	. . . . .	,, SS. Vincent and Anastasius	177
ROVEIHA (¹)	. . . .	Church	94

S.

SAFA	. . . . . .	Ancient Castle	89
S. GEORGE OF VALPO-LICELLA	. . . .	Church	97–102

(¹) Syria.

			PAGE
S. ANGELO IN FORMIS	Church	. . . .	163
S. HILARY (Venetian)	. Abbatial Church		276
SERDJILLA (¹) . . .	. . A House		89
SOUEIDEH (²) . .	. . Church		171
SPALATRO . . .	. . Baptistery	. . .	216
SPOLETO	. Belfry of the Cathedral		158, 197
„	. . Communal *Pinacoteca*		158–9
„ . . .	. . Church of S. Saviour		160 (in note)
„ . . .	. . Temple of Clitumnus	. .	160 (in note)

T.

THESSALONICA (³) .	Church of S. Demetrius	.	68
TORCELLO .	. . Cathedral		73, 75, 309
„ .	. . Baptistery		75–6
„	. . . . Church of S. Fosca		311
„	. . . . Provincial Museum		119, 311
„	. . . . Museum of the Estuary		311, 337
TURIN . . .	. . . Palace of the Towers		56
TOSCANELLA .	. Church of S. Maria Major		196
TREVES (⁴) .	. Gate of the City		56
TREVISO . .	. . . Museum		118, 209
„	. . . . Cathedral		209
TRIESTE	. Cathedral		118
„ . . .	. . Winckelmann Museum		210

V.

VENASQUE .	. . . Church of the Minims		164
VENICE . .	Church of S. Mark . 70, 83 (et seq.), 285 (et seq.), 336		
„	„ S. Zachariah		279, 303
„	„ SS. John and Paul		71, 296
„	„ S. Gregory (Cloister)		297
„	„ the Virgins		326
„	„ S. John-the-Baptist		325–6
„	„ del Carmine		298
„	„ S. Euphemia at Giudecca		325
„	„ S. Augustine		120
„	. . . . . Bembo Palace on the Grand Canal		298, 326
„	. . . . . Da Mosto Palace on the Grand Canal		298
„	. . . Malipieri Palace at S. Samuel		327
„	. . . . . House in the Calle Lunga S. Simeon piccolo . .		296
„	. . . . . „ on the Rio del Beccarie (Quay of the Shambles)		298
	. . . . . . „ ex Favretto on the Grand Canal		298

(¹) Syria.   (²) Syria.   (³) Asia Minor.   (⁴) Germany.

			PAGE
VENICE	. . . . . .	House near the Prefecture on the Grand Canal	298
"	. . . . .	" on Ponte Widmann at S. Canciano . .	326
"	. . . .	" at Ponte Storto S. Apollinaris . . .	326
"	. .	" Corte del Milione at S. John Chrysostom .	326
"	. . . .	Houses on the Riva del Carbon . . .	298
"	. . . .	Corte Battagia ai Birri	304
"	. . .	Museum of the Ducal Palace	72, 307
"	. . . .	Civic Museum 121, 277, 297–8, 307
"	. . . .	Patriarchal Seminary	307
"	. . . .	State Record Office at the Frari	297, 301
"	. . . .	Well-mouth in possession of the Chevalier Guggenheim	121, 305
"	. . . .	Depôt of Signor Marcato	304, 306
"	. . . . .	" Signor Dorigo	120
"	. . . . .	Ponte della Frescada at S. Thomas	121
"	. . .	Door of the Arsenal	326
VERONA	. . . .	Cathedral of S. Maria Matricolare	205
"	. . . . .	Church of S. John-in-Fonte	206
"	. . . .	" S. Stephen . .	125, 206-7, 274
"	. .	" S. John-in-Valle . . .	207
"	. . . .	" S. Maria-in-Organo . . .	207
"	. . . .	" S. Teuteria	125
"	. . .	" S. Zeno Major	207
"	. .	Lapidary Museum	97
"	. . .	Archæological Museum	125
"	. . .	Gates of the City	56
VICENZA	. . . .	Museum	127
"	. . . .	Palazzo Orgian	127
"	. . . .	Church of SS. Felix and Fortunatus .	266
VILLANOVA (Veronese).	Church	208
VOGHENZA	. . . .	Fragments now in the University of Ferrara . .	131

Z.

ZARA	. . . . . .	Church of S. Donato	216
"	. . . . .	Museum	216

INDEX OF THE MONUMENTS

STUDIED IN THIS VOLUME
ACCORDING TO THEIR CLASS AND CHRONOLOGY.

CHURCHES

STILL EXISTING WHOLLY OR IN PART.

		CENTURY	FIG.	PAGE
ROME	S. Stephen-on-the-Cœlius	V	6	37
„	S. Laurence-beyond-the-Walls	VI	9, 10	47, 53
GRADO	Cathedral	VI	12, 13	61, 65
„	S. Maria	VI	14, 15	66, 69
ROME	S. Agnes-beyond-the-Walls	VII		53, 189
„	S. George-in-Velabro	VII		41, 48, 55, 187
TORCELLO	Cathedral	VII	156	308
VALPOLICELLA	S. George	VIII	30	101
VERONA	S. Teuteria	VIII	48	126
BRESCIA	S. Saviour	VIII	61-68	144-52
PAVIA	S. Maria-delle-Caccie	VIII	70	154
ROME	S. Maria-in-Cosmedin	VIII	80-82	171-4
„	S. Saba	VIII	83	175
„	S. Praxedis	IX	87-89	180-2
„	S. Maria-in-Domnica	IX	90, 91	183-4
„	S. Cecilia	IX		54-189
„	S. Mark	IX		185
CAPUA	S. Michael	IX	100	194
S. HILARY	Abbey	IX		276-7
VENICE	S. Mark	IX	139-146	288-94
„	S. Zachariah	IX		279-303
TORCELLO	Cathedral	IX	156, 157	73, 308, 310
	S. Fosca	IX		311

		CENTURY	FIG.	PAGE
MILAN	S. Ambroise . . .	IX	117–122	230–45
„	. . S. Vincent in Prato	IX	123, 124	250–1
„	. . S. Satyrus . .	IX	125–127	254–6
„	. S. Calimero	IX		248
„ . .	S. Eustace . . .	IX	133	266
ALLIATE . .	. Parish Church	IX	128–130	257–9
MILAN .	S. Celso	X		269
VICENZA .	. . . SS. Felix and Fortunato . .	X	134, 135	268–9
VERONA .	S. Stephen	X	136	271
VENICE	. . S. John the Baptist .	XI		325–6
TORCELLO	Cathedral	XI	Frontispiece and 161-166	330–7
CAORLE	. Cathedral . .	XI		338
PADUA .	. S. Sophia	XI		340
AQUILEIA	. Cathedral	XI	168, 169	341–2

DOORS AND PORTICOS.

		CENTURY	FIG.	PAGE
SYRIA	. Churches, Houses, and Castles	VI or VII	21–24	86–89
CIMITILE	S. Felix	VIII	27	93
ROME	. . S. Clement-on-the-Cœlius .	IX	91	189
ALLIATE . . .	Parish Church	IX		258
TORCELLO	Cathedral .	IX		75
VENICE . .	S. Mark . . .	IX	139	288
AQUILEIA	. . . Cathedral . .	XI	169	242

PRESBYTERIAL CRYPTS.

		CENTURY	FIG.	PAGE
BRESCIA	S. Saviour	VIII	63, 64, 68	147–8, 152
„	. . Rotunda	VIII	112, 113	219, 220
VENICE .	. S. Mark	IX		285
MILAN .	. . . . S. Vincent-in-Prato . . .	IX		252
ALLIATE.	Parish Church . . .	IX	129	258
CAPUA .	. . S. Michael	IX	101	195
VENICE . .	S. Zachariah .	IX or X		279

PRESBYTERIAL CHANCELS.
(PARAPETS, LITTLE PILASTERS, FRIEZES, ETC.)

		CENTURY	FIG.	PAGE
ROME	. S. Clement-on-the-Cœlius .	VI	8	42
„	. . S. Maria-in-Cosmedin .	VI		170
MONZA . . .	. . S. John	VII	11	59

		CENTURY	FIG.	PAGE
VENICE . . .	S. Mark	VII	18	83
ATHENS	Old Cathedral	VIII	19	85
CIMITILE	S. Felix	VIII	28	94
CIVIDALE	Cathedral	VIII	35	106
,, ...	S. Maria-in-Valle .	VIII	38, 39	114-5
TORCELLO	Provincial Museum	VIII	41	117
VENICE	S. Augustine	VIII	42	119
,, ...	Depot of Signor Dorigo .	VIII		120
MONSELICE	Communal Museum . .	VIII	49	127
VERONA	Archaeological Museum	VIII		125
VICENZA . . .	Museum	VIII		127
BRESCIA	Christian Museum . . .	VIII	65, 67	150-2
MILAN	Museum of Brera .	VIII	58	141
ALBENGA	Baptistery	VIII	72	156
FERRARA . . .	University	VIII	52	132
MODENA	Cathedral	VIII		133
SPOLETO	Belfry of the Cathedral . .	VIII	74	159
NARNI	S. Oreste	VIII		160
VILLANOVA	Church of S. Peter . . .	VIII	108	208
ROME	Holy Apostles	IX		189
,, ...	S. Maria-in-Trastevere . .	IX	93 a-c	186-7
,, ...	S. Mark	IX		185
,, ...	S. Maria-in-Ara Cœli . .	IX		192
,, ...	S. Agnes-beyond-the-Walls	IX	95	190
,, ...	S. Saba	IX		175
,, ...	SS. Quattro Coronati . .	IX		189
,, ...	S. John Lateran . . .	IX		178
,, ...	S. Sabina	IX	92	181
,, ...	S. George-in-Velabro . .	IX		187
,, ...	S. Clement-on-the-Cœlius .	IX		188
,, ...	S. Laurence-beyond-the-Walls	IX		193
,, ...	Lateran Museum . . .	IX		161
,, ...	Roman Forum	IX		190
CAPUA	Campano Museum	IX	99	194
TOSCANELLA . . .	S. Maria Major . . .	IX		196
ASSISI	S. Maria-of-the-Angels . .	IX	102	197
SPOLETO	Belfry of the Cathedral . .	IX		197
ORVIETO	Museum	IX		197
ANCONA . .	Cathedral . .	IX		197
PISA	Cathedral .	IX		198
RAVENNA . . .	Museum . .	IX		201
TREVISO	Museum	IX		209

		CENTURY	FIG.	PAGE
CIVIDALE . . .	Cathedral	IX		209
TRIESTE	Winckelmann Museum	IX		210
MUGGIA VECCHIA .	S. Maria	IX		210
POLA	Cathedral . .	IX		211
„	Museum	IX		214
„ . .	S. Maria Formosa (or of the Canneto)	IX		214
OSSERO	Parish Church	IX		215
NOVEGRADI	Parish Church .	IX		216
ZARA . .	Museum .	IX		216
SPALATRO . . .	Baptistery	IX		216
RAGUSA	S. Stephen . . .	IX		216
COMO .	S. Abbondio .	IX	114	221
MILAN . .	S. Ambroise	IX	119	236
GRADO	Cathedral . . .	IX	137	283
VENICE .	S. Mark	IX	140-144	290-1
„	S. Gregory	IX		297
„ . . .	SS. John and Paul	IX		296
„	Civic Museum	IX		297
„	Houses in Calle lunga S. Simeon	IX		296
CONSTANTINOPLE .	Church of the Theotocos .	IX	148-151	296-7
„	Museum	IX	147	295
ATHENS	Museum . .	IX	153	299
„	Old Cathedral	IX		85
BOLOGNA	Civic Museum	IX		303
ANCONA . .	S. Maria-in-Piazza . . .	IX		303
TORCELLO . . .	Cathedral	IX	157	310
„	Provincial Museum . . .	IX		311
„ . . .	Museum of the Estuary . .	IX		311
MURANO .	Cathedral	IX		312
„	Communal Museum . . .	IX		312
CONCORDIA	Baptistery	IX		313
VICENZA . .	SS. Felix and Fortunatus .	X		267
VENICE .	S. Mark	X	159	321
PADUA	Cloister of S. Anthony . .	X	167	339
TORCELLO	Cathedral . . .	XI	163-166	332-7
AQUILEIA . .	Cathedral . .	XI	168, 169	341-2

AMBOS.

		CENTURY	FIG.	PAGE
RAVENNA	SS. John and Paul	VI	1	28
„	Rasponi Palace . .	VI	2	30

		CENTURY	FIG.	PAGE
ANCONA	Church of the Misericordia	VII		96
VALPOLICELLA	S. George	VIII		99
GRADO	Cathedral	VIII	46	121
CONCORDIA	Baptistery	VIII		123
FERRARA	University	VIII		131
MODENA	Cathedral	VIII		132
BRESCIA	S. Saviour	VIII	66	151
VENICE	S. Mark	X		319
TORCELLO	Cathedral	XI		336

CIBORIA.

		CENTURY	FIG.	PAGE
ROME	S. Clement-on-the-Coelius	VI	7	39
AIN SULTAN	Christian Ruins	VII		91
VALPOLICELLA	S. George	VIII	29	98
CIVIDALE	S. Maria-in-Valle (?)	VIII	40	116
„	Museum	VIII		118
BAGNACAVALLO	Pieve	VIII	50, 51	129–30
BOLOGNA	Piazza of Dominic	VIII	53	133
ALBENGA	Baptistery	VIII	72	156
PERUGIA	Museum	VIII		157
ROME	Lateran Museum	IX	86	178
„	S. Maria-in-Trastevere	IX		185
„	S. Maria Major	IX		189
„	S. Maria-in-Ara Coeli	IX		192
TOSCANELLA	S. Maria Major	IX		196
RAVENNA	S. Apollinaris-in-Classe	IX	104, 106	202–4
„	Holy Spirit	IX		204
ARBE	Cathedral	IX		215
CATTARO	Cathedral	IX	111	217
MILAN	S. Ambroise	IX	122	245
GRADO	S. Maria	IX	138	281
MURANO	Cathedral	IX		312
„	Communal Museum	IX		312
TORCELLO	Museum of the Estuary	X		337

ALTARS.

		CENTURY	FIG.	PAGE
ORLEANSVILLE	Christian Ruins	VII	26	91
FERENTILLO	Abbey	VIII		102
CIVIDALE	S. Martin	VIII	37	109
„	S. Maria-in-Valle (?)	VIII		114

			CENTURY	FIG.	PAGE
PERUGIA	. . .	Museum . . .	VIII		158
COMO	. . . .	. S. Abbondio	IX	115	222
MILAN		S. Ambroise .	IX		224

EPISCOPAL SEES.

			CENTURY	FIG.	PAGE
RAVENNA .	. . . .	. Cathedral .	VI		34
VENICE .	. .	. . S. Mark . .	VII		70
PARENZO .	. . .	. Cathedral .	IX		38
MILAN	. . . . .	S. Ambroise .	IX	120	237

BAPTISTERIES.

			CENTURY	FIG.	PAGE
AQUILEIA .	. . . .	. Near the Cathedral .	IV		342
GRADO	. . . .	Near the Cathedral	VI		60
TORCELLO	. . . .	. Near the Cathedral . . .	VII	156	308
POLA .	. . .	. . Formerly near the Cathedral	IX		213
ALLIATE	. . . . .	. Near the Parish Church .	IX	128, 131	257–8
BIELLA	. . . . .	Near the Cathedral	IX or X	132	261

BAPTISMAL FONTS.

			CENTURY	FIG.	PAGE
CIVIDALE .	. . . . .	. Cathedral	VIII	31	103
VENICE .		Museum	VIII	44	122
ADRIA .	. . . .	. . Church of the Tomb .	VIII		128
TOSCANELLA .	. . .	S. Maria Major . . .	IX		180

BAPTISMAL CIBORIA.

			CENTURY	FIG.	PAGE
CIVIDALE .	. .	. . Cathedral	VIII	31–34	103–5
POLA		Once in the Baptistery . .	IX	110	214

BELFRIES.

			CENTURY	FIG.	PAGE
RAVENNA .	. . . . .	. Of several Churches	VI		255
MILAN .		S. Satyrus . .	IX	127	256
CAORLE	. . . . .	. Cathedral . .	IX		339

363

SARCOPHAGI AND EPITAPHS.

		CENTURY	FIG.	PAGE
VENICE . . . . . S. Mark		VI		69-70
RAVENNA . . . . . S. Vitale		VI		32
,, ... Cathedral		VI		32
,, ... S. Apollinaris-in-Classe .		VI or VII	3	31
VENICE . . . . . SS. John and Paul . . .		VI or VII	16	71
,, ... Museum of the Ducal Palace		VII	17	72
RAVENNA . . . . S. Apollinaris-in-Classe . .		VIII	4, 5, 103	{ 34, 35, 199
PAVIA . . . . . . Malaspina Palace .		VIII	69	153
MURANO . . . . . Cathedral		VIII	45	123
OSIMO . . . . . . Cathedral (?)		VIII		157
RAVENNA . . . . S. Apollinaris-in-Classe . .		IX	105	203
,, ... Archiepiscopal Museum .		IX		200
,, ... Tomb of Braccioforte . .		IX		204-5
MILAN . . . . . . S. Ambroise		IX	116	223
VENICE . . . . . Ducal Palace		IX		307
,, ... Patriarchal Seminary . .		IX		307
MURANO . . . . . Museum		IX		313
JESOLO . . . . . Cathedral		IX		313
POLA . . . . . . Cathedral		IX		212

www.ingramcontent.com/pod-product-compliance
Lightning Source LLC
Chambersburg PA
CBHW020231240426
43672CB00006B/483